WATER SHORTAGE

Richard A. Berk
C. J. LaCivita
Katherine Sredl
Thomas F. Cooley

WATER SHORTAGE

Lessons in
Conservation
from the Great
California
Drought,
1976-1977

Abt Books · Cambridge, Mass.

Library of Congress Cataloging in Publication Data
Main entry under title:

Water shortage.

Includes index.
1. Water conservation—California. 2. Droughts—
California. I. Berk, Richard A.
TD224.C3W37   333.91′16′09794   81-3651
ISBN 0-89011-560-5   AACR2

Printed in the United States of America

Book design by Martha Scotford Lange

CONTENTS

Preface .... *vi*

Acknowledgments .... *vii*

ONE
Some preliminaries on water shortages and their
consequences *1*

TWO
Theories of water consumption and conservation .. *19*

THREE
Local responses to the drought *35*

FOUR
What works: time series analyses of local water
consumption *89*

FIVE
What works better in some communities than
others: differential effects across communities *125*

SIX
Summary, conclusions, and policy recommendations *143*

APPENDIX 1
Data collection instrument *165*

APPENDIX 2
Some theoretical considerations in water pricing ... *178*

APPENDIX 3
Time series results for the full sample *183*

Code sheet for treatments 1–4 .... *191*
NOTES *192*
REFERENCES *198*
INDEX *202*

PREFACE

In 1976 and 1977 the state of California experienced its worst drought of the century. In the pages that follow we examine how the local communities in California altered their water management policies in response to the drought, and why some of these changes were effective but others were not.

Although our report rests on underpinnings from economics, social psychology, and sociology, it is an effort in applied social science, and we have drawn on these other disciplines only to the extent required to tackle the problems at hand. In other words, we did not set out to test one or more social science theories. For example, we were more concerned with determining how well water conservation programs worked than with advancing current thinking on the dilemma of the commons. Similarly, we were more interested in estimating price elasticities for various kinds of consumers than in developing elaborate disequilibrium models of the market for water.

In this context, we have tried to write in a manner that will be accessible to a diverse audience: academic social scientists, urban planners, water management specialists, public officials, and consumer organizations interested in water management policy. Nevertheless, some technical questions, particularly with respect to statistical procedures, are considered, and readers interested in such matters will require a background in applied econometrics. However, the final chapter has been written as an independent summary of findings, conclusions, and policy recommendations. Some readers may find it helpful to read the final chapter first, and then decide which issues they wish to pursue in more depth.

ACKNOWLEDGMENTS

Our interest in water conservation began with the experience of the water district serving the University of California at Santa Barbara. During a graduate seminar on evaluation research, we learned of local efforts to conserve water and decided to undertake an assessment of those efforts. Judith Maki and Donnie Hoffman, the prime movers in this study, deserve credit for an excellent pilot evaluation and for laying much of the groundwork for the study reported here. Equally important was the excellent cooperation provided by the staff of the Goleta County Water District and particularly Laura Malcolm and Robert Paul.

As the plans for an evaluation of water conservation programs across the state were evolving, we received assistance from a number of colleagues at UCSB. Douglas Morgan, Lloyd Mercer, and Alan Wyner were especially helpful even when their views differed from ours.

We contacted several federal agencies about support for the evaluation and received enthusiastic encouragement from Dr. Katharine Lyall, then the Deputy Assistant Secretary for Economic Affairs at HUD. She also provided excellent technical advice as we moved from a preliminary to a final proposal. It is doubtful that the research would have gotten off the ground without her significant contributions.

Generous funding was provided by HUD (grant no. H-2980-RG), and it fell to David Puryear to serve as project monitor. He took on the job with uncommon sensitivity and sophistication in matters of both bureaucratic maneuvering and social science technology. As the months progressed he became an enormously helpful colleague to whom we are genuinely indebted.

The fieldwork undertaken during our first summer was orchestrated by Donnie Hoffman and Rebecca Cannon. They deserve much of the credit for what turned out to be an efficient and relatively painless data collection enterprise. Fieldwork staff included Ai Chao, Miriam Chaiken, Glen Culbertson, Hollis Jackson, William Viergever, and Elizabeth Vogel. Each brought enthusiasm and intelligence to the task and went well beyond the level of effort we had any right to expect. Still, the research might well have foundered at this point had we not received such excellent cooperation from water district personnel throughout the state. They gave freely of their time and expertise when there was certainly no requirement that they do so. We also appreciate the cooperation of staff at the California Department of Water Resources when we troubled them for suggestions on how best to proceed.

The field operation generated an enormous amount of data that required difficult manipulations as statistical analyses were undertaken. In these efforts, Anthony Shih, Stanley Parker, and David Rauma provided essential assistance despite a number of competing commitments. Much of the credit for the timely completion of this research belongs to these three individuals.

A number of people participated in the preparation of the final manuscript. Trina Miller, Leslie Wilson, Claire Donahue, and Cathy Fitzmaurice typed various parts of the text and what turned out to be long and tedious tables. They also made a number of helpful suggestions along the way, particularly when our writing was far less than perfect.

Finally, Marilynn Brewer made major contributions to the research design and proposed analyses during the project's first year. Unfortunately, she was out of the country for much of the second year, and we sorely missed her contribution; we suspect that she would have provided a number of helpful suggestions. She deserves much of the credit for the project's initial formulation and is in no way responsible for any failures to carry out the project properly.

Richard A. Berk
C. J. LaCivita
Katherine Sredl
Thomas F. Cooley

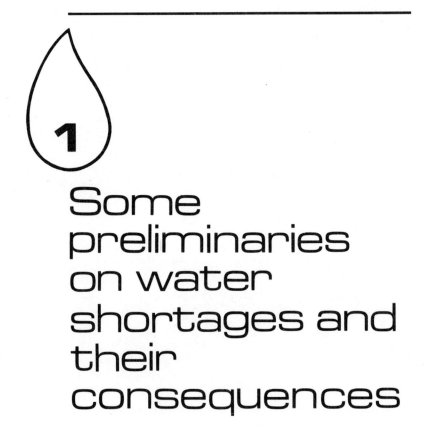

Some preliminaries on water shortages and their consequences

Introduction

During the twenty-five months between November of 1975 and December of 1977, the state of California experienced its most severe drought in this century. As one "God damned beautiful" day followed another, the grim statistics piled up. Precipitation in 1977 was but 35 percent of normal totals, the accumulation of snow at higher altitudes was, with a few exceptions, the lowest in forty-seven years, and the water content of California's snowpack was only 25 percent of the usual levels (Kahrl et al. 1979, pp. 76–77). The year of 1976 was the fourth driest on record, and the following year's shortfall rewrote the record books.[1]

The day-to-day consequences were equally dramatic. Karhl et al. report that runoffs from rivers and streams were 76 percent below average, and by August 1977 total storage in the state's 143 reservoirs was 61 percent lower than normal reserves (1979, p. 77). Graphic illustrations of such statistics could be found throughout the state: dry riverbeds, exposed lake bottoms, and falling water tables.

However, the drought's consequences varied enormously by locale and kind of water user. A large part of southern California, for example, was able to draw on entitlements from the Colorado River, thus releasing for use elsewhere much of the water routinely imported from northern regions. In contrast, Marin County, just north of San Francisco, faced a genuine crisis in which it appeared to some that Marin residents would soon have no water at all. In a parallel fashion, agricultural users relying on irrigation were initially able to proceed almost as usual, thanks to water from the massive supply systems contained within the State Water Project and the Central Valley Water Project. Agricultural users wedded to more traditional watering methods (based on local sources) were far less fortunate. Nonirrigated agriculture accounted for 90 percent of the estimated $510 million in crop losses during 1976 and the $800 million in crop losses during 1977 (Kahrl et al. 1979, p. 78).

Consistent with the wide variation in the drought's impact across

1

different locales and different kinds of users, a diverse set of conservation measures was adopted. For example, assuming that the typical urban dweller uses 150 gallons of water per day, Marin County restricted its residential users to a daily allotment of 45 gallons and doubled the price. In contrast, San Diego, relying heavily on imported water from the Colorado River, confined its efforts to a single educational leaflet. Similarly, while some agricultural users were able to proceed largely unaffected, others decreased the acreage allocated to water-intensive crops, turned to more efficient irrigation systems, dug new wells, drew on deeper (and more expensive) groundwater, and/or simply accepted smaller crop yields.

Within this context of enormous local variation, our study considers whether public policies responding to the drought had their intended effects, that is, whether water consumption differed as a result of these policies. In short, this is a book about water conservation.

At first blush, the answers to such questions are clear. According to official aggregate statistics, urban water use (including residential, commercial, industrial, and public consumers) during the height of the drought dropped substantially across the state (Kahrl et al. 1979, pp. 77–78). Using the six-month period from January through June of 1976 as a benchmark, urban water use declined by 21 percent over the same interval the following year. Agricultural consumption also declined, although precise figures are difficult to obtain because of water drawn from wells and other private sources (for example, riparian rights to river water).

However, such aggregate assessments are at best incomplete for several reasons. First, California routinely experiences enormous variation in precipitation between its wet and dry seasons (roughly November through April and May through October, respectively) and substantial variation from year to year. For example, the mean annual rainfall in Los Angeles is 14.8 inches, but precipitation above 20 inches and below 10 inches is quite common (Kahrl et al. 1979, p. 7); variation of plus or minus 33 percent is almost routine. Eureka enjoys an average of 38.3 inches of rainfall per year, but precipitation above 45 inches and below 30 inches occurs with some regularity (Kahrl et al. 1979, p. 7); thus, 20 percent variation is hardly unusual. Moreover, there is apparently some serial correlation in precipitation across the state such that good years and bad years tend to come in clusters. The result is that the yearly consequences of too much or too little precipitation are compounded. Natural and artificial storage can of course moderate the impact of nature's capriciousness, but cannot eliminate the substantial variation in rainfall.

In view of such variation, the very concept of a drought seems ambiguous. Indeed, Howe defines a drought as "a shortage of precipitation of seasonal or longer duration relative to the expectations of users" (1979, p. 280). Hence, droughts are defined only on a comparative basis and then through complicated subjective processes under what sociologists study as "social problem definition" (Spector and Kitsuse 1977). Put a bit crudely, a drought is whatever relative shortage in precipitation people choose to call a drought. In practical terms, then, the 1976–1977 precipitation shortfall must be studied within the range of naturally occurring variation over a period of years. In addition, whatever the changes in consumer behavior, these too can be properly understood only in comparison to consumer behavior over a longer interval. Without such anchors, it is impossible to determine what was special about the 1976–1977 period and whether the drop in water consumption was in some sense unusual. Note that the issues are both substantive and statistical: were the drought years really different, and, if so, were the differences real or artifactual? If, for example, a series of conservation measures was instituted in reaction to several years of unusually high consumption (irrespective of the drought) and in service of more general concerns about the adequacy of existing supplies, the apparent reductions during the drought could perhaps be explained by regression to the mean (Campbell and Stanley 1963, pp. 10–12).

Second, estimates of aggregate water reduction neglect the relative importance of a variety of factors that might alter consumption. Surely water consumption responds to monthly variation in rainfall and temperature, along with human intervention in the form of conservation efforts and normal variation in price (for example, see Berk et al. 1980; Hirshleifer, DeHaven, and Milliman 1969; and Howe 1979). Estimates of aggregate reductions are no substitute for a causal model of water use; they offer little insight into underlying mechanisms and provide an inadequate basis for making policy recommendations. For example, can adequate savings be obtained through price increases alone, or must educational efforts be launched as well? Can one expect such measures to compensate fully for water shortages, or are they more properly viewed as temporary holding actions until supplies can be increased?

Third, aggregate figures ignore variation in responses to the drought by different kinds of users and in different locales. Assuming that a credible causal model of water use can be built, one might well want to determine, for instance, whether residential users were less responsive to price increases than commercial users. Similarly, one might wonder whether communities in which residents have achieved a high educational level were especially good sites for conservation campaigns. Again, the benefits of such comparisons are both substantive and practical: a broader understanding of factors affecting water use may be forthcoming, and there is the prospect that future drought responses could be tailored to different users and different communities.

Finally, just as one might be interested in responses during the drought, one might be concerned about responses after the drought. Did the drought-related conservation measures have a lasting effect, or did consumption return to former levels? If former levels were approached, how rapidly did this occur and through what causal factors? In short, was the drought but a passing crisis that Californians managed to survive, or were there long-term consequences?

It is important to stress that, despite the focus on conservation in response to the 1976–1977 drought, the material discussed in this book has broader implications for understanding water use in California. Californians (and all Americans) use enormous amounts of water both in direct consumption and indirectly in production. For example, while average per capita use in urban households is about 150 gallons per day, suburban users in the hot Central Valley may consume over four times that amount (Kahrl et al. 1979, p. 1). These figures may seem striking, but they pale in comparison to total water use per day when indirect consumption is considered; estimates of overall daily per capita consumption run as high as 1,800 gallons, and over time consumption has been increasing (Kahrl et al. 1979, p. 1). The wheat in one pound of bread, for instance, requires approximately 136 gallons of water, and a pound of steak represents consumption of 2,500 gallons to sustain the steer, produce the feed, maintain the rancher's facilities, and the like (Kahrl et al. 1979, p. 1).

Coupled with the enormous demand for water is an escalating concern about the viability of existing supplies. Population growth has increasingly taxed available groundwater (Berk et al. 1980), and efforts to insure local water supplies through large public works projects have of late faced several obstacles. The real costs of constructing elaborate supply systems are apparently increasing, and large-scale public works may be facing diminishing marginal returns. Equally important, environmental groups question the wisdom of making further incursions upon California's natural system of rivers, lakes, and water-bearing aquifers. And linked to these local problems are the complications produced by even a modest dependence on water imported from the Colorado River. In view of recent economic development in the western states served by the Colorado River, California's entitlements certainly cannot be increased, and they may well have to be reduced (Kahrl et al. 1979, pp. 38–45). Finally, with increasing demands being placed on current water supplies, California's long and acrimonious experience with the politics of water continues to this day. For example, a series of recent articles appearing in the *Los An-*

geles Times (Jones 1980) chronicles the efforts to expand the California State Water Project, which for fifteen years were mired in a heated controversy about who should bear the enormous capital costs, how water resources should be equitably distributed among users in the northern and southern parts of the state, what means should be used to prevent further environmental damage to affected watersheds in Northern California, and conflicting projections about future demand for water.

Related to the problem of insuring adequate water supplies is the concern with water quality. Water imported from the Colorado River contains large amounts of natural salts, which accumulate in irrigated farm land over time and affect crop yields. Similarly, large withdrawals of groundwater in coastal regions often lead to the incursion of ocean water so that local wells become unusable. Finally, local water supplies are frequently contaminated with pollutants from sewage systems and/or industrial production. For instance, burgeoning development along the shores of Lake Tahoe (the largest North American alpine lake) has led to serious problems in water quality. Air-borne pollutants have caused siltation and the growth of algae along the shoreline, particularly around the mouths of tributary streams. Moreover, the ability to handle local sewage has been outstripped. Even with generous discount rates to calculate the present value of a clean Lake Tahoe for future generations (Howe 1979, pp. 295–297), it is hard to imagine that anything close to optimal social policy is being implemented.

On the other hand, California is not in immediate danger of running out of water nor of polluting existing supplies to the extent that de facto shortages would materialize. Rather, what California faces are the worsening consequences of long-standing economic inefficiencies.[2] First, there is good reason to expect that the real marginal cost of water will continue to rise. Given increasing demand, supply systems must contend with natural limits on the availability of cheap water: groundwater must be drawn from deeper aquifers, river water must be transported over longer distances, water carried by newer aqueducts must be pumped over higher elevations, and the like. In addition, there seem to be few prospects for developing innovative technology that will significantly moderate the increasing costs of constructing new supply systems or providing water from existing facilities. There is nothing on the horizon, for instance, suggesting that new technology will significantly reduce the enormous costs of dam construction. Finally, the costs of maintaining or improving water quality are growing. Recognizing that water laced with pollutants may be next to useless (or actually harmful), government has established firm standards for water quality. Thus, current consumers must pay for the earlier sins of others and live with increasing marginal costs, even in instances where ameliorative efforts have been underway for some time.

If the rising real cost of water were accurately translated into per unit (marginal) prices, there might be no special cause for alarm. The higher marginal price would reduce the quantity demanded and allocate water efficiently.[3] However, for several reasons the real price of water is not effectively captured by current pricing policies.

First, as we will consider in some depth later, the price of water is rarely consistent with its marginal cost. At best, consumers are asked to cover lower average costs. This leads to the inefficiencies that a number of economists have stressed (for example, see Hirshleifer, DeHaven, and Milliman 1969, pp. 88–92).

Second, the prices paid by consumers do not reflect the full marginal cost because of local, state, and federal subsidies. Consequently, water is "too cheap," which in turn leads to additional inefficiencies.

Third, water use creates substantial externalities that current pricing policies typically ignore. For example, a series of municipal wells will often extract groundwater not only from lands held by the community, but from outlying areas belonging to others. Similarly, the environmental consequences of water overdrafts are rarely captured in the prices paid by consumers. Again, inefficiencies result.

Finally, to the degree that some water supplies are nonrenewable (for example, in the case of aquifers that are not recharged by rainfall), that the environmental consequences of extensive water use are not reversible (or are reversible only at considerable cost), and that current use increases the price of water consumed in the future (for example, by requiring deeper wells), pricing practices that fail to incorporate these "scarcity rents" (Howe 1979, pp. 75–79) neglect significant costs. Once again, the prices paid by consumers today are too low, and inefficiencies follow.

In short, an excellent case can be made that current pricing policies, which in effect make water too cheap, are producing a host of distortions leading to inefficiencies and "overconsumption." One solution is to make the prices paid by water consumers more consistent with the real marginal cost of water. Unfortunately, an enormous number of political and legal reforms would be necessary before efficient pricing policies could be implemented. All of these in turn would require a fundamental change in the current public view of access to cheap water as a right not subject to market forces. Moreover, technical means need to be found to price accurately the future consequences of today's water use and construct an appropriate discount rate. Without such advances, there is no way to estimate the current discounted price of water.[4]

Where does that leave us? Perhaps most important, even if the price mechanism could in principle match consumer demand for water with available supplies, market mechanisms currently in practice are insufficient and will remain so for some time to come.[5] Hence, water consumption will have to be regulated in part through other instruments, and conservation programs relying on noneconomic principles are clearly one important option. Among the central concerns of the study reported in this volume are the impacts of conservation programs of various types and the kinds of communities in which they are more or less effective. Presumably, our findings will therefore be useful not only for an assessment of how well conservation programs worked during the 1976–1977 drought, but for judgments about the feasibility of water conservation programs in general.

Moreover, our findings need not be limited to the California experience nor even to water consumption. There is no particular reason to assume that our models of water consumption are especially different from models appropriate for other regions. While parameter estimates might differ in detail, signs and orders of magnitude should be roughly comparable; that is, the *causal relationships* among these variables will be similar. Thus, other states can learn something of value from the California experience.

Of course, differences between the means and variances of the important variables studied in California and those in other areas do raise the question of relevance. In particular, regions experiencing substantial precipitation with little variation from month to month may not have to worry about water conservation.

From our perspective, this view is shortsighted. Even areas blessed with adequate endowments of water increasingly must face serious water quality problems. Untreated sewage has fouled drinking water. Industrial wastes and pesticides have turned groundwater into a genuine health hazard. Acid rain has seriously contaminated an enormous number of freshwater lakes. In short, while the overall amount of water may be adequate, the amount of water with the requisite quality is probably far less than imagined. For example, a recent issue of the *Los Angeles Times* (July 24, 1980) reports on a study undertaken by the Environmental Protection Agency in which it was found that industrial wastes were "threatening the drinking water at more than 3,600 locations" across the country (Hume 1980, p. 1). In addition, "preliminary studies of 11,000 industrial sites show that about half contain 'potential hazardous waste' and a third are located above aquifers (layers of water-bearing rock) or near drinking wells" (Hume 1980, p. 1). In this context, many areas may be forced to conserve water until its quality is improved.

Equally important, many regions previously rich in water supplies face significant changing circumstances in the near future. Expanding efforts to exploit domestic stocks of timber, minerals, and energy pose a serious risk of damage to productive watersheds, and crash programs to extract gas and oil from coal and oil-bearing shale will require enormous amounts of water (for example, see Miller 1979, pp. 176–177). Some experts have estimated, for example, that each barrel of oil obtained from oil-bearing shale will require an input of two barrels of water. Consequently, many parts of the country face a double bind of mounting threats to existing water supplies and a dramatic leap in demand.[6] Indeed, it is perhaps not too alarmist to assert that the energy crisis of the 1980s will be followed by the water crisis of the 1990s. Again, in the short run at least, conservation becomes a critical element of public policy.

Finally, the all too painful experiences of the summer and fall of 1980 clearly indicate that serious droughts can occur almost anywhere in the country; the southwestern United States is not the only vulnerable region. December 1980 found New York City's reservoirs at a fifteen-year low that was so serious, massive conservation efforts were initiated. In addition, contingency plans were announced permitting restriction of industrial water use should the drought conditions not improve. More generally, the drought in the East dramatized the inadequacy of existing systems for the supply of water. As one informed observer noted, "New Jersey's water supply system constantly stands on the brink of disaster" (Adler and Agrest 1981, p. 20).

Our models of water consumption may also be relevant to other issues. Consider current policy surrounding energy use. The newspapers are full of fervent calls for a variety of rather draconian measures to limit consumption of fossil fuels: gasoline rationing, systems of heating oil allocations, forbidding driving one day each week, tough regulations governing the window area and insulation of new buildings, and the like. While such proposals are typically well-intentioned and certainly genuine policy options, they are hardly trouble-free. In addition to the inevitable bureaucratic complications and enormous policing costs, there is the likely prospect of substantial distortions in a range of markets. The perverse consequences of such distortions are well known.

Our examination of factors affecting water use in California provides a unique opportunity to evaluate the effectiveness of less intrusive means of altering consumption. Despite the severity of the 1976–1977 drought, California communities typically resorted to rather mild measures, such as allowing water to be priced at levels closer to its real marginal cost. While a few communities instituted strict rationing plans, most relied on educational appeals stressing the seriousness of the problem and suggesting ways to reduce consumption (for example, fix leaky faucets). If interventions of this sort were effective in reducing water consumption, why not use them to reduce energy consumption as well? On the other hand, if increases in the price of water and well-orchestrated publicity campaigns had negligible effects (or low benefit-cost ratios), perhaps the time is right for dramatic government intervention.

What is a water shortage?

As we noted earlier, the meaning of the term "drought" is at best relative; indeed, since the amount of precipitation varies from season to season and from year to year, a drought is (in a hydrological sense) nothing more than a point on a distribution (Ward 1975, pp. 16–30). Moreover, even several years with unusually low levels of precipitation may be of no practical concern except insofar as the reduced availability of water has important social consequences. In particular, low levels of precipitation must raise the prospect of water shortages (either real or imagined) before a "drought" materializes.

No one would dispute that in the two years during which California experienced its record-breaking precipitation shortfall, there was a widespread belief that water shortages were in the offing. And it was this belief that presumably mobilized conservation efforts throughout the state. However, without additional clarification, it is difficult to know precisely what the spectre of water shortages really entailed. Clearly, enormous stocks of water remained even near the end of the second year, and many regions enjoyed significant precipitation over the entire two-year interval. So what was the problem?

We can say intuitively that a water shortage has something to do with a mismatch between the demand for water and the available supply. However, it is possible to be far more precise, and in the interest of laying a sound conceptual foundation for the analyses to be presented later, it will perhaps prove useful to consider briefly a more formal perspective on water shortages.

Building on the conceptual approach used by Hirshleifer, DeHaven, and Milliman (1969, pp. 10–21), the "hydrologic balance" in some period of time (t) for a given geographic area can be modeled as a function of the following variables:

(1) total withdrawals (W_t) that can be separated into (a) consumptive withdrawals, in which water leaves the particular phase of the hydrologic cycle (for example, free-standing water) through evaporation, transpiration, chemical recombination, and the like, and (b) nonconsumptive withdrawals, in which used water is recycled for use by others;

(2) new water (N_t), which is liquid water received by the area from precipitation and inflow (via rivers, streams, underground flows, aqueducts, and so forth);

(3) the sum of losses from liquid water (T_t) through transpiration and evaporation other than water vapor losses associated with withdrawal uses; [7]

(4) liquid discharge (D_t) away from the area through surface streams, underground flows, storm drains, sewers, and the like;

(5) the net change in the liquid water stored (r_t) either on the surface or underground through natural or artificial means (for example, underground aquifers or reservoirs); and

(6) the amount of effluent withdrawals in the form of recycled water (E_t), what we called nonconsumptive withdrawals above.

Given these variables, an equation for total withdrawals in a given period (t) can be written as:

$$W_t = N_t - T_t - D_t - r_t + E_t$$

This equation implies that the total withdrawals in any given period (W_t) and for some particular geographic area increase (other things being equal) with increments in new water (N_t) and with increments in the amount of recycled water (E_t), but decrease with increments in water vapor losses (T_t), increments in liquid discharge (D_t) from the area to other areas, and increments in the amount of water stored (r_t). Thus, the first general point is that variation in precipitation by itself is only one of several factors affecting the amount of water withdrawn; precipitation is an important variable, but not the only variable.

The variables on the right-hand side of the equation are differentially manipulable, especially in the short run. At one extreme, there is little that can be done to alter the amount of precipitation, while at the other extreme one can rather easily vary the amount of water stored. Changing the area inflows and outflows may be easily accomplished if water transportation systems are under human control (for example, in the case of dammed rivers), but bringing more transported water under control typically requires large capital investments and considerable lead time. Similarly, if water-recycling facilities are already in place, it may be relatively easy to alter the amount of water that is recycled, but construction of new facilities (or expansion of existing facilities) entails time delays and capital costs.

From these observations it is apparent that a precipitation shortfall does not necessarily force reductions in water use; there exist both short-term and long-term ways to compensate. In the short run, for example, a decline in precipitation can be balanced by an increase in the use of stored groundwater. In the long run a decline in precipitation can be balanced by the construction of water-recycling plants and other means. What then was the problem created by the 1976–1977 drought?

In brief, the dramatic reduction in precipitation during 1976 and 1977 required that *if the demand for water stayed at existing levels,* compensatory changes were necessary from one or more of the variables in the right-hand side of the above equation. And given the size of the two-year precipitation shortfall, only variables subject to short-term manipulation could be considered. Clearly, the construction of new water transportation systems, for instance, would not help maintain existing withdrawal rates. However, in some locales, at least, short-run alterations in such things as the amount of water stored appeared to be insufficient. Moreover, there was the possibility that heavy reliance on short-term solutions would create serious difficulties in the future. If too much groundwater was extracted in coastal areas, for example, the remaining groundwater might be fouled by inflows from the ocean.

In this context, the meaning of "shortages" associated with the drought becomes more clear. The marked reduction in precipitation during 1976 and 1977 required that short-run ways to increase the supply of water had to be found *if current water use levels were to be maintained.* In some areas, however, these short-run options were soon outstripped and each additional month of drought raised the prospect that other areas would experience the same fate. It was possible, therefore, that a time would come in which previous withdrawal levels could *not* be maintained; withdrawals would necessarily have to decline.

But does a reduction in withdrawals mean that a shortage has occurred? The answer is that it depends on whether the reduction in withdrawals is associated with a reduction in the demand for water. If the demand for water declines commensurate with the available supply, there is no shortage. *Only if demand does not decline (or does not decline sufficiently) can it be said that there is a shortage.* What this means is that the water shortages associated with the 1976–1977 drought were in fact *expectations* that if the demand for water was not reduced, short-run supplies would be insufficient. It was these expectations, in turn, that presumably led to the adoption of a variety of efforts to alter the *demand* for water.

In summary, the 1976–1977 drought brought a dramatic reduction in precipitation. The precipitation shortfall, in turn, forced many areas throughout the state to employ short-term solutions in meeting the existing demand for water. However, as the drought continued, it appeared that these solutions could not by themselves fully compensate for the reduction in precipitation (and hence, the reduction in "new water"), or even if they could, disproportional long-term costs would be incurred (for example, the fouling of remaining underground supplies). In other words, there was the real prospect that the short-run demand for water would substantially exceed the short-run supply. It was this expectation that qualified as a "water shortage" and prompted efforts to reduce demand.

Data base and data collection procedures

In the chapters that follow, we will consider in depth the kinds of conservation efforts undertaken in response to the 1976–1977 drought and the effects of those efforts on water consumption. We will develop the relevant theory and then turn to a variety of empirical analyses. However, since our ultimate aim is to build and estimate the parameters for causal models of water consumption, both the theoretical and empirical work must respond to the kinds of data available. It is all well and good, for example, to propose elegant theories explaining variation in water consumption, but at some point these theories need to be operationalized. Similarly, when the time comes to interpret our empirical results, the kind and quality of available data must be seriously considered. Therefore, in anticipation of these concerns, we turn to an overview of our data base and the methods used to collect data.

The data base is derived from a sample of fifty-seven geographic areas, most of which are public water districts—"public agencies with authority over some aspect of water supply, delivery, use and treatment" (Kahrl 1979, p. 63). Much like school districts, public water districts are typically given substantial discretion in how they conduct their affairs, including the kinds of goods and services provided, the financing of their activities, and their form of governance (as long as these are consistent with state and federal law, administrative regulations from such bodies as the California Water Resources Control Board, and a corpus of legal precedents).

We will be focusing on urban water districts providing water to residential consumers, although many also provide water to commercial, industrial, agricultural, and public users. Such districts are the most common type of water agency among the diverse set of over 800 existing during the period for which data were collected (Kahrl 1979, p. 63).[8] They are also the local administrative units for which data of high quality are likely to be available. In short, the emphasis on public water districts servicing residential consumers (and others) reflects not only the single most important urban water purveyor, but the existence of appropriate and readily available data to study water consumption during the 1976–1977 drought.

Water district data will be complemented by information about smaller areas *within* water districts, such as communities. This is particularly important in the case of large water districts composed of heterogeneous elements (for example, the Metropolitan Water District in the Los Angeles area).

Our sample reflects considerable variation in water district climate, location, economic base, and size. Included in the sample are districts in coastal and inland regions and in the northern, central, and southern parts of the state; some are urban or suburban areas, others are rural. We also considered using formal probability sampling, but rejected such procedures as impractical. We knew in advance that districts varied enormously in the kinds and quality of data that were readily available, but we did not know a priori which districts were likely to have data of the requisite quality. In other words, we could not construct in advance a sampling frame that took into account data availability. Therefore, we established quotas for the different kinds of districts we wanted to study and then filled the quotas by selecting appropriate districts in which empirical analyses were feasible. To the degree that our purposive sample affects our ability to generalize, we will address specific concerns as they arise in our empirical results. Suffice it to say that our empirical work rests on a larger and more varied sample of districts than is typically available for studies of water consumption.

It is important to stress that since initially we planned to analyze each water district separately, the most important sample size issues involved the number of observations *within* each water district. In this context, our design called for the collection of longitudinal data and a time series perspective in which longitudinal variation in water consumption was of primary concern. We anticipated a large number of time series analyses in which consumption figures were to be "regressed" on a variety of exogenous variables, including measures of local conservation efforts. This implied the need for many lengthy time series bracketing the drought. Earlier pilot work indicated that it was possible to obtain the requisite time series data organized by month (Berk et al. 1980), and with this in mind, we settled on trying to get monthly data from January 1970 to June 1978. The goal was to obtain about 100 longitudinal observations for each district.

At the same time, we were concerned about the total number of districts, if for no other reason than to get an overall picture of urban conservation efforts across the state. We initially set a target of fifty water districts, although the exact number was far less important than the need to obtain data from a diverse set of districts.[9] In other words, we viewed the sample of districts as a vehicle for a large number of *replications* in which the critical question was whether findings for one kind of district would surface in other kinds of districts. If the findings differed, we hoped that explanations could be found in the varying characteristics of each district. In any case, practical constraints intervened before we could obtain data from fifty water districts, and our sample therefore includes only thirty districts.[10]

While the reduced sample of districts may be somewhat disappointing, we managed nevertheless to generate the variation in district characteristics we were seeking. In addition, several of our districts contained within their boundaries diverse geographic units (communities) for which the necessary data were often available. We treated these smaller units as separate entities for purposes of analysis, and the result is an effective sample of 57 districts and communities. Finally, the majority of districts or communities were able to provide data for different kinds of consumers: residential, commercial, industrial, agricultural, and public.[11] These breakdowns in turn enormously increased the possibilities for comparative analyses, or replications. Indeed, we envisioned undertaking nearly 200 time series analyses across geographic units and across different kinds of users.

We began the data collection in the summer of 1978. The letter initially sent to prospective water districts explained the general purpose of the study. The letter was followed by a phone call in which details were provided and information was sought about the kinds of data that were available. We explained that we were seeking information about the number of accounts served, monthly consumption figures, prices charged, and the timing and content of water conservation programs, as well as climatic and other characteristics of the area. Fortunately, the majority of districts contacted had the necessary data, although in widely varying formats. Some districts had the information in machine-readable form, while others could only suggest that if we culled through their records, we might be able to extract what we wanted. In nearly every case, the water district personnel were extremely cooperative and even enthusiastic.

Once we established that the necessary data were available, we arranged to send research assistants to each of the districts that agreed to cooperate (and most did). We had recruited and trained as fieldworkers eight graduate students from the sociology, anthropology, psychology, and economics departments at the University of California at Santa Barbara. They visited the districts and communities in two-person teams and collected data using questionnaires that we had provided (see Appendix 1).[12] Sometimes the information was obtained in as little as a few hours. In other cases, several days of hard work were required.

Each team was in the field for about a week at a time, during which several areas were visited. After each trip, field-workers were debriefed at some length, and the information obtained was examined for missing data and inconsistencies. Before going out into the field again, each team edited and coded the information it had obtained. This contributed to quality control since, with their firsthand knowledge of the water districts and data sources, team members were uniquely qualified to identify and solve problems. Difficulties that could not be handled on the spot were resolved by making phone calls to the areas just visited. Often ambiguities and confusions were straightened out during these phone calls, and, if necessary, additional information from water district personnel was mailed to the university. Problems that surfaced later were typically resolved the same way.

Most of the fieldwork was completed during the summer of 1978, but some of it continued over the next twelve months. In particular, we obtained access to data from one very large water district during the following summer and dispatched a single research assistant in the same manner as before. Also, we re-established contact with most of the districts and communities by mail and phone during the summer of 1979 in order to update information.

In summary, thanks to the cooperation of local water agencies and the efforts of a talented and energetic group of field-workers, we were able to obtain the data required by our research design. That design rested on thirty water districts with diverse characteristics, a total of fifty-seven geographic areas, and up to five kinds of water consumers in each. Data were collected for approximately an eight-year period bracketing the drought and were organized by month. This material forms the data base for all that follows.

An overview of the volume

No single social science discipline has the full story on water conservation. Microeconomic theory has a great deal to say about the impact of price on consumption (of both a normative and positive nature), for example, concerning the consequences of marginal versus average cost pricing. Similarly, there are rich insights to be gained from studies of public goods, the optimal use of natural resources, and the role of water as a production factor. Yet, by and large, microeconomics takes the preferences of optimizers as given and thus neglects the ways in which instruments of public policy can be used to shift the demand curve. Since many conservation programs are aimed directly at changing consumer preferences, this is a serious flaw.

Perhaps the most important scholarship relevant to changing consumer preferences can be found within social psychology. Whether drawn from sociological or psychological traditions, social psychology addresses such issues as the role of commitment to group welfare, notions of equity in the distribution of public goods, and the kinds of information required to inform decision making. Clearly, these are the kinds of concerns that should be critical in understanding the effectiveness of many kinds of conservation programs.

Therefore, in Chapter Two we will turn to theory from both microeconomics and social psychology in order to help us formulate causal models of water consumption. From the former we will consider such questions as how to anticipate the impact of surcharges for water use in excess of some fixed allotment, compared to an overall increase in the price schedule for water. From the latter, we will extract ideas about the kinds of conservation appeals that are likely to be effective.

The third chapter addresses local responses to the 1976–1977 drought, examining in depth the sorts of conservation efforts undertaken. The analysis is based on aggregate statistics concerning water consumption, the number of water accounts, pricing practices, the timing and content of water conservation programs, and several control variables for climatic factors relevant to water use.

Chapter Four explores the impact of these conservation efforts on water consumption. For each geographic unit and each kind of user (to the degree that data are broken down by kind of user), a number of month-by-month aggregate indicators are arrayed over time and analyzed primarily through Box-Jenkins time series techniques. Each time series reflects approximately eight years of monthly data (depending on availability) in which water consumption, standardized for the number of water accounts, is regressed on various indicators of conservation programs, a measure of the per-unit price of water, and several variables controlling for seasonal and climatic variation. The results of approximately 200 such time series analyses are reported. Finally, we consider differences in the time series results for various kinds of consumers, in part to address the differential impact by consumer type (for example, residential versus commercial) of conservation programs and pricing practices.

Considering the variety of geographic units and consumers studied, there is good reason to anticipate a range of findings from the time series analyses. In Chapter Five we turn to an examination of the variation in time series results and discuss why some communities may have had greater success with their conservation programs than others. One of the key questions is whether it pays to undertake a large number of conservation programs or whether the returns are subject to rapid marginal declines.

In the final chapter we summarize the results of our study and consider their implications. Both theoretical and practical concerns are discussed with an eye to policy recommendations. In addition, we note the limitations of our research and suggest areas in which future research should be fruitful.

2

Theories of water consumption and conservation[1]

Introduction

Applied problems rarely evolve in a form that can be effectively addressed from the perspective of any single academic discipline. Empirical processes almost inevitably unfold with no concern for the convenience of researchers, let alone the organizational boundaries that separate different bodies of thought. Consequently, as we turn to social science theory to inform the analyses that follow, we will draw on the perspectives of social psychology and microeconomics. We will argue that rather than offering conflicting views, social psychology and microeconomics provide important insights that complement one another rather nicely.

Microeconomics will be used to formulate an overall theoretical framework for water conservation programs and especially to characterize the impact on consumption of variation in the price of water. With this in mind, it is important to emphasize that the price of water can vary not only as a function of conservation programs, but also in the normal course of events as water districts attempt to cover their costs. Social psychology will be used primarily to articulate "tastes" for conservation and how the demand curve may be shifted by appeals to such concerns as group welfare. Our overall goal is to develop several somewhat general models to explain variation in water consumption over time, taking into account variation in kinds of consumers and communities.

The social psychological perspective

Programs designed to control water use typically rely on voluntary measures, and therefore, water conservation can be examined by considering the societal dilemmas that are created when short-run self-interest conflicts with long-run public welfare. Such problems, variously characterized as "commons dilemmas" (Dawes 1975, Hardin 1968), the "new Malthusianism" (Schelling 1971), or "social traps" (Platt 1973), typically arise when some publicly provided good is scarce.[2] An individual has little incentive to reduce his or her consumption, and in the aggregate the good is rapidly depleted. Consequently, no one's self-interest is ultimately served. With respect to water use in particular, Schelling observes:

> What we are dealing with is the frequent divergence between what people are individually motivated to do and what they might like to accomplish together. . . . We are warned of water shortages; leaky faucets account for a remarkable amount of waste, and we are urged to fit them with new washers. There just cannot be any question but what, for most of us if not all of us, we are far better off if we *all* . . . repair the leaky faucets, let the lawns get a little browner and the cars a little dirtier, and otherwise reduce our claims on the common pool of water . . . But . . . [mine] is an infinitesimal part of the demand for water . . . and while the minute difference that I can make is multiplied by the number of people to whom it can make a difference, the effect on me of what I do is truly negligible. . . . (Schelling 1971, pp. 63–69, emphasis in the original)

While Schelling (1971) and Hardin (1968) provide numerous graphic illustrations of such dilemmas, more formal models have been proposed by Dawes (1975) and Messick (1973, 1974), based on n-person extensions of the prisoner's dilemma decision structure. Messick's (1974) analysis, for example, demonstrates that in large groups and the absence of coercion, the dilemma is solvable if and only if a nonnegative "group interest" term is added to economic self-interest in the individual decision maker's utility function. Such models provide a framework for considering a number of empirical studies, briefly summarized below.

Laboratory experiments on the commons dilemma have confirmed that self-interest is a more powerful determinant of behavior than group interest and that, in general, the greater the incentive for engaging in self-interested behavior, the greater the number of people who choose this course of action (Kelley and Grzelak 1972, Talarowski 1977). However, certain interventions have been shown to influence subjects' propensities to further group welfare. In a study by Dawes, McTavish, and Shaklee (1977), for example, subjects given an opportunity to communicate freely about the dilemma chose the cooperative response more often than subjects who were not allowed to communicate or who communicated about some irrelevant topic. The researchers note that the subjects allowed to communicate freely often spontaneously brought up moral aspects of the dilemma (that is, appeals to social responsibility) in the course of discussion. Talarowski (1977) subsequently demonstrated that a strong moral plea delivered directly by the experimenter increased cooperation. Similarly, Marwell and Ames (1979) found that moral concerns (that is, what constitutes a "fair" contribution to the groups) are critical. Education has also been demonstrated to be effective, if it takes the form of information about the undesirable long-term consequences of self-interested choices (Stern 1976).

Studies by Linder (1977) and Brechner (1977) are particularly germane to the analysis of water conservation, since both use a setting in which a limited quantity of a partially renewable resource is available for "consumption" by subjects. The quantity of the resource diminishes as a function of consumption, but the resource is also "replenished" at a rate proportional to the amount of resource remaining in the pool—the larger the pool at any given point in time, the faster the replacement rate. However, if the pool reaches zero as a result of overconsumption, the resource is exhausted and the game ends. A large initial pool, open feedback among game players, and feedback about resource level were all demonstrated to prolong the life of the pool in these simulation studies.

Another relevant issue is the individual's beliefs about the attitudes of others in the group. Dawes, McTavish, and Shaklee (1977) found that people who pursue self-interest in a laboratory commons dilemma tended to believe that most other group members would behave similarly. Those who acted cooperatively expected more cooperation from others. Related research on "ingroup" formation suggests that the salience of membership in a common group and the perception of a shared dilemma increase the belief that others in the group will behave cooperatively (Brewer forthcoming).

While laboratory commons dilemmas or social traps bear many resemblances to real-world conservation dilemmas (particularly in their motivational structure), they must ignore numerous complexities. For example, the rules of the game are explicitly defined in a laboratory commons dilemma; in the real world participants may only gradually become aware of the existence of a dilemma. Yet in real world settings the conditions under which awareness is reached and response habits previously established can all be expected to be important.

A recent survey on energy-related issues, for instance, provides support for a direct relationship between the belief that shortages exist and conservation behavior. Thompson and McTavish (1976) found that only 20 percent of the respondents in their Grand Rapids, Michigan, survey indicated that they believed in present or future energy shortages. These individuals (who, compared to the rest of the respondents, were generally better educated; had higher socioeconomic status;

and relied more on newspapers, magazines, and research reports for their information about energy) reported practicing significantly more conservation measures than the remainder of the sample.

Belief in a resource shortage, however, is apparently only a necessary condition. Perceived effort and inconvenience have also been related to conservation behavior (Lipsey 1977). As part of an ongoing energy conservation project, Seligman, Darley, and Becker (forthcoming) surveyed fifty-six couples living in identical townhouses in Twin Rivers, New Jersey. Husbands and wives responded separately to twenty-eight energy-related attitude scales. A factor analysis of their responses yielded four factors: (1) beliefs about personal comfort and health, (2) beliefs about the relationship between personal effort (in conservation) and personal benefit, (3) opinions about a single individual's ability to have an impact on the energy crisis, and (4) beliefs about the legitimacy of the energy crisis. A regression analysis relating the four factor scores to actual electricity consumption of the households surveyed yielded an R^2 of .55, with the factor of personal comfort and health having the largest single impact on usage. Those who believed decreased energy use would lead to discomfort or ill health used more electricity than respondents who did not share this belief.

There has also been survey research on attitudes toward water conservation (Watkins 1974, Bruvold 1978). Perhaps most informative is a recent survey in which 195 residential consumers in Goleta, California (Talarowski and McClintock 1978) were grouped as overusers, on-target users, and conservers (defined in terms of consumption levels relative to quotas established by the water district). Questionnaire items were derived from three social-psychological models of behavior—the Bystander Intervention Model (Latané and Darley 1968), the Information Processing Model of Attitude Change (McGuire 1969), and Leventhal's (1970) Fear Arousal Model. Consumers who had exceeded their district-imposed water allotments perceived the California drought as less serious than did other respondents, and also were more likely to view the drought and resulting water shortages as the responsibility of the local water district.

Based on these survey results, Talarowski and McClintock concluded that overusers, on-target users, and conservers differ not so much in the types of information they possess, nor in the conservation methods they eventually use, but rather in their perception of the need to conserve and in their motivation to do so. Those who conserve water displayed both substantial concern for the drought's effects and above-average knowledge of water conservation techniques. Those who exceed their water consumption allotments show only knowledge, only concern, or neither.

To summarize, we have focused largely on research addressing the impact of attitudes on the commons dilemma, since attitudes are among the most critical targets of typical water conservation campaigns. Available theory and data suggest at least five social-psychological factors influencing conservation: (1) a belief that a resource shortage exists and constitutes a problem for a group with which an individual identifies, (2) a moral commitment to "fair" contributions to group welfare, (3) a belief in the efficacy of personal efforts to achieve a collective solution, (4) a belief that the personal cost or inconvenience resulting from conservation efforts will not be great, and (5) a belief that others in the relevant group will also conserve. We will see in Chapter Three that in many of the California communities we studied, "common sense" led to conservation programs that relied on similar conclusions.

The microeconomic perspective

While attitudes no doubt alter the demand for it, water is a market commodity; it must be purchased at a price. When viewed solely from this perspective, there is no "commons dilemma" inherent in water shortages. In a competitive market, if a commodity is in short supply at the existing price, the price should rise to equilibrate supply and demand. However, in the California market price is not simultaneously determined by supply and demand; it is *exogenously* determined (in the short run) by water suppliers, subject to public review. Nevertheless, in principle a municipality faced with a water shortage need only set the price at a sufficiently high level to effect the desired reduction in consumption.

Practice, of course, is rarely this simple, and the issues are important enough to warrant some elaboration. (A more detailed discussion of water pricing is presented in Appendix 2.) One of the basic principles of economic theory holds that the most efficient use of resources occurs when the price of a good is equal to the marginal (additional) cost of producing one more unit of the good.[3] As noted earlier, shortages created by droughts (or, in the case of oil, because the resource is depletable) arise because the quantity demanded exceeds the quantity supplied at the existing price. In a competitive market excess demand will provide incentive for producers to supply more of the good, which in turn will increase the marginal cost of production,[4] and suppliers will raise their price. The higher price will cause consumers to reduce consumption. Thus, the price will rise until an equilibrium is reached, and resources will be allocated efficiently.

Unfortunately, this principle is rarely acknowledged in water pricing, and government-mandated departures from it characterize a large number of commodities. It may be that elected officials fear the distributional consequences of relying on the price mechanism; indeed, this is the reason often cited.[5] In addition, accurate marginal cost pricing requires consideration of a host of externalities and future consequences defying any simple formulation. As we noted in Chapter One, even though water is typically a renewable natural resource, temporal models of optimal use may rely on Ricardian perspectives in which current water use increases the real price of water for future generations. This in turn produces technical difficulties that enormously complicate efforts to generate accurate estimates of marginal cost. Finally, marginal cost pricing entails myriad practical problems, given the patchwork of agencies with overlapping responsibilities for water supply and the almost inevitable conflict surrounding water management policy. Apart from these difficulties, the use of price as an allocation mechanism is effectively undercut by the fact that water is generally regarded as a basic necessity—even a right—not as an economic good.

Most nonprivate water purveyors determine their prices by using the average-cost pricing scheme devised by the American Water Works Association (AWWA). The sole purpose of this scheme, called the declining-block rate structure, is to recover the historical costs incurred in operating the system. Total annual historical costs are allocated among three different cost categories: customer, capacity, and commodity. These costs are then used to determine a fixed fee and a schedule of marginal prices.

Customer costs are those costs associated with the number of customers served (for example, meter installation, meter reading, and billings). Capacity costs are the capital costs associated with the size of the water supply system. Commodity costs are the costs incurred in actually delivering the water. However, in allocating capital costs, the AWWA guidelines distinguish between the amount of capacity necessary to meet peak demand and that necessary to meet average demand. Because water is supplied on demand, the water supply system must be large enough to deliver an adequate supply at those times of the year when demand is highest. These peak demand periods usually occur during hot, dry spells in the summer. Thus, the system must be designed to meet both average demand throughout the year and peak demand in summer months. Accordingly, the AWWA recommends that part of the capital costs be allocated to capacity costs and the remainder to commodity costs. Noting that the peak demand is usually twice the average demand, the recommendation is to allocate 50 percent to each.

Once all the costs have been allocated, capacity and customer costs are added together to determine a minimum fixed monthly fee for each

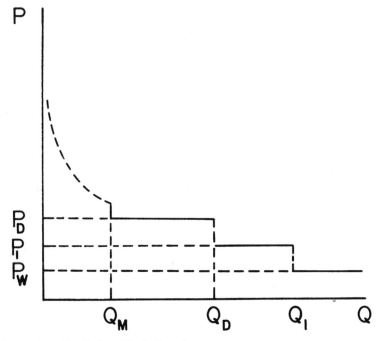

Figure 2.1 Declining Block Rate Structure

customer, based on the customer's meter size. This fixed fee usually
entitles the customer to a small amount of water that is less than his
or her normal monthly consumption. The marginal (per-unit) price for
quantities in excess of the fixed fee entitlement is then determined by
using commodity costs (including 50 percent of the capital costs) and
the expected yearly quantities of water used by wholesale, intermedi-
ate, and domestic users. The result is a three-price system in which
the marginal price depends on the amount of water used. Thus, the
individual consumer faces a price structure like that depicted in Figure
2.1. Here Q_m is the water allotted under the minimum charge. Since
the minimum charge is fixed, the price per unit for any amount less
than Q_m depends only on the quantity used (the curve is a rectangular
hyperbola between the origin and Q_m). Between Q_m and Q_D, the customer pays P_D per unit; between Q_D and Q_I the price drops to P_I; and
for quantities in excess of Q_I, the price drops further to P_W.

In short, the price structure is typically determined by a scheme
that reflects fixed, historical costs. Since these costs constitute the bulk
of the costs of supplying water, the price structure is rather unresponsive to changes in water quantities used, particularly in the short run,
when the size of the supply system is fixed. Furthermore, even when
the system is operating at or beyond its designed capacity, price is
rarely used to decrease demand. Instead, water agencies rely on such

devices as moratoriums on new hookups, rationing, and pleas for conservation, while plans are made to increase capacity. Therefore, the water supply and demand process is, in the short run, one in which the individual consumer, faced with *a given price structure,* must decide how much water to consume.

The total demand on a water supply system is the sum of the individual demands of the different types of consumers. Since the water demanded by these consumers is used for different purposes, the determinants of demand for each type of consumer will differ. The types of water users in our sample of districts and communities include residential, commercial, industrial, agricultural, and public authority consumers. In the theoretical development to which we now turn, we will consider each type separately.

The typical residential consumer is a household living in a one-family dwelling. The amount of water demanded by such a household is determined by the intersection of its demand curve with the price structure discussed above. Assuming that this demand curve lies to the right of Q_m, as in Figure 2.2, the price on which the consumer bases his or her decision is the real marginal price of water. The fixed minimum is a price that must be paid to receive any water at all and is not marginal to the consumer's decision.

The position of the demand curve depends on the price of water, consumer tastes, household characteristics, and income. The income elasticity of demand for water may be significant, because as family income increases, households typically purchase water-using devices, such as garbage disposals and, for the very wealthy, swimming pools. They also buy larger houses on larger lots.

Climate also plays an important part in determining the position of the demand curve. Areas with hot, dry climates will, ceteris paribus, demand more water than other areas. Climate also creates seasonal variations in water demand, with greater demand in the summer, when temperatures are higher and rainfall lower than at other times of the year. We see, then, that we can write that $q_r^i = f(P, Y_i, S)$, where q_r^i is the quantity of water demanded by residential household i, P is the real marginal price of water, Y_i is the disposable income of the ith household, and S represents seasonal factors, such as rainfall and temperature.

The other types of water users have in common the fact that the water demanded is an input in the production of goods and services; the main differences among them are the nature of the good or service produced and the production technology. Commerical users demand water for indirect input into the selling of goods and services; industrial users, for direct input into the production of goods; public authority users, for input into the production of public goods and services; and irrigational users, for direct input into the production of

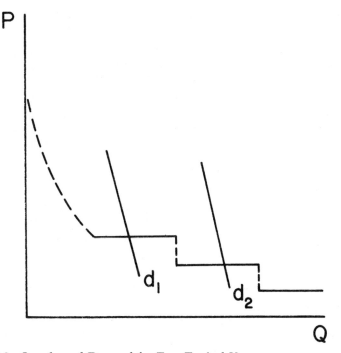

Figure 2.2   Supply and Demand for Two Typical Users

agricultural goods. Water demanded by these users is a derived demand,[6] and in analyzing this demand we must consider the quantities of the final goods and services produced, as well as the prices of the other inputs to production.

A typical commercial consumer is more difficult to define than a residential consumer, because the commercial category includes such diverse businesses as restaurants, medical offices, and retail stores of various types. The factors that affect the demand for water in these establishments are the quantities of the goods and services they provide, the price of water, and the prices of other inputs. For example, water is demanded by restaurants for preparation of food and drinks, cleaning of equipment, and use of restrooms by customers and employees. Obviously, the volume of business the restaurant is doing has a large influence on the amount of water that it will use.

The price of inputs other than water and the demand for the final goods and services also influence the amount of water used. To continue with the restaurant example, suppose the price of water goes up. Then, ceteris paribus, one would expect the quantity of water demanded by the restaurant to decrease. Conversely, if the prices of other inputs for which water is a substitute or complement in production go up while the price of water remains constant, the amount of water demanded will increase or decrease depending on whether water is a substitute or complement (respectively). For example, when the price of ground coffee increased dramatically several years ago, many restaurants raised the price of coffee and limited (or charged for) refills. If this led to a decrease in coffee sales, as expected, then the quantity of water demanded by a restaurant probably also decreased, since water is a complement to ground coffee in the production of a cup of coffee. Hence, the price of water relative to the prices of other inputs is also important in determining the demand for water by a restaurant.

Finally, the level of output of the goods and services provided (determined by demand) affects the quantity of water demanded, because the higher this level, ceteris paribus, the more incentive there is to employ larger quantities of all inputs. In this respect, the demand for water can be thought of as a derived demand. To summarize, if q_c^i is the quantity of water demanded by commercial user i, P_w is the real marginal price of water, P_s is a vector of real prices for the relevant substitutes and complements of water, and Q is the quantity of the final goods and services provided, then, $q_c^i = f(P_w, P_s, Q)$.

The factors affecting the demand for water by the typical industrial user are much the same as those for commercial users. The only real differences between commercial water use and industrial water use are the way water is used in the final production process and the quantities of water demanded. Thus, for industrial users, $q_m^i = f(P_w, P_s, Q)$, where q_m^i is the quantity of water demanded by industrial user i, and the other variables are as defined above.

Unfortunately, some of the variables discussed above for commercial and industrial users are almost impossible to calculate on an aggregate basis. For example, the cost of obtaining monthly measures of the output for the diverse commercial establishments in any city would be prohibitive. In fact, the only variable readily available is the price of water. However, some water use by the commercial or industrial user may be seasonal in nature. To the extent that this holds true, seasonal variables will contain some of the cyclical variation that would have been captured by Q, the volume of output. Of course, seasonal variables will not capture variation caused by other factors, such as an economic recession.

Public authority water use differs from commercial and industrial use in that the goods and services produced are publicly provided at no profit. The government can be viewed either as a producer earning no profit or as an entity that produces a target level of output and is constrained by the amount of tax dollars available. If the government acts as a producer of goods, then it is still presumably interested in supplying these goods and services in the most efficient manner; therefore, public authority users should respond to changes in the price of water, ceteris paribus, as well as to changes in the prices of substitutes and complements for water in the production of public goods and services. Moreover, since government expenditures are financed by taxes, the more tax dollars available, ceteris paribus, the greater the incentive to use more of all inputs, including water. Some public authority water use is also seasonal in nature, for example, the quantity of water demanded for watering highway rights-of-way and landscaping around government buildings; consequently, seasonal variables should be included as a determinant of public authority water demand.

If the government is viewed as a producer of a target level of goods operating under a tax budget constraint, the consequences of an increase in the price of water are basically the same: less water will be used, taxes will be raised, or the target level of output will be lowered. Price increases for substitutes and complements of water will have the same results. Therefore, regardless of which view we take, $q_p^i = f(P_w, P_s, T, S)$, where q_p^i is the quantity of water demanded by public authority user i; P_w, P_s, and S are as defined above, and T is real tax dollars available to the particular public authority account. Once again, some of the variables—in this case, P_s and T—are not readily available.

The determinants of the agricultural demand for water include the price of water; the price and quantities of the crops it is used to produce; the type of crop grown; environmental characteristics, such as soil condition and climate; technical determinants, such as water quality; and the prices of other factors of production.

Climate has much the same effect on agricultural demand for water as on residential demand. Users in hot, dry areas will demand more water, ceteris paribus, and more water will be demanded in the summer months than in the cooler months. Moreover, crop rotations are seasonal, and seasonal variables, such as rainfall and temperature, should partly capture these effects. Since soil conditions and water quality are constant in the short run for any given water supply system, $q_a^i = f(P_w, P_s, Q, P_o, S)$, where q_a^i is the water demanded by the ith agricultural consumer; and P_w, P_s, Q, P_o, and S are as defined above. Again, P_s, Q, and P_o, are not readily available.

Given this framework, we turn to the price elasticities for the different types of water use. In brief, the demand for water by residential users should be price-inelastic for two reasons. First, there is no close substitute for water in most of its uses. A certain minimum amount of water is necessary to sustain human life and for human hygiene and health. Washing dishes and watering lawns also require water. Second, the amount of money spent on water is usually a very small percentage of the average family budget.

In contrast, since water is an input to production for the other user

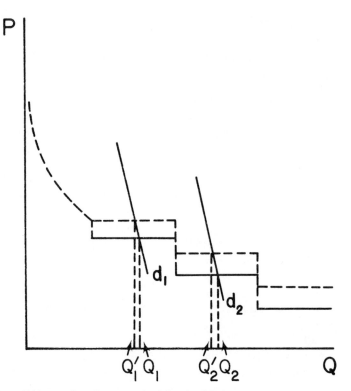

Figure 2.3   Effects of an Increase in Marginal Prices

categories, the price elasticity of water may be higher than for residential users. For example, the elasticity of demand for agriculture may be higher, because in the long run crops that are less water-intensive can be substituted for current crops. The demand characteristics, however, depend on the elasticity of demand for the crops that can be grown, as well as on the characteristics of the aggregate supply.

What then is the role of conservation measures? In principle, conservation measures are of two types: those that alter supply conditions and those that attempt to reduce demand "artificially." The former include raising marginal prices, imposing surcharges for water consumed in excess of an allotted amount, rationing consumption, and imposing moratoriums on new hookups to the system. Raising marginal prices will reduce water demand as long as the price elasticity of water is less than zero, as shown in Figure 2.3. Surcharges also alter the price structure but in a different manner. The usual practice is to offer a certain amount of water at the prevailing marginal prices and then to increase sharply the marginal price for units of water in excess of the base amount, as shown in Figure 2.4. Rationing limits water use by threatening to eliminate all water deliveries if the user consumes more than an allotted amount. A moratorium does not directly

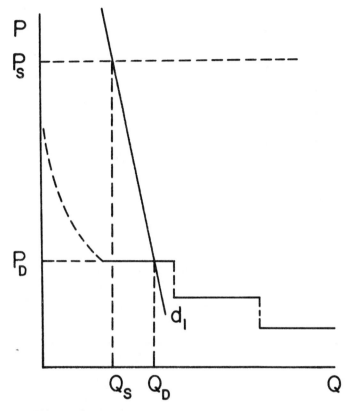

Figure 2.4 Effects of a Surcharge

affect users who already have water service, but it prevents additional hookups to the system. Moratoriums, however, may affect the water consumption of present users indirectly by providing information that water is in short supply.

Conservation measures that affect demand include advertising to inform consumers of the water shortage and to promote conservation, educating consumers in how to conserve water, and passing legislation to prohibit certain uses of water (such as car washing) under threat of punishment. All of these measures attempt to reduce demand by shifting the demand curve, as shown in Figure 2.5. Thus, the demand functions derived earlier must be modified to include the appropriate conservation measures.

Earlier we reviewed research on altering the demand curve by changing consumer attitudes. What is the empirical evidence for the impact of changes in price?

Economic incentives have been shown to have a modest impact on water consumption. Metered as opposed to flat-rate billing appears to discourage gross wastefulness, according to the results of a time series

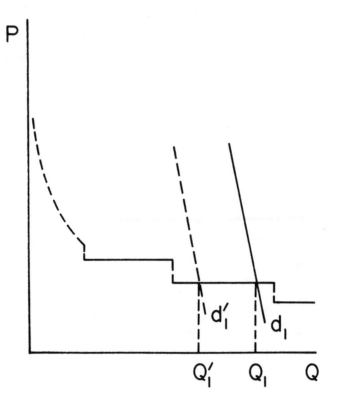

Figure 2.5   Effects of Nonprice Conservation Measures

natural experiment conducted in Boulder, Colorado (Hanke and Boland 1971). In 1961 Boulder switched from flat-rate to metered billing,
resulting in an immediate decrease in residential water consumption.
Moreover, consumption had not climbed back to previous levels after
seven years. Despite this encouraging finding, variations in rates with
the metered system do not appear to have large effects (for example,
see Hanke and Boland 1971 and Turnovsky 1969), perhaps because the
rates charged for water have generally been relatively low. It is only
recently that purveyors in the West have been forced by drought conditions to experiment with new and higher rate structures.

Apart from the economic incentives associated with it, metered billing acts as a monitoring device; it can serve both to enhance awareness of consumption and to provide feedback on attempts to alter
usage. However, water (and other utility) bills have at least two draw-
backs as a source of feedback. First, they report only the total amount
of resource used in a way that cannot be disaggregated by specific
sources of consumption within households. Second, the feedback is
delayed since bills are typically received long after the consumption
behavior has taken place.

The second of these problems can be alleviated by providing the consumer with more frequent feedback. In one study involving energy consumption, Seligman, Darley, and Becker (forthcoming) asked two groups of Twin Rivers, New Jersey, residents (living in identical housing units) to conserve. Members of the control group received no indication of how well they were doing, while members of the experimental group were supplied with a daily percentage score that informed them whether they were consuming electricity at a higher, lower, or equivalent rate compared to the previous month's consumption (adjusted for temperature fluctuations). The experimental group reduced electricity consumption by 10.5 percent, relative to the control group. In a subsequent study residents who were given an explicit, difficult conservation goal (to reduce electricity usage by 20 percent), in addition to feedback, achieved an energy savings of 13 percent.

While individual feedback can be used to compare consumption to standards or goals based on previous personal usage, its effectiveness may be reduced if the individual realized how minute, in absolute terms, such savings actually are. McClelland (1977) has experimented with group feedback and its effect on energy consumption. Four groups of student-housing residents at the University of Colorado were offered a competitive incentive to conserve, and feedback was provided to all of the groups about the performance of each. The group that conserved the most electricity over a month received $80. It was found that the group feedback, coupled with the incentive, resulted in a large reduction of energy consumption by one of the groups, but no appreciable reduction by the others. Apparently, the competitive feedback served to reinforce the most successful group in its efforts, but at the same time indicated to the other groups that their attempts were ineffective, and hence discouraged continued effort.

Where does this leave us? Perhaps most important, in analyzing water conservation campaigns, we must recognize that the market for water is one in which price is exogenously determined. Social-psychological perspectives and research suggest that conservation campaigns addressing appropriate consumer attitudes should affect the demand curve for water and consequently alter consumption. Economic theory and research suggest that consumers should respond to the price of water and that conservation campaigns aimed at changing the supply curve should alter consumption. In addition, the market model shows how consumption may be affected by income and seasonal factors. With these preliminaries in hand, we can turn to our data and the story they tell.

3

Local responses to the drought

Introduction

One has only to scan local newspapers published during the 1976–1977 drought to discover that the adequacy of water supplies was a common concern prompting numerous efforts to reduce consumption. Beyond such general observations, there is little documentation of the conservation programs that were actually implemented and how they varied across the state. Moreover, given the substantial decentralization of water-related public policy, there is good reason to expect significant variation in the ways water districts responded. Indeed, we have already hinted at the diversity of programs in earlier chapters.

In this chapter we describe the range of conservation programs undertaken in our sample of water districts. We will see that local programs varied enormously in both conservation strategies and tactics. While a description of these programs should be of considerable interest in its own right, the material presented in this chapter provides an essential foundation for the causal analyses that follow.

Readers unfamiliar with social policy and programs surrounding water use may feel a bit overwhelmed by our detailed description of programs. Consequently, we will start by examining two large water districts that differed enormously in their conservation efforts. At the very least, this comparison will suggest the extent of local variation in conservation programs.

The Marin Municipal Water District (MMWD) serves twelve communities in Marin County, and its conservation efforts have been cited by the California Department of Water Resources (CDWR 1977) as the most successful in the state. MMWD initiated a water supply management program in June 1973, when it issued a moratorium on new service connections, in part to insure equity between present and future generations of water users. Following a series of workshops launched in the spring of 1974, a Water Supply Task Force was formed to collect information in four areas: wastewater reuse, desalinization, conservation, and natural supply. Efforts to educate the public included newspaper advertisements informing consumers about avail-

35

able supplies and discouraging waste, a poster contest for children, a calendar containing conservation hints and a booklet on conservation gardening, and a two-acre drought-tolerant demonstration garden. The MMWD continued these efforts throughout 1975.

In a cooperative effort with large users, MMWD studied the use of mechanical devices to curtail water consumption. The results of these studies formed the basis of Marin's "retrofit program," which has been widely praised by the Department of Water Resources (CDWR 1976a, 1976b). In practice, the retrofit program evolved from a field experience which enlisted the aid of college students to distribute and install dye pills and plastic toilet bottles, low-flow shower heads, and pressure-reducing valves. These initial efforts were judged so success-ful that Marin used billing inserts to encourage additional customers to participate in this free program. Other provisions (CDWR 1976b) in Marin's predrought program were:

1. Evaluation of landscaping plans in specified areas, particularly for government agencies and large users; in such areas, irriga-tion systems had to be approved by the district.
2. Evaluation of all proposed conservation measures.
3. Recycling requirements for car-washing facilities.
4. Required use of reclaimed wastewater when available at reason-able cost, reducing potable water consumption.
5. Required use of recycling and water-saving devices as made possible by new technology.
6. Provision of technical help to large public/private irrigation con-sumers and recommendations for improving irrigation practices and/or landscape alterations.
7. Provision of technical help to industrial/commercial users upon consideration of their unique conditions.
8. Seminars and conferences on water-saving gardening tech-niques.
9. Other educational programs, e.g., extensive literature distribu-tion, restaurant cooperation, and programs designed for multi-family dwellings and apartment complexes.
10. Performance review of MMWD water supply system.

Some specific instances of public education included presentation of the film "Water Follies—A Soak Opera" at schools, community gath-erings, and colleges; a slide show on drought-tolerant gardening given by the Environmental Forum (a private group); a water conservation county fair; information displays at libraries, city hall, and other pub-lic offices; and production of promotional stickers and buttons.

With the onset of the drought, Marin turned to rationing as an im-mediate method of reducing consumption and prepared a set of guide-lines for water agency personnel:

1. Designate a coordinator of all rationing/conservation activities.
2. Define the water supply situation and give notice as early as possible to consumers of rationing requirements.
3. Insure positive and complete exposure by maintaining good relations with communications media.
4. Check your distribution system for operational changes, i.e., interties, fire protection, decreased hydraulic peaking requirements, supplemental water movement requirements, etc.
5. Consumer accounts—define classifications and special needs.
6. Prepare for an increase in consumer phone calls, investigation requests, consumers coming to office, water saving ideas, and bill disputes.
7. Define essential (sanitary or domestic) water needs from non-essential (turf irrigation—non-commercial).
8. Consider alternate water supplies for non-essential needs and implement their uses, i.e., wastewater truck hauling programs.
9. Prepare for variations in quality. Additional testing may be required for stagnant conditions in storage tanks, salinity, etc.
10. Prepare for use of all available water, i.e., recreation lakes, fishery enhancement, etc.
11. Anticipate a greater reduction in usage and revenue than required.

In February 1976 Marin introduced an ordinance establishing procedures for service disconnection in cases of wasteful water use. Mandatory rationing followed in March 1976. Marin also invoked watering restrictions with the goal of a 25 percent reduction in consumption through the prohibition of nonessential use (for example, employing hydrant water for fire drills or construction, refilling swimming pools, washing hard surfaces).

During the second year of the drought, when it became apparent that the original rationing program was insufficient, Marin designed an entirely new approach to attain a necessary 57 percent cutback. Rather than directly control how consumers used water, MMWD decided to establish consumer water allotments for each billing period, with severe penalty rates charged to violators: $10.00/HCF (hundred cubic feet) if over the first level, $50.00/HCF if over the second. Customers received explicit information about these rationing procedures, along with a host of conservation suggestions. MMWD staff believe the modified rationing program was well received by consumers.

Coupled with these rather stringent measures, MMWD's 1977 annual progress report states that an estimated 90 percent of district customers obtained conservation kits. Further actions included the construction of an intertie with the East Bay Municipal Utility District (EBMUD) to provide an emergency source of water, and the expanded use of wastewater.

These conservation efforts were probably the most aggressive in the state. In marked contrast, San Diego, with a population six times as large, simply mailed with the July 1976 bills a leaflet recommending both energy and water conservation. These leaflets were the sum total of San Diego's conservation program.

While it would no doubt be interesting to explore why Marin and San Diego differed so greatly in their conservation programs and more generally to consider explanations for the diversity in conservation programs across the state, several serious obstacles prevent us from doing so. The causal processes are quite complex, involving a mixture of objective factors, such as the sufficiency of supplies, the environmental consequences of alternative water policies, sources of revenue, and the costs of providing water. Political aspects that must be considered include the membership of water district governing boards and the links between water policy and local growth. In this context, a rather different research design would have been required with data collected well before the 1976–1977 drought. At the very least, we would have had to be in the field during the early 1970s or have undertaken a large number of retrospective interviews with the principal actors. For many of the most important political considerations, archival material (for example, in newspapers) is at best incomplete. Therefore, the adoption of alternative water conservation programs will not be the main concern here, although later in this chapter we will make a few observations in this respect. Rather, taking the content and timing of conservation programs as given, we will document their nature, and in the next chapter examine their impact on water consumption.

A typology of water conservation programs

Conservation programs, according to the California Department of Water Resources, can be organized into three broad categories in terms of how they are instituted (CDWR 1976b):

1. *Voluntary* action by individual users.
2. *Institutional* action by government or water agencies (for example, pricing, educational programs, and leakage repair programs).
3. *Proscriptive* action (that is, the imposition of laws and regulations).

Table 3.1 classifies particular water conservation practices according to the type of implementation (voluntary, institutional, or proscrip-

Table 3.1 **Methods of Implementation for Various Conservation Techniques**

	Voluntary	*Institutional*	*Proscriptive*
TECHNIQUES THAT REDUCE WATER CONSUMPTION	Education Retrofitting Recycle water Restrict outside use	Education Retrofitting Recycle water Restrict outside use Rationing Warnings and citations Service shutoffs Prohibitions on new connections Metering Pricing	Education Retrofitting Recycle water Restrict outside use Rationing Warnings and citations Service shutoffs Prohibitions on new connections Plumbing code changes

tive). Although this is only one of many forms in which water conservation programs can be conceptually organized, the three implementation mechanisms reflect in part the thinking of the California Department of Water Resources and, therefore, presumably represent important categories for public policy. Note that several conservation practices are listed in more than one category (for example, education and prohibitions on new connections).

It should be immediately apparent that the three implementation forms cannot be placed along any single substantive dimension. Moreover, it is difficult to imagine a multidimensional scheme in which one approach dominates the other two. That is, it is extremely unlikely that any single implementation form will be superior across all of its net benefits, especially when future consequences are taken into account (Howe 1979, 151–168). For example, voluntary implementation lacks formal sanctions, although significant peer pressure of various sorts may materialize. Yet voluntary programs are not necessarily less expensive to launch, and their impact on consumption is difficult to anticipate. Alternatively, under institutional implementation, increases in the unit price of water may actually reduce water district revenues and consequently may be rather costly from the district's perspective. However, the impact of price increases is probably more predictable. In this context, the California Department of Water Resources suggests the trade-offs involved in different kinds of conservation programs but offers little firm guidance on which mix of approaches to implement. Table 3.2 summarizes this information.

Consider the first four methods to reduce water consumption: water-saving plumbing, retrofitting, new technology, and efficient ir-

Table 3.2 Methods of Urban Water Conservation: Implementation, Advantages, and Disadvantages

Means to Reduce Water Consumption	*Implementation*	*Advantages*	*Disadvantages*
Water-saving plumbing fixtures in new and replacement construction	Proscriptive	1. Mechanical devices render savings despite user habits. 2. Reduced wastewater conveyance and treatment load.	1. Possible resistance to redesign and retooling to manufacture water-conserving devices. 2. Drain pipe slope tolerances are more critical. 3. Initially, consumers may resist acceptance. 4. Higher unit cost of water-saving devices, until demand increases production and reduces cost. 5. May cause blockage problems in marginal sewage collection systems.
Modification (retrofit) of existing plumbing fixtures	Proscriptive, voluntary, institutional	1. Many devices are nominal in cost. 2. Conservation of water and energy in existing facilities makes rapid, widespread savings possible.	1. Inconsistent effectiveness of retrofit devices because of variable design and construction of existing fixtures. 2. Consumer removal or tampering with retrofit

		Advantages	Disadvantages
		3. Water savings mechanically effected. 4. Reduced wastewater conveyance and treatment load.	devices because of suspected poor performance. 3. Some devices require skilled installation and/or follow-up adjustment. 4. May cause blockage problems in marginal sewage collection systems.
New technology	Voluntary, institutional	1. Greater water and energy savings than conventional devices. 2. Reduced wastewater conveyance and treatment load.	1. Uncertain long-term effectiveness. 2. Consumer and institutional resistance to innovations. 3. Higher initial costs. 4. Conformance with existing codes and regulations may require changes or variations. 5. May cause blockage problems in marginal sewage collection systems.
Efficient irrigation using automatic devices	Voluntary	1. Healthier plants. 2. Decreased maintenance. 3. Mechanical type savings.	1. Periodic adjustments required. 2. High initial cost.

Table 3.2 Methods of Urban Water Conservation: Implementation, Advantages, and Disadvantages (*Continued*)

Means to Reduce Water Consumption	*Implementation*	*Advantages*	*Disadvantages*
Native and other low-water-using plants in landscaping	Voluntary, institutional	1. Established native and other low-water-using plants need little or no irrigation. 2. Established plants need little care.	1. General preference for exotic plants. 2. Narrow selection of native plants in nurseries. 3. Difficulty establishing some low-water-using plants and lack of knowledge about care. 4. Somewhat higher costs because native and other low-water-using plants are not readily available.
Leak detection and repair of water agencies' distribution system	Institutional	1. Reduces unaccounted water losses. 2. Reduces undermining damage to streets, sidewalks, and other structures.	1. Because leaking water often percolates to usable groundwater, water agencies sometimes ignore losses. 2. Low cost of lost water may not equal cost of detection and repair.
Leak detection and repair of consumers' systems	Voluntary, institutional	1. Can reduce other home repair costs, such as those from wood rot. 2. Many leaks are simple	1. Difficult to induce flat-rate consumers and apartment dwellers to repair leaks.

Method	Type	Advantages	Disadvantages
		and inexpensive to repair. 3. Reduces operational costs.	2. Could be expensive if consumer needs professional service.
Metering	Institutional	1. Easier to implement than some of the other methods. 2. May induce consumers to begin conserving water.	1. Consumer objection. 2. High capital cost. 3. Requires changes in rate structure and billing.
Pricing	Institutional	1. May be relatively easy to implement. 2. Affects all customers. 3. Potentially strong inducement for consumers to save.	1. Consumer objection. 2. Requires well-designed pricing structure to achieve effective, equitable pricing. 3. Often require changes in rate structure, meter reading, and billing.
Sewer service charges based on water consumption	Institutional	1. More equitable than flat-rate basis to pay operational cost of sewage treatment. 2. Dual benefits of reduced water consumption and wastewater flow.	1. Requires well-designed rate structure. 2. Inside and outside water consumption must be segregated.

Table 3.2 Methods of Urban Water Conservation: Implementation, Advantages, and Disadvantages (*Continued*)

Means to Reduce Water Consumption	Implementation	Advantages	Disadvantages
Education	Voluntary, proscriptive, institutional	1. Induces voluntary water conservation. 2. Changes wasteful consumption habits. 3. Achieves long-lasting results by influencing younger generation. 4. Ensures greater success and acceptance of other water-saving means.	1. Requires coordinated efforts of local and state agencies.

Source: California Department of Water Resources, "Water Conservation in California," Bulletin 198, May 1976.

rigation. All involve some mechanical solution that, once introduced, automatically reduces water use regardless of consumers' habitual practices; this is an obvious asset. However, such built-in conservation means require professional installation and/or maintenance of both equipment and the water system. Furthermore, technical "fixes" often require that consumers bear the large capital costs. The few communities in our sample that chose these techniques generally did so in response either to severe drought effects or to substantial, ongoing supply problems.

Detection and repair of leaks in agencies' distribution systems and/or consumers' water systems may result in large water savings, considering the East Bay Municipal Utility District's (EBMUD) estimate that over 1,000 gallons of water per day can pour through a leak only $1/16$ inch in diameter. However, in many cases the inconvenience and cost make such measures unpopular. Only a few large districts in our sample (e.g., EBMUD, Los Angeles, Ventura) initiated leak detection programs. High costs relative to agency budgets apparently eliminated this option for smaller districts. However, several smaller agencies offered their customers free technical assistance in leak detection and repair.

The additional institutional means of metering, pricing, and sewer charges typically result in immediate and direct costs to consumers. Consequently, they are often resisted by public officials and users. Yet metering and price increases in particular have been found to be quite effective in inducing water conservation; several communities in our sample incorporated effective pricing schemes into their conservation programs.

Native landscaping and education appear to be among the most readily accepted conservation methods; this and their other advantages are quite compelling. Both methods are believed to stimulate public awareness, with comprehensive educational efforts possibly having the greatest potential for far-reaching effects. Many communities used these techniques throughout the 1970s to increase consumer awareness of the need to conserve.

In summary, it should now be readily apparent that the institution of water conservation programs typically involves a complicated mix of costs and benefits. Measuring and weighing the trade-offs are extremely difficult, and even with these tasks accomplished, there may well be no single strategy that excels. Moreover, all conservation programs must run the gauntlet of local politics, while at the same being subjected to a variety of legal and administrative constraints. In this context, we are unaware of any formal plan to guide local water districts in their decision making and suspect that the patchwork pattern of programs instituted across the state results from uncertainty about how best to proceed. Indeed, one of the critical reasons for undertaking the impact analyses presented later is to improve the quality of information available to local water districts. At the very least, we hope to provide some systematic insights into what works.

Characteristics of the geographic sample

Table 3.3 presents characteristics of the fifty-seven geographic units whose conservation programs we will discuss. The sample represents a cross-section of areas of California across a variety of parameters: location, population, income, education, and climate. Figure 3.1 locates the units in terms of hydrologic and geographic regions. Note that, in most instances, water district boundaries correspond closely to the boundaries of communities, towns, or cities.

The northern community of Cutten had the smallest number of residents (2,228); Los Angeles was the most populous, with 2,816,061 residents. Within these limits population figures vary widely. Palm Springs had the smallest number of people per household (2.21), while Coachella had the largest (4.49). In twenty-seven communities median family income was less than $10,000 annually; in twenty-six communities, median family income was more than $10,000. Limiting our attention to persons twenty-five years of age or older, in only eight communities was the median number of years of schooling less than twelve.

The southern desert communities and the northern Humboldt County communities represent the extremes of the climate continuum. The desert communities averaged less than 0.40 inch of rain per month, and average monthly temperatures hovered in the low 70s. In Humboldt County nearly ten times as much rain fell each month, and average monthly temperatures were almost twenty degrees lower.

While these characteristics of our sample provide a good sense of the variation in the areas where the impact of conservation programs will be explored, their main import will be apparent somewhat later. We will use these and other community characteristics to help us understand the differential effects of local conservation programs. For example, one might anticipate that district populations characterized by high socioeconomic status (SES) may be more responsive to educational conservation programs than low-SES districts.

Figure 3.1 Major Hydrologic and Geographic Regions of California

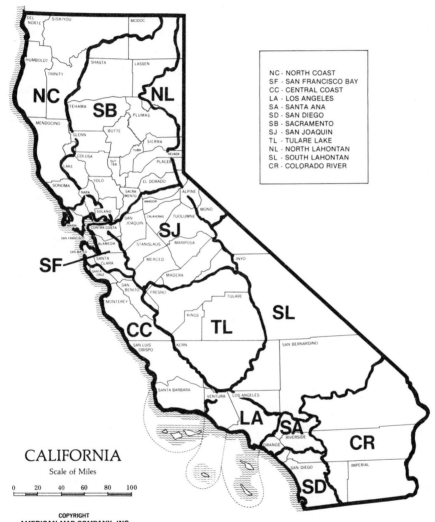

NC · NORTH COAST
SF · SAN FRANCISCO BAY
CC · CENTRAL COAST
LA · LOS ANGELES
SA · SANTA ANA
SD · SAN DIEGO
SB · SACRAMENTO
SJ · SAN JOAQUIN
TL · TULARE LAKE
NL · NORTH LAHONTAN
SL · SOUTH LAHONTAN
CR · COLORADO RIVER

CALIFORNIA

Scale of Miles

0   20   40   60   80   100

Contract No. 18638

TABLE 3.3

CHARACTERISTICS OF THE SAMPLE DISTRICTS

COMMUNITY	HYDROLOGIC REGION[1]	POPULATION[2]	PERSONS/ HOUSEHOLD[2]	MEDIAN FAMILY INCOME (DOLLARS)[2]	MEDIAN # OF SCHOOL YEARS COMPLETED[2][3]	AVERAGE MONTHLY RAIN (INCHES)[6][7]	AVERAGE MONTHLY TEMP. (°F)[6][7]
Humboldt County							
Eureka	North Coastal	24,337	2.67	9,108	12.3	3.21	51.64
Arcata	North Coastal	8,985	2.90	10,141	12.6	3.21	51.64
Cutten	North Coastal	2,228	3.20	N.A.	N.A.	3.21	51.64
Northern Inland Comm.							
Susanville	North Lahontan	6,608	2.81	9,965	12.3	0.97	48.45
Marysville	Sacramento Valley	9,353	2.71	8,746	12.4	1.69	62.23
Grass Valley	Sacramento Valley	5,149	2.37	7,555	12.1	4.24	55.00
Paradise	Sacramento Valley	14,539	2.44	6,729	12.2	4.17	59.70
Central Valley							
Madera	San Joaquin Valley	16,044	3.18	7,846	10.7	0.87	61.32
Merced	San Joaquin Valley	22,670	3.04	8,323	12.3	0.98	61.33
Woodland	Sacramento Valley	20,677	3.09	9,635	12.3	1.64	60.53
West Sacramento[4]	Sacramento Valley	23,752	2.99	9,009	11.7	1.30	60.58
Davis	Sacramento Valley	23,488	3.02	11,858	16.1	1.37	59.35
San Francisco Bay Area							
San Jose W.W.[4]	San Francisco Bay	499,518	3.37	15,886	13.4	1.17	59.29
Marin Municipal W.D.[4]	San Francisco Bay	115,490	2.83	16,481	14.0	3.88	58.32
East Bay M.U.D. Includes:							
San Leandro	San Francisco Bay	68,698	2.85	11,938	12.2	2.04	56.50
Alameda Co. Inside[5]	San Francisco Bay	N.A.	N.A.	N.A.	N.A.	2.04	56.50
Oakland	San Francisco Bay	361,561	2.53	9,626	12.2	1.50	57.54
Emeryville	San Francisco Bay	2,681	2.41	9,548	10.4	1.95	57.27
Piedmont	San Francisco Bay	10,917	3.06	20,017	15.1	1.50	57.54
Berkeley	San Francisco Bay	116,716	2.32	9,987	14.3	1.95	57.27
Albany	San Francisco Bay	14,674	2.48	10,206	12.7	1.95	57.27
Walnut Creek	San Francisco Bay	39,844	2.81	14,647	13.2	2.25	56.47
Lafayette	San Francisco Bay	20,484	3.12	17,635	14.2	2.24	56.47
Contra Costa Co. Inside, Walnut Creek Office[5]	San Francisco Bay	N.A.	N.A.	N.A.	N.A.	2.25	56.47
Alameda	San Francisco Bay	70,968	2.70	10,674	12.4	1.50	57.54
Richmond	San Francisco Bay	79,043	3.00	10,363	12.1	1.76	58.08
El Cerrito	San Francisco Bay	25,190	2.76	13,358	12.8	1.76	58.08
San Pablo	San Francisco Bay	21,461	2.79	9,057	11.2	1.76	58.08
Pinole-Hercules[5]	San Francisco Bay	16,102	3.55	13,113	12.5	1.44	60.19
Crockett	San Francisco Bay	3,698	2.68	11,181	12.1	1.44	60.20
Contra Costa Co. Inside, Richmond Office[5]	San Francisco Bay	N.A.	N.A.	N.A.	N.A.	1.76	58.08

TABLE 3.3
(CON'T)
CHARACTERISTICS OF THE SAMPLE DISTRICTS

COMMUNITY	HYDROLOGIC REGION [1]	POPULATION [2]	PERSONS/HOUSEHOLD [2]	MEDIAN FAMILY INCOME (DOLLARS) [2]	MEDIAN # OF SCHOOL YEARS COMPLETED [2,3]	AVERAGE MONTHLY RAIN (INCHES) [6,7]	AVERAGE MONTHLY TEMP. (°F) [6,7]
Monterey Bay Area							
Watsonville	Central Coastal	14,569	2.83	8,993	11.3	1.71	55.84
Santa Cruz	Central Coastal	32,076	2.41	8,516	12.4	2.33	56.62
Monterey[4]	Central Coastal	50,136	2.56	11,594	13.3	1.40	56.18
Santa Barbara County							
Carpinteria	Central Coastal	6,982	3.22	9,152	12.3	1.57	60.00
Summerland	Central Coastal	2,741	2.51	10,864	12.9	1.54	60.18
Montecito	Central Coastal	8,027	2.69	14,746	14.4	1.54	60.06
Goleta[4]	Central Coastal	63,077	3.12	11,670	13.5	1.56	60.19
Ventura County							
Santa Paula	Los Angeles	18,001	3.16	8,941	11.5	1.57	59.75
Port Hueneme	Los Angeles	14,295	3.29	8,360	12.2	1.22	60.88
Oxnard	Los Angeles	71,225	3.48	9,892	12.1	1.17	60.85
Ventura	Los Angeles	55,797	2.96	11,552	12.5	1.30	60.91
Greater Los Angeles							
Pomona	Los Angeles	87,384	3.04	10,014	12.2	1.48	62.50
Burbank	Los Angeles	88,871	2.55	11,502	12.4	1.48	63.56
Alhambra	Los Angeles	62,125	2.43	11,004	12.4	1.52	64.04
Los Angeles	Los Angeles	2,816,061	2.68	10,535	12.4	1.28	65.11
Greater San Diego							
San Diego	San Diego	696,769	2.80	10,166	12.5	0.82	63.80
Escondido	San Diego	36,792	2.85	9,066	12.4	1.22	62.38
Imperial Beach[4]	San Diego	88,145	3.20	9,177	12.3	0.82	63.77
Oceanside	San Diego	40,494	2.98	8,184	12.3	0.99	60.98
Desert Communities							
El Centro	Colorado River	19,272	3.32	10,011	12.2	0.17	71.08
Blythe	Colorado River	7,047	3.47	9,808	12.1	0.31	70.87
Coachella	Colorado River	8,353	4.49	6,993	8.2	0.30	72.69
Indio	Colorado River	14,459	3.41	9,615	11.7	0.30	72.69
Palm Springs[4]	Colorado River	27,314	2.21	8,447	12.3	0.39	72.50

TABLE 3.3

(CON'T)

CHARACTERISTICS OF THE SAMPLE DISTRICTS

1. Refer to Figure 3.1 to locate the various hydrologic regions.

2. We obtained the population, persons per household, median family income and median number of school years completed figures from the 1970 federal census.

3. The median number of school years completed figure represents the median for persons twenty-five years of age or older.

4. These sample communities service additional area/communities outside their city limits. We calculated the census variables by matching census tract information with each water district's service area to the best of our ability.

5. These are four East Bay Municipal Utility District service area classifications. We computed all available census information.

6. We recorded the climatological information from monthly reports prepared by the National Oceanic and Atmospheric Administration for the Department of Commerce's National Climatic Center.

7. We selected the climatological data from the nearest National Weather Service Station for the communities without their own.

8. N.A. = not available.

An overview of conservation programs adopted

The first year for which we have conservation information is 1970, and for most communities, the data extend through June 1978. Tables 3.4, 3.5, and 3.6 show each community's actions during three distinct time periods, labeled predrought, drought, and postdrought. The pre-drought period (Table 3.4) begins in January 1970 and ends in December 1975. To capture the full range of programs instituted when genuine drought conditions began, we define the drought (Table 3.5) as extending from January 1976 through December 1977. The postdrought period (Table 3.6) starts in January 1978 and lasts until the last month for which data are available, usually June 1978.

The conservation technique of metering is used in 86 percent of our sample communities (see the bottoms of Tables 3.4, 3.5, and 3.6). This statistic is not surprising, since metering has long been acknowledged as a prerequisite for per-unit pricing practices, and these, in turn, are more likely than other pricing schemes to yield economic efficiencies.

The percentage of metered districts did not change over time; 86 percent of the districts had introduced metering long before the drought. Among those communities that had unmetered accounts, some have reportedly considered meter installation but have apparently met with consumer opposition.

Conservation education encompasses a broad spectrum of approaches. The California Department of Water Resources, in conjunction with the American Water Works Association, has published a catalog of educational materials available to water agencies planning conservation programs. (Figure 3.2 shows two pages from this catalog on bumper stickers and school programs.) Educational programs also can be implemented voluntarily, institutionally, or proscriptively. Many district officials believe that educational programs are quite effective, which perhaps explains why education was an extremely popular conservation technique, especially in response to the drought. Prior to the drought, 39 percent of the communities in our sample employed multimedia efforts to increase consumer awareness of water consumption; during the drought, 91 percent of the communities distributed educational literature, while other media efforts and educational programs were undertaken by 72 and 70 percent of the districts, respectively. Even communities experiencing few of the drought's effects typically initiated some form of an educational program. It is also interesting to note that, in contrast to metering, investment in conservation education dropped substantially after the drought. Only about

Figure 3.2   **Bumper Stickers and School Programs**

SAVE WATER SOAP TOGETHER
NATIVE PLANTS CONSERVE WATER
DIRTY CARS SAVE WATER

East Bay Municipal Utility District, P.O. Box 24055, Oakland, CA 94623 (415) 835-3000

CONSERVE WATER, SHARE A TUB WITH A FRIEND . . .
GROW GREENIES THAT DRINK LESS
GUTTER FLOODERS ARE ALL WET!
WATER IS LIFE . . . DON'T WASTE IT

Santa Clara Valley Water District, 5750 Almaden Expressway, San Jose, CA 95118 (408) 265-2600

SAVING WATER SAVES ENERGY
DO A GOOD TURN. SAVE WATER

Metropolitan Water District of Southern California, P.O. Box 45153, Los Angeles, CA 90054 (213) 626-4282

PEEL-OFF STICKERS

Four to seven mini-posters in two colors on one 3½" x 8" sheet.

Santa Clara Valley Water District, 5750 Almaden Expressway, San Jose, CA 95118 (408) 265-2600

North Marin County Water District, 999 Rush Creek Place, Novato, CA 94947 (415) 897-4133

A How You Can Help–Coloring Book
City of San Buenaventura

SAVE EVERY DROP

A 47 page 8½" x 11" black and white educational guide to water conservation for grades 1 through 3. Six pages of background information for the teacher and the remainder lesson plans and work sheets on all aspects of water use. Includes teacher's answer sheet and teacher's evaluation. Copyrighted by:

Goleta County Water District, P.O. Box 788, Goleta, CA 93017 (805) 967-6761

SAVE EVERY DROP

A 47 page 8½" x 11" black and white educational guide to water conservation for grades 4 through 6. Six pages of background information for the teacher and the remainder lesson plans and work sheets on all aspects of water use. Includes teacher's answer sheet Copyrighted by:

Goleta County Water District, P.O. Box 788, Goleta, CA 93017 (805) 964-6761

A CONSERVATION CERTIFICATE FOR ELEMENTARY SCHOOL USE

This is a three color 9 x 6" certificate with a conservation logo enlivening the diploma-like format. Also, a WATER CONSERVATION INSPECTOR'S card, 1¼ x 3½, for student.

Goleta County Water District, P.O. Box 788, Goleta, CA 93017 (805) 964-6761

THE OFFICIAL CAPTAIN HYDRO WATER CONSERVATION WORKBOOK

Multi-color cover and 32 pages of black and white comic book style story and student projects in water conservation. This 8½" x 11" booklet was enthusiastically received by students and teachers everywhere. Some orientation toward East Bay area. Suitable for upper elementary and above. A teachers'edition gives added projects and a large bibliography.

East Bay Municipal Utility District, P.O. Box 24055, Oakland, CA 94623 (415) 835-3000

WATER PLAY

Fourteen 8½" x 11" pages of puzzles and projects for the primary grade student. Half in full color, the remainder suitable for coloring.

East Bay Municipal Utility District, P.O. Box 24055, Oakland, CA 94623 (415) 835-3000

THE AMAZING WATER CONSERVATION ADVENTURES OF SUPERDROP – A COLORING BOOK

Every other page, a water-wasting monster and facing page, a water conservation message for both children and adults, cover red and blue on white. 12 black and white pages, 8½ x 11.

City of San Buenaventura, P.O. Box 99, Ventura, CA 93001 (805) 648-7881

TABLE 3.4

PREDROUGHT CONSERVATION PROGRAMS

COMMUNITY	METERING[1] A	B	C	CONSERVATION EDUCATION[2] A	B	C	CONSERVATION RETROFIT KITS PROVIDED	RECYCLED WATER USED	PLUMBING CODE CHANGES	RESTRICTED OUTSIDE USE	WARNINGS AND CITATIONS	SERVICE SHUTOFFS	RATIONING	WATER RATE SURCHARGE	PROHIBITIONS ON NEW CONNECTIONS	OTHER
Humboldt County																
Eureka	X															
Arcata	X															
Cutten	X															
Northern Inland Comm.																
Susanville	X															
Marysville		X														
Grass Valley			X													
Paradise	X															
Central Valley																
Madera						X										
Merced		X														
Woodland[4]		X														
West Sacramento[4]		X														
Davis		X														
San Francisco Bay Area																
San Jose W.W.[3][4]	X			X												
Marin Municipal W.D.[4]	X			X	X	X	X	X	X						X	X[6]
East Bay M.U.D. Includes:																
San Leandro	X			X	X	X		X								X[7]
Alameda Co. Inside[5]	X			X	X	X		X								X[7]
Oakland	X			X	X	X		X								X[7]
Emeryville	X			X	X	X		X								X[7]
Piedmont	X			X	X	X		X								X[7]
Berkeley	X			X	X	X		X								X[7]
Albany	X			X	X	X		X								X[7]
Walnut Creek	X			X	X	X		X								X[7]
Lafayette	X			X	X	X		X								X[7]
Contra Costa Co. Inside,	X			X	X	X										
Walnut Creek Office[5]	X			X	X	X										X[7]
Alameda	X			X	X	X		X								X[7]
Richmond	X			X	X	X		X								X[7]
El Cerrito	X			X	X	X		X								X[7]
San Pablo	X			X	X	X		X								X[7]
Pinole-Hercules[5]	X			X	X	X		X								X[7]
Crockett	X			X	X	X		X								X[7]
Contra Costa Co[5] Inside,	X			X	X	X										
Richmond Office	X			X	X	X		X								X[7]

TABLE 3.4
PREDROUGHT CONSERVATION PROGRAMS
(CON'T)

COMMUNITY	METERING[1] A	B	C	CONSERVATION EDUCATION[2] A	B	C	CONSERVATION RETROFIT KITS PROVIDED	RECYCLED WATER USED	PLUMBING CODE CHANGES	RESTRICTED OUTSIDE USE	WARNINGS AND CITATIONS	SERVICE SHUTOFFS	RATIONING	WATER RATE SURCHARGE	PROHIBITIONS ON NEW CONNECTIONS	OTHER
Monterey Bay Area																
Watsonville[5]	X															
Santa Cruz	X															
Monterey	X														X	
Santa Barbara County																
Carpinteria	X															
Summerland	X														X	
Montecito	X			X										X	X	
Goleta[4]	X			X	X				X						X	X[8]
Ventura County																
Santa Paula	X															
Port Hueneme		X														
Oxnard	X			X	X	X										
Ventura	X			X	X	X		X								X[9]
Greater Los Angeles																
Pomona	X															
Burbank	X															
Alhambra	X															
Los Angeles	X			X												
Greater San Diego																
San Diego	X															
Escondido	X															
Imperial Beach[4]	X															
Oceanside	X															
Desert Communities																
El Centro	X															
Blythe	X															
Coachella	X			X	X	X		X								
Indio	X			X	X	X		X								
Palm Springs[4]	X			X			X									X[10]

TABLE 3.4

PREDROUGHT CONSERVATION PROGRAMS
(CON'T)

COMMUNITY	METERING[1]			CONSERVATION EDUCATION[2]			CONSERVATION RETROFIT KITS PROVIDED	RECYCLED WATER USED	PLUMBING CODE CHANGES	RESTRICTED OUTSIDE USE	WARNINGS AND CITATIONS	SERVICE SHUTOFFS	RATIONING	WATER RATE SURCHARGE	PROHIBITIONS ON NEW CONNECTIONS	OTHER
	A	B	C	A	B	C										
Total number of communities = 57																
Number of communities for each category	49	5	3	22	22	22	2	21	2	0	0	0	0	1	5	21
% of total number of communities	85.9	8.8	5.3	38.6	38.6	38.6	3.5	36.8	3.5	0	0	0	0	1.8	8.8	36.8

1. METERING: A = almost all accounts are metered; B = only commercial, industrial and other nonresidential accounts are metered; C = almost all accounts are unmetered.

2. CONSERVATION EDUCATION: A = printed literature; B = other media, e.g., radio, T.V., newspaper; C = educational programs for children and/or adults.

3. These agencies record consumption figures for inside/outside city limits. We analyzed inside/outside consumption separately, as though each represented a community.

4. The service areas for these water districts include more than one additional neighboring community. Unless consumption figures were recorded individually, e.g., East Bay Municipal Utility District, we analyzed the entire water district as one unit.

5. These are four East Bay Municipal Utility District service area classifications. We analyzed them as though they represented four communities.

6. Organized a Water Supply Task Force in 1974, offered technical assistance to large users and planted a conservation garden.

7. Devised a Water Management Plan in 1972, sponsored the leak detection program and planted a conservation garden.

8. Monitored bills and offered technical assistance to users.

9. Participated in two fairs by sponsoring conservation exhibits.

10. Conducted a pilot residential conservation program and an in-house conservation program, and offered help to large users.

TABLE 3.5
DROUGHT CONSERVATION PROGRAMS

COMMUNITY	METERING[1] A	B	C	CONSERVATION EDUCATION[2] A	B	C	CONSERVATION RETROFIT KITS PROVIDED	RECYCLED WATER USED	PLUMBING CODE CHANGES	RESTRICTED OUTSIDE USE	WARNINGS AND CITATIONS	SERVICE SHUTOFFS	RATIONING	WATER RATE SURCHARGE	PROHIBITIONS ON NEW CONNECTIONS	OTHER
Humboldt County																
Eureka	X	X	X	X	X	X										X[6]
Arcata	X	X	X	X	X	X				X						X[6]
Cutten	X	X	X	X	X	X										X[6]
Northern Inland Comm.																
Susanville	X			X	X	X	X									
Marysville		X		X	X	X	X									
Grass Valley	X		X	X	X	X				X	X	X		X		
Paradise	X			X	X					X	X	X	X	X		X[7]
Central Valley																
Madera	X			X	X		X			X	X	X				
Merced	X	X		X												X[8]
Woodland	X	X		X											X	
West Sacramento[4]	X	X	X	X	X		X			X	X	X				
Davis	X	X	X	X	X		X		X	X	X	X				X[9]
San Francisco Bay Area																
San Jose W.W.[3][4]	X	X		X	X			X	X	X	X	X	X	X	X	X[10]
Marin Municipal W.D.[4]	X	X		X				X	X	X	X	X	X	X	X	X
East Bay M.U.D. Includes:																
San Leandro	X	X		X	X	X		X		X	X	X	X	X	X	X[11]
Alameda Co. Inside[5]	X	X		X	X	X		X		X	X	X	X	X	X	X[11]
Oakland	X	X		X	X	X		X		X	X	X	X	X	X	X[11]
Emeryville	X	X		X	X	X		X		X	X	X	X	X	X	X[11]
Piedmont	X	X		X	X	X		X		X	X	X	X	X	X	X[11]
Berkeley	X	X		X	X	X		X		X	X	X	X	X	X	X[11]
Albany	X	X		X	X	X		X		X	X	X	X	X	X	X[11]
Walnut Creek	X	X		X	X	X		X		X	X	X	X	X	X	X[11]
Lafayette	X	X		X	X	X		X		X	X	X	X	X	X	X
Contra Costa Co. Inside, Walnut Creek Office[5]	X			X	X	X		X		X	X	X	X	X	X	X[11]
Alameda	X	X		X	X	X		X		X	X	X	X	X	X	X[11]
Richmond	X	X		X	X	X		X		X	X	X	X	X	X	X[11]
El Cerrito	X	X		X	X	X		X		X	X	X	X	X	X	X[11]
San Pablo	X	X		X	X	X		X		X	X	X	X	X	X	X[11]
Pinole-Hercules[5]	X	X		X	X	X		X		X	X	X	X	X	X	X[11]
Crockett	X	X		X	X	X		X		X	X	X	X	X	X	X
Contra Costa Co. Inside, Richmond Office[5]	X			X	X	X		X		X	X	X	X	X	X	X[11]

TABLE 3.5

DROUGHT CONSERVATION PROGRAMS

(CON'T)

COMMUNITY	METERING[1] A	B	C	CONSERVATION EDUCATION[2] A	B	C	CONSERVATION RETROFIT KITS PROVIDED	RECYCLED WATER USED	PLUMBING CODE CHANGES	RESTRICTED OUTSIDE USE	WARNINGS AND CITATIONS	SERVICE SHUTOFFS	RATIONING	WATER RATE SURCHARGE	PROHIBITIONS ON NEW CONNECTIONS	OTHER
Monterey Bay Area																
Watsonville	X			X	X	X										
Santa Cruz[3]	X			X	X	X			X	X	X	X	X	X		
Monterey[4]	X			X	X	X	X			X	X	X	X	X	X	
Santa Barbara County																
Carpinteria	X			X	X		X									X[12]
Summerland	X			X	X										X	X[13]
Montecito	X				X	X								X	X	
Goleta[4]	X			X	X	X	X		X	X	X			X	X	X[14]
Ventura County																
Santa Paula	X			X	X		X									
Port Hueneme	X		X	X	X	X										X[15]
Oxnard	X			X	X	X	X									
Ventura	X			X	X	X	X	X	X							X[16]
Greater Los Angeles																
Pomona	X			X	X		X									X[17]
Burbank	X			X	X		X									X[18]
Alhambra	X															X[19]
Los Angeles	X			X	X	X	X			X	X	X	X	X		
Greater San Diego																
San Diego	X			X	X	X										
Escondido	X			X	X	X	X									
Imperial Beach[4]	X			X	X	X	X									
Oceanside	X			X	X	X										X[20]

TABLE 3.5

DROUGHT CONSERVATION PROGRAMS

(CON'T)

COMMUNITY	METERING[1] A	B	C	CONSERVATION EDUCATION[2] A	B	C	CONSERVATION RETROFIT KITS PROVIDED	RECYCLED WATER USED	PLUMBING CODE CHANGES	RESTRICTED OUTSIDE USE	WARNINGS AND CITATIONS	SERVICE SHUTOFFS	RATIONING	WATER RATE SURCHARGE	PROHIBITIONS ON NEW CONNECTIONS	OTHER
Desert Communities																
El Centro	X															
Blythe	X			X												X[2,1]
Coachella	X			X	X			X								X[2,1]
Indio	X			X	X			X								X[2,2]
Palm Springs[4]	X			X	X											
Total number of communities = 57																
Number of communities for each category	49	5	3	52	41	40	33	21	6	31	27	26	23	28	23	36
% of total number of communities	85.9	8.8	5.3	91.2	71.9	70.2	57.9	36.8	10.5	54.4	47.4	45.6	40.3	49.1	40.3	63.1

1. METERING: A = almost all accounts are metered; B = only commercial, industrial and other non-residential accounts are metered; C = almost all accounts are unmetered.

2. CONSERVATION EDUCATION: A = printed literature; B = other media, e.g., radio, T.V., newspaper; C = educational programs for children and/or adults.

3. These agencies record consumption figures for inside/outside city limits. We analyzed inside/outside consumption separately, as though each represented a community.

4. The service areas for these water districts include more than one additional neighboring community. Unless consumption figures were recorded individually, e.g., East Bay Municipal Utility District, we analyzed the entire water district as one unit.

5. These are four East Bay Municipal Utility District service area classifications. We analyzed them as though they represented four communities.

TABLE 3.5

DROUGHT CONSERVATION PROGRAMS

(CON'T)

6. Joined the Humboldt Bay Municipal Users Association.

7. Restricted water use by laundromats and car washes.

8. Asked for a voluntary 10% reduction in water use.

9. Offered water consultation.

10. Constructed intertie with EBMUD.

11. Built an emergency water supply facility, continued leak detection program.

12. Offered leak detection assistance.

13. Worked individually with abnormally high users.

14. Offered technical assistance.

15. Used media spinoffs from Oxnard, Ventura and Los Angeles.

16. Offered help to large users.

17. Requested parks to reduce consumption and curtailed hydrant flushing.

18. Used Los Angeles media campaign and asked for a voluntary 10% reduction in water use.

19. Sponsored a leak detection program.

20. Monitored bills and used them as feedback devices.

21. Relinquished 1977 entitlement of State Water Project water.

22. Relinquished 1977 entitlement of State Water Project water, conducted residential conservation program and offered help to large users.

TABLE 3.6

POSTDROUGHT CONSERVATION PROGRAMS

COMMUNITY	METERING[1] A	B	C	CONSERVATION EDUCATION[2] A	B	C	CONSERVATION RETROFIT KITS PROVIDED	RECYCLED WATER USED	PLUMBING CODE CHANGES	RESTRICTED OUTSIDE USE	WARNINGS AND CITATIONS	SERVICE SHUTOFFS	RATIONING	WATER RATE SURCHARGE	PROHIBITIONS ON NEW CONNECTIONS	OTHER
Humboldt County																
Eureka	X	X														
Arcata	X	X														
Cutten	X	X														
Northern Inland Comm.																
Susanville	X			X	X	X	X		X							
Marysville		X		X	X	X	X		X							
Grass Valley			X	X		X			X							
Paradise	X			X	X				X							
Central Valley																
Madera			X	X	X				X	X	X	X				
Merced	X	X							X			X				
Woodland	X	X							X						X	
West Sacramento[4]	X	X		X	X		X		X							
Davis	X	X							X							
San Francisco Bay Area																
San Jose W.W.[3][4]	X	X							X					X	X	X[6]
Marin Municipal W.D.[4]	X	X		X				X	X		X	X	X	X	X	X[6]
East Bay M.U.D. Includes:																
San Leandro[5]	X	X		X	X	X		X	X	X	X	X	X	X	X	X[6]
Alameda Co. Inside[5]	X	X		X	X	X		X	X	X	X	X	X	X	X	X[6]
Oakland	X	X		X	X	X		X	X	X	X	X	X	X	X	X[6]
Emeryville	X	X		X	X	X		X	X	X	X	X	X	X	X	X[6]
Piedmont	X	X		X	X	X		X	X	X	X	X	X	X	X	X[6]
Berkeley	X	X		X	X	X		X	X	X	X	X	X	X	X	X[6]
Albany	X	X		X	X	X		X	X	X	X	X	X	X	X	X[6]
Walnut Creek	X	X		X	X	X		X	X	X	X	X	X	X	X	X[6]
Lafayette	X	X		X	X	X		X	X	X	X	X	X	X	X	X[6]
Contra Costa Co. Inside, Walnut Creek Office[5]	X	X		X	X	X		X	X	X	X	X	X	X	X	X[6]
Alameda	X	X		X	X	X		X	X	X	X	X	X	X	X	X[6]
Richmond	X	X		X	X	X		X	X	X	X	X	X	X	X	X[6]
El Cerrito	X	X		X	X	X		X	X	X	X	X	X	X	X	X[6]
San Pablo	X	X		X	X	X		X	X	X	X	X	X	X	X	X[6]
Pinole-Hercules[5]	X	X		X	X	X		X	X	X	X	X	X	X	X	X[6]
Crockett	X			X				X	X	X	X	X	X	X	X	X[6]
Contra Costa Co, Inside, Richmond Office[5]	X			X				X		X	X	X	X	X	X	X[6]

TABLE 3.6

POSTDROUGHT CONSERVATION PROGRAMS
(CON'T)

COMMUNITY	METERING[1] A	B	C	CONSERVATION EDUCATION[2] A	B	C	CONSERVATION RETROFIT KITS PROVIDED	RECYCLED WATER USED	PLUMBING CODE CHANGES	RESTRICTED OUTSIDE USE	WARNINGS AND CITATIONS	SERVICE SHUTOFFS	RATIONING	WATER RATE SURCHARGE	PROHIBITIONS ON NEW CONNECTIONS	OTHER
Monterey Bay Area																
Watsonville	X	X		X	X				X							
Santa Cruz[3]	X	X		X	X				X							
Monterey[4]	X	X				X			X	X	X	X			X	
Santa Barbara County																
Carpinteria	X	X		X	X		X		X							X[7]
Summerland	X	X							X							
Montecito	X	X		X	X				X					X	X	
Goleta[4]	X	X		X	X		X		X					X	X	
Ventura County																
Santa Paula	X								X							
Port Hueneme			X						X							
Oxnard	X	X		X	X	X			X							
Ventura	X	X		X	X	X	X	X	X							X[8]
Greater Los Angeles																
Pomona	X	X		X					X							X[9]
Burbank	X	X							X							
Alhambra	X	X		X	X	X			X							
Los Angeles	X	X		X	X	X	X		X	X						X[10]
Greater San Diego																
San Diego	X	X							X							
Escondido	X	X		X					X							
Imperial Beach[4]	X	X							X							
Oceanside	X	X							X							
Desert Communities																
El Centro	X	X		X					X							
Blythe	X	X							X							
Coachella	X	X						X	X							
Indio	X	X						X	X							
Palm Springs[4]	X	X		X	X	X	X		X							X[11]

TABLE 3.6

POSTDROUGHT CONSERVATION PROGRAMS

(CON'T)

COMMUNITY	METERING[1]			CONSERVATION EDUCATION[2]			CONSERVATION RETROFIT KITS PROVIDED	RECYCLED WATER USED	PLUMBING CODE CHANGES	RESTRICTED OUTSIDE USE	WARNINGS AND CITATIONS	SERVICE SHUTOFFS	RATIONING	WATER RATE SURCHARGE	PROHIBITIONS ON NEW CONNECTIONS	OTHER
	A	B	C	A	B	C										
Total number of communities = 57																
Number of communities for each category	49	5	3	33	28	24	7	21	57	22	21	21	18	22	23	22
% of total number of communities	85.9	8.8	5.3	57.9	49.1	42.1	12.3	36.8	100.0	38.6	36.8	36.8	31.6	38.6	40.3	38.6

1. METERING: A = almost all accounts are metered; B = only commercial, industrial and other nonresidential accounts are metered; C = almost all accounts are unmetered.

2. CONSERVATION EDUCATION: A = printed literature; B = other media, e.g., radio, T.V., newspaper; C = educational programs for children and/or adults.

3. These agencies record consumption figures for inside/outside city limits. We analyzed inside/outside consumption separately, as though each represented a community.

4. The service areas for these water districts include more than one additional neighboring community. Unless consumption figures were recorded individually, e.g., East Bay Municipal Utility District, we analyzed the entire water district as one unit.

5. These are four East Bay Municipal Utility District service area classifications. We analyzed them as though they represented four communities.

6. Continued leak detection program.

7. Offered leak detection assistance.

8. Organized conservation task forces, offered leak detection assistance and started a conservation program aimed at apartment, condominium and mobile home residents.

9. Used a conservation process called water spreading.

10. Modified their water system operations, offered consultation to large users and devised their eleven-point long-range conservation program.

11. Offered help to large users.

half the districts continued their educational efforts. Clearly, such measures were linked to the drought.

During the drought, 58 percent of the districts in our sample provided conservation/retrofit kits for consumers. This is a dramatic change from both the predrought period, when only two districts distributed kits, and the postdrought period, when only 12 percent did so. Once again, use of the conservation device appears to be linked to the drought.

Over the three time periods, twenty-one communities (37 percent of the sample) actively recycled water. This figure primarily reflects the practices of the East Bay Municipal Utility District, which served seventeen of these twenty-one communities. Other communities reported research in wastewater reclamation and related areas, and perhaps this portends well for the future of wastewater reclamation.

Before the drought, two agencies, or 4 percent of the sample, enacted changes in the plumbing code. This increased slightly to 11 percent during the drought. On January 1, 1978, a new section of California's Health and Safety Code mandated the installation of conservation devices in new construction, resulting in 100 percent participation—an excellent example of the state exercising its proscriptive power.

Other conservation methods frequently implemented by institutional or proscriptive means included restriction of outside water use, issuance of warnings and citations, service shutoffs, rationing, and water rate surcharges. Water districts and local governments usually resorted to such potent measures during the drought to induce rapid reductions in water use. In the predrought period only one of the communities in our sample used any of these techniques: Montecito initiated a water rate surcharge system in 1973 as part of its water management policy. But the severe water shortages of 1976–1977 forced many communities to institute more radical conservation measures. In many cases agencies launched several measures in concert, perhaps hoping for synergistic effects (for example, imposing stiff water rate surcharges to discourage rationing violations, issuing warnings and citations prior to service shutoffs for continued violations, and restricting outside use in conjunction with rationing). A comparison of Tables 3.4 and 3.5 shows dramatic increases in the popularity of these techniques during the drought: 54 percent of the communities restricted outside water use during the drought, 47 percent issued warnings and citations, 46 percent provided for termination of water service (shutoffs), 40 percent imposed rationing, and 49 percent instituted water rate surcharges (see Table 3.5). Closer inspection reveals a concentration of these measures in the San Francisco Bay area communities, perhaps the most severely threatened in California. Interestingly, the postdrought popularity of these five conservation measures did not drop dramatically (see Table 3.6). The postdrought percentages ranged between 32 and 39 percent, compared to the drought range of 40 to 54 percent. This stems from the initial reluctance of Bay area communities to return to business as usual. They did, however, lift many of these harsh measures early in 1978, a fact not revealed in Table 3.6.

Prohibitions on new connections (moratoriums), the final institutional/proscriptive technique, followed a different implementation pattern over the three time periods. Note that moratoriums are unlikely to have immediate effects; they only prevent extension of service to new customers. Thus, rather than remedying short-term water shortages caused by droughts, moratoriums are useful as part of a long-range management policy (for example, to avoid overdrafts of local supplies). Perhaps this explains the higher predrought participation rate of 9 percent, compared to the predrought rate for the five measures noted above. The drought still increased the popularity of moratoriums, with 40 percent of the communities using this device during and after the drought. Some communities lifted their moratoriums early in 1978, but a few have retained them through 1979.

Before the drought, 37 percent of the sample used miscellaneous conservation techniques (the "other" category in Tables 3.4, 3.5, and 3.6). The drought and postdrought rates were 63 and 39 percent, respectively.

Several important conclusions follow from these findings. First, there was apparently some concern about water conservation in a significant proportion of our sample well before the onset of the drought. In particular, approximately 40 percent of the communities had instituted educational campaigns, wastewater recycling, or one of the programs listed under our "other" category. However, almost all of these communities fell within the East Bay Municipal Utility District, suggesting that predrought conservation efforts were in fact a highly localized affair.

Second, the onset of the drought triggered a wide variety of conservation programs. Discounting metering, which was commonly used before 1976, eleven of the thirteen conservation approaches enjoyed a dramatic increase in utilization. (The two exceptions were wastewater recycling and changing plumbing codes.) Approximately 80 percent of the sample initiated one of the three educational options, and about half implemented one or more of the remaining ten conservation mechanisms.

Third, all of the conservation approaches that increased in popularity during the drought showed a reduction in use after the drought ended. Twelve of the sixteen conservation approaches seemed to be especially linked to the drought.

Fourth, the patterns of use across the three time periods suggest that four of the sixteen conservation strategies were used in response to other water-related issues, perhaps to remedy long-term supply problems and assure the adequacy of water district revenues. More specifically, the use of metering, wastewater recycling, plumbing code changes, and moratoriums were not clearly associated with the drought.

Finally, given the changing use patterns over time, it is apparent that for the time interval over which we have data, conservation efforts varied considerably. This is critical if we are in later chapters to examine the differential effectiveness of local conservation programs.

These conclusions can be extracted by simply examining Tables 3.4 through 3.6. In addition, however, we succumbed to the temptation of applying more formal statistical procedures to the patterns of conservation programs adopted, despite the risk of either restating the obvious or pushing the data beyond its limits.

To begin, it is apparent from an inspection of Tables 3.4 through 3.6 that communities involved in a few conservation activities tended to institute many others. This follows from the practices in the Bay area, if for no other reason. It is less clear from inspection whether similar conclusions obtain over time. In particular, were communities undertaking several conservation activities before the drought also more likely to institute programs during the drought and perhaps afterward as well? To try to answer these questions we constructed three variables for each community ($N = 57$) measuring the *sum* of the conservation programs undertaken in each of the three periods. The number of predrought programs correlated over .82 with the number of drought programs. The number of drought programs correlated over .92 with the number of postdrought programs (see Table 3.7). Finally, the number of predrought programs correlated nearly .87 with the number of postdrought programs. In short, areas heavily involved in conservation programs during one time period are likely to be heavily invested during the other two time periods. Perhaps such communities are in especially tenuous positions with respect to their water supplies and/or having initiated conservation activities, they generate a continued commitment to conservation. We will return to these possible explanations below.

One difficulty with relying only on correlations between the *number* of conservation programs is that the absolute number may not be sensitive to change over time. Programs launched before the drought may simply be carried over into later periods; that is, the correlations may reflect responses to long-standing problems with water supply or general awareness of the need to conserve water rather than drought responses per se. With this in mind, we constructed two *change* variables for each community reflecting the change in the number of programs launched during the drought and the change in the number

Table 3.7   Correlations Among Measures of Conservation Programs
            (N = 57)

	(1)	(2)	(3)	(4)	(5)
No. of Predrought Programs (1)	1.00	.82	.87	.38	.32
No. of Drought Programs (2)		1.00	.92	.84	.03
No. of Postdrought Programs (3)			1.00	.67	.41
Drought Change Score (4)				1.00	−.25
Postdrought Change Score (5)					1.00

of programs launched after the drought. In the first instance the number of predrought programs was subtracted from the number of drought programs, and in the second instance the number of drought programs was subtracted from the number of postdrought programs; thus, both are "gain scores."

The correlation between the total *number* of predrought programs and the *change* in the number of programs associated with the drought is .38 (see Table 3.7). Hence, areas that were more committed to conservation activities before the drought were more responsive during the drought. Since the mean of the drought change score is 4.7, it is apparent that, on the average, the change score was positive. The correlation between the number of predrought programs and the postdrought change score is positive, with a value of .32. However, since the postdrought change score has a mean of −1.2, the positive correlation implies that communities with greater involvement in water conservation programs before the drought experienced, on the average, smaller declines after the drought. While this finding also suggests greater commitment to water conservation, the commitment translates into a brake on the postdrought withdrawal from conservation activities.

The correlation between the number of drought programs and the postdrought change score is only .03; that is, a greater investment in water conservation activities during the drought seems to have no impact on postdrought behavior; a larger number of water conservation programs during the drought does *not* check the postdrought decline. Moreover, since the correlation between the drought and postdrought change scores is −.25, greater gains during the drought are associated with greater losses after the drought.

Taken as a whole, the data in Table 3.7 suggest that conservation activities respond to three somewhat different factors. First, compared to areas with few predrought conservation measures, communities strongly committed to water conservation before the drought undertake more conservation activities during the drought and postdrought periods, make greater gains during the drought, and experience smaller declines after the drought. In other words, there is a pervasive influence of conservation-mindedness. Second, whatever the other factors are that stimulate conservation activities during the drought (more on those shortly), they seem to have little effect on postdrought behavior. Once the crisis passes, investment in drought-related conservation programs does little to check the decline in the number of postdrought programs. Finally, the negative correlation between the two change scores may mean that unusual efforts (as measured by large gains during the drought) sap a community's will thereafter. Perhaps dramatic gains made during the drought severely tax local resources, making it necessary to beat a rapid retreat once normality returns.

With some hesitation, we turn now to a brief consideration of community characteristics that might explain commitment ot water conservation. As mentioned earlier, we have little data suggesting why some areas are more conservation-oriented than others. Nevertheless, we regressed each of the variables just discussed on a number of community characteristics. To be more specific, we regressed the number of predrought programs, the number of drought programs, the number of postdrought programs, the change in the number of drought programs, and the change in the number of postdrought programs on subsets of the following exogenous variables:

1. population,
2. median income,
3. minimum average annual runoff,
4. maximum average annual evaporation rate,
5. total groundwater available,
6. minimum rainfall and snowpack in 1976 as a percentage of normal totals,
7. minimum rainfall and snowpack in 1977 as a percentage of normal totals, and
8. East Bay Municipal Utility District as a dummy variable.

We used the first variable, population, as a rough gauge of the total resources available to each area (for example, total revenues). Median income was deemed a measure of aggregate socioeconomic status. We also had several measures of overall educational level, such as median number of school years completed, but these were highly correlated with median income (around .80). Therefore, we could not use them in the regression analysis without the risk of serious collinearity. Minimum average annual runoff and total groundwater available were used to tap (in part) the local endowment of water and, hence, the adequacy of local supplies. Maximum average annual evaporation rate is one important indicator of need, since areas with higher evaporation rates require more water, other things being equal. The two percentage variables measure the local shortfall in precipitation for 1976 and 1977, the two years of the drought. Finally, the EBMUD dummy variable captures all of whatever is unique about that district (which had invested heavily in water conservation).

We had access to a much larger number of community and water-related measures but were seriously constrained by the small sample size (few degrees of freedom) and very high correlations between these variables and the ones included. For example, the correlation between the minimum average annual runoff and the maximum average annual runoff was .99. Therefore, we make no great claims for the specification of our models.

It should also be kept in mind that our model does not meet the usual statistical assumptions of ordinary least squares. In particular, since many of our geographic units are nested within larger water districts, cross-sectional serial correlation is likely. This is known to yield inefficient estimates of regression coefficients and inconsistent standard errors. However, we decided not to use generalized least squares, because we knew of no way to estimate accurately the covariance matrix of the errors. With one exception, we did not include dummy variables for the larger districts in which communities were nested because to do so would have entailed substantial losses in degrees of freedom. Thus, on top of specification problems, our significance tests present certain difficulties.

Beginning with the number of predrought programs, we specified a model including all of the exogenous variables listed above, except for the two drought shortfall indicators. Clearly, these were irrelevant to predrought conservation efforts. The story that emerged was straightforward: the EBMUD dummy variable explained 75 percent of the variance by itself, and when the other variables were added, only 2 percent more variance was accounted for. Consistent with these results, only the EBMUD dummy variable had a statistically significant effect (at the .05 level) in the full model (that is, with all but the two drought variables). Finally, holding all of the other variables constant the regression coefficient indicated that EBMUD communities had an average of 4.5 more conservation programs before the drought than did communities that were not part of the EBMUD.

A slightly more complicated pattern surfaced when the number of drought conservation programs was considered. First, the EBMUD dummy variable dominated, much as it had before; it explained 74 percent of the variance by itself. However, when we included all of the variables listed above (with the exception of the 1977 shortfall indicator, which correlated .82 with the 1976 shortfall indicator), the variance explained increased to 79 percent, and two other variables had statistically significant effects at the .05 level. Every 10 percent increment in the precipitation shortfall led to an additional .20 water conservation programs. Since 50 percent shortfalls were hardly unknown, communities that experienced substantial shortfalls had an average of one more conservation program. In addition, cities with large populations instituted more conservation programs, other things being equal. The regression coefficient for our population variable indicated that for every increment of 100,000 residents across locales, about .16 more water conservation programs were in place. This implies that, on the average, cities with 600,000 people had approximately one more conservation program during the drought than cities with 100,000 people. Finally, communities in the EBMUD instituted an average of 7.4 more programs. In short, while most of the variation in the number of drought-related conservation programs can be attributed to the activities of the EBMUD, one measure of drought severity and one measure of district resources proved useful.

Consideration of the change in the number of water conservation programs during the drought produced similar results. The same three variables attained statistical significance at the .05 level: the EBMUD dummy, the 1976 precipitation shortfall, and population. Each 10 percent increment in precipitation shortfall led to an average gain in conservation activities of .37, and each increment of 100,000 in population led to an average gain of .15. Compared to other communities, those in the EBMUD launched an average of 2.7 more new water conservation programs. Perhaps the only twist is the improved performance of the shortfall measure, coupled with a decline in importance for the EBMUD dummy. Indeed, of the 60 percent variance that was explained, these two variables made approximately equal contributions. This means that EBMUD membership was somewhat less important when the *gain* in programs was examined, using the findings for the *total number* of drought programs as a yardstick. At the same time, the impact of the drought itself was somewhat more important. Put in other terms, once one adjusts for the EBMUD's long-standing involvement in water conservation efforts by focusing only on the gain in programs during the drought, local drought severity is important, as are district resources. Nevertheless, the efforts of the EBMUD were exemplary.

Turning to the postdrought period, one can employ much the same regression model with the exception that it probably makes sense to replace the 1976 shortfall indicator with the 1977 shortfall indicator. While one might not expect drought severity to influence the postdrought period, any effects would most likely derive from more recent experiences.

Beginning with the total number of postdrought water conservation programs, the findings look almost exactly the same as those for the predrought period. Eighty-eight percent of the variance was explained, and virtually all of that can be attributed to the EBMUD dummy variable. Moreover, the EBMUD dummy variable was the only variable to attain statistical significance at the .05 level. On the average, communities within the EBMUD had 8.9 more water conservation programs in place. Moreover, the story did not vary much when the change in water conservation programs was examined. While only 24 percent of the variance was explained, the only statistically significant effect was for the EBMUD dummy variable. Compared with the other communities, those within the EBMUD initiated about two more new programs, although it should be kept in mind that fewer programs were in place after the drought than during it.

In summary, whatever the weaknesses of our multivariate analyses, the results do not seem particularly unreasonable and are consistent with the story that emerged from an examination of the correlations among our endogenous variables. That is, there are effects from a long-standing commitment to water conservation, and there are effects associated with the drought. Note that a priori one could have anticipated both effects, one of them, or neither.

Conservation programs enacted by our sample communities

Humboldt County The first three sample communities, Eureka, Arcata, and Cutten, are located in Humboldt County. Although northern California apparently suffered more from the drought than other regions, many coastal communities experienced somewhat less adverse effects. This may explain the relatively mild conservation programs enacted by these three northern communities.

All three locales belong to the Humboldt Bay Municipal Water District. The district reduced its supply by 10 percent in June 1977, and at this point the three communities became members of the Humboldt Bay Municipal Users Association, which was established to increase cooperation among communities.

Literature campaigns were begun during the summer of 1977. The Eureka Department of Public Works designed and mailed a conservation pamphlet to its customers. Arcata's meter readers distributed the same pamphlet by hand. Cutten utilized the American Water Works Association (AWWA) pamphlet, which included suggestions for voluntary conservation. At about the same time, local newspapers published a table that listed suggested water use quantities as a function of family size.

On July 20, 1977, Arcata drew up an ordinance for emergency water rationing, but it was never implemented. During the same summer, only Eureka restricted use of outside water; this was the most severe conservation measure employed by any of the three communities to cope with the drought.

Northern Inland Communities Severe drought effects were experienced by some inland communities, in particular, Susanville, Marysville, Grass Valley, and Paradise. Even though Susanville reported no actual water shortage, it carried out a general media campaign encouraging conservation, and distributed conservation kits. Similar programs are still in place.

Since 1977 the water company in Marysville has had brochures available to advise customers of ways to avoid waste. In addition, the film "Water Follies" was shown to the Rotary Club in March 1977 and to high school students in June 1977. That year, the water company also distributed 600 to 800 free toilet kits, and they are still widely available. To protect the current water supply, Marysville distributes literature reinforcing the good habits users presumably learned during the drought.

More stringent conservation measures were initiated by Grass Valley and Paradise. Declaring a water shortage emergency in March 1977, Grass Valley adopted new ordinances regulating and restricting certain types of water use, such as watering lawns; washing autos, recreational vehicles, or hard surfaces; and filling swimming pools. Grass Valley also restricted water consumption by commercial car washes and laundromats. Violations and/or neglected system reparations could result in the termination of water service.

In December 1976 the Paradise Irrigation District (PID) adopted restrictions governing water use, and strict rationing was imposed from April through September of 1977. PID launched its literature campaign in 1977, disseminating conservation handouts through stores and businesses. The district also enclosed conservation pamphlets in customer bills.

The PID attempted to educate children, as well as adults, through drought and postdrought activities conducted at local schools. The conservation program staff used a range of creative pedagogical devices, including crossword puzzles, illustrations showing the "water cycle," and a slide show for viewing and discussion by fourth, fifth, and sixth grade children. In the postdrought period PID personnel sponsored a contest involving games and activity sheets (abbreviated diaries of water use) to reinforce continuing conservation. Unfortunately, the staff reported this contest to be less successful than they had hoped. From the state department of water resources (DWR), the PID purchased the Captain Hydro (a water conservation superhero) series and a booklet entitled, "California Water Works."

Central Valley The five sample communities in Central Valley are Madera, Merced, Woodland, West Sacramento, and Davis. Both Madera and Merced distributed educational literature. Madera enclosed conservation bulletins and copies of the irrigation watering restrictions (for example, lawn watering two days per week) in customer bills. The first set was sent with the May 1977 bills, and the second set in June 1978. Merced enclosed fliers with the March and May 1977 bills and asked customers to reduce their water use by 10 percent.

Woodland enclosed conservation literature with bills from April 1977 through September 1977 and offered conservation kits for toilets and shower heads. A moratorium on the development of new properties was imposed in response to a significant drop in the water table. Throughout the duration of the moratorium, which lasted from April 1977 through April 1978, Woodland honored only those construction plans already in effect.

Users in West Sacramento were notified by mail that water conservation pamphlets and kits could be procured from the agency office. In cooperation with the Sacramento Water Works Association the local agency publicized water conservation over the radio and on bus placards. In addition, community participation was elicited through cards on restaurant tables stating that water would be served only upon request, free "how to save water" consultation to customers, and enforcement of water use rules (for example, prohibiting car washing).

Davis's conservation program began in 1976. Boy Scouts delivered pamphlets door-to-door, and the local newspaper published advertisements and biweekly reports on water consumption to encourage conservation and show how well the community was doing. In addition, personnel from the Office of Economic Opportunity went door-to-door handing out conservation kits provided by the water agency.

In September 1976 Davis adopted a general code controlling water use. Under this code, consumers who neglected plumbing reparations risked having their water service discontinued. Another section prohibited water waste and provided suggestions for restricting certain uses. On March 16, 1977, Davis passed an ordinance requiring installation of water-saving plumbing devices in new buildings. Finally, the February 1977 *Water Bulletin* published in Davis requested citizens to review their water practices, particularly exterior uses, and to continue to eliminate waste voluntarily.

San Francisco Bay Area The water districts that constitute our sample from the San Francisco Bay Area are San Jose Water Works (SJWW), servicing roughly 80 percent of San Jose and several nearby communities; Marin Municipal Water District (MMWD), whose efforts we noted earlier; and East Bay Municipal Utility District (EBMUD), servicing approximately eighteen communities in the East Bay area. The San Francisco Bay Area is the second largest urban area in California (Hoffman, Glickstein, and Liroff 1979), and it encompasses one of the most complex and extensive water conveyance systems in the world.

Water suppliers in the Bay Area varied enormously in their vulnerability to the drought and, hence, in the aggressiveness of their responses (Hoffman, Glickstein, and Liroff 1979). San Jose Water Works, for example, apparently obtained adequate supplies by pumping water from its own wells and purchasing additional amounts from the Santa Clara Valley Water District, a private wholesaler with abundant supplies. Thus, SJWW primarily relied upon voluntary conservation efforts. In 1977 customers received literature encouraging conservation, and SJWW presented a few public lectures. A water rate surcharge for overconsumers served as a temporary conservation measure lasting from August 1977 through January 1978. Finally, SJWW followed the county ordinance, which regulated outside water use.

The East Bay Municipal Utility District enacted an exemplary conservation program, perhaps because this water service area has long suffered many of the same problems as Marin's. In 1972 the EBMUD Water Board adopted a Water Management Plan to reduce long-term per capita consumption by encouraging consumer "water conscience," rather broadly defined as "an awareness of, and responsibility for, the water supply."

Attending to its own water conscience as well, EBMUD improved its internal conservation practices. Most noteworthy was its leak survey program, born in mid-1973 from concern about resource use, energy conservation, and facility costs. Research, self-scrutiny, perseverance, and improved technology resulted in a savings of 4 million gallons per day, or a total of 1.5 billion gallons per year—enough water to make a good-sized lake (DWR 1976a). For its efforts, the EBMUD leak survey program has achieved international fame. EBMUD also chose to reduce directly its own water use (DWR 1976b). Employees were schooled in the utility's internal conservation program, and stricter accounting measures were instituted.

Along with its 1972 Water Management Plan, the EBMUD Water Board presented the district's commercial, industrial, and public authority users (DWR 1976b) with seventeen recommendations for identifying and correcting excessive water use. Carelessness, leakage, and other causes of waste were strongly discouraged; public agencies were asked to reduce water use, particularly for street cleaning; and the district promoted recycling and wastewater reclamation. EBMUD also informed major users about all applicable codes and regulations, and endorsed the use of less water-intensive plants in public areas.

Programs for the general public that evolved from the Water Management Plan were primarily educational (DWR 1976b). For example, a mobile van carrying exhibits toured local schools on a regular basis, and a demonstration garden used native plants requiring little water. The district also redesigned water bills to better inform users of their water habits, established a speaker's bureau, and distributed literature extensively.

Another frequently cited facet of EBMUD's conservation program was "PROJECT WATER—Water Awareness Through Education and Research" (DWR 1976a). The program rested on at least four justifications. First, there was virtually no adequate educational material on urban conservation, especially in the context of EBMUD's special situation. Second, acknowledging the difficulty involved in changing people's long-standing habits, EBMUD hoped that children would be the easiest to reach. Third, EBMUD realized that parents could be reached through their children, if the conservation message was made sufficiently salient. Finally, many concerned educators were eager to cooperate so that several practical barriers were eliminated.

The pedagogical strategy behind PROJECT WATER capitalized on ongoing classroom subjects and employed practical applications to water and water conservation (DWR 1976a). Conservation material was designed for various grade levels with the objective of instilling an understanding of hydrological principles, alternative solutions to water supply problems, and the application of such knowledge in the community. EBMUD produced printed curricula and audiovisual materials for the project, which have subsequently been translated into Spanish.

Among the printed conservation materials EBMUD has sent its customers intermittently since 1973, posters, decals, brochures, and fliers have been particularly popular. Examples are literature on leak detection (1974) and on selection of low-water plants, irrigation, and gardening tips (1976); and toilet-dam kits and instructions (1977). The most recent piece is a comprehensive review of PROJECT WATER, with advice on using it in other areas.

As part of the Water Management Plan, EBMUD enacted many resolutions throughout the 1970s to govern water service. To cope with the drought, the district supported ordinances imposing rationing and a moratorium. Allotments for inside and outside water use were determined for each customer according to classifications based on inferred need. EBMUD concurrently restricted the use of water for landscaping and prohibited decorative fountains, among other things. Nevertheless, the original goal of a 25 percent reduction in water consumption needed to be increased to 35 percent in April 1977. Rationing began in February 1977 and lasted until February 1978. Finally, EBMUD rejected applications for annexation of territory outside district boundaries when additional demand for water was involved. This moratorium lasted from February 1977 to April 1978.

Other EMBUD actions stemming from new ordinances included filing applications for federal funding of drought projects under the Community Emergency Drought Relief Act of 1977; endorsing expenditures for emergency supplies from the Middle River facility; hiring a consultant to prepare the Water Education Program; selling educational materials to other agencies; and distributing and using reclaimed wastewater. This by no means exhaustive list of EBMUD's additional conservation efforts demonstrates the almost limitless possibilities available to agencies endowed with sufficient financial support and a will to conserve.

Monterey Bay Area   Watsonville, Santa Cruz, and Monterey are the three sample communities located in the Monterey Bay area, most of which was seriously affected by the drought. Nevertheless, each community responded differently in the conservation measures taken. Watsonville did the least, apparently only sending informative literature with customers' bills during the summer of 1977.

Santa Cruz, in contrast, launched a multimedia conservation program. The literature sent periodically to customers in 1976 and 1977 promoted conservation and explained a variety of techniques to conserve water inside and outside the home (meter reading; water-saving tips; conservation rules; water-energy-saving suggestions for large buildings; decals for major users, such as public facilities, hotels/ motels, restaurants, schools, and businesses; and bumper sticker advertisements).

On May 25, 1976, Santa Cruz declared a water shortage emergency and passed an ordinance restricting water use (for example, outside watering only on particular days and at certain hours), coupled with fines for violations. During the next eighteen months, as the drought grew more severe, the city passed seven ordinances amending the original declaration (that is, additional prohibitions and regulations, along with stiffer penalties). For example, hotels and motels were required to install water-restricting equipment before April 1, 1977. Moreover, penalty rates of $25.00/HCF were introduced to discourage excessive use, and previously disconnected violators were charged high reconnection rates. The March 1977 ordinance promulgated a rationing scheme that attempted to define equitable allotments.

In the autumn of 1977 a water conservation film was shown at local theaters. From February 1977 through January 1978, Santa Cruz issued periodic press releases in conjunction with educational literature on conservation and ordinance compliance. Rationing was rescinded on November 8, 1977, but water use regulations remained in force. Customers were asked to evaluate the rationing program by responding to a questionnaire sent by the city.

Monterey also enacted an extensive conservation program. The California-American Water Company (Cal-Am) enforced service restrictions ordered by the Public Utility Commission (PUC). First, on May 30, 1973, PUC ordered a moratorium on extension of water mains to new developments that were not already in the final planning stage. Second, PUC prohibited new service connections, but modified this order in January 1977 to allow service to single-family dwellings with low water use requirements. The moratorium was totally lifted on September 8, 1978.

Cal-Am developed its own rationing program in July 1976, with the implementation of successive phases dependent upon the groundwater level. A more suitable long-term rationing plan was enacted in February 1977.

In addition to enforcing these rather stringent measures, Monterey sponsored a variety of less draconian activities. Three local radio stations broadcasted conservation messages, beginning in July 1976. Initiated at the same time and lasting until March 1977 were more than seventy public addresses given to various groups. Throughout the 1977 school year, children saw classroom demonstrations and participated in water-related field trips. Other actions included installing more than 42,000 water-saving toilet devices (August and September 1976), presenting a cable TV program on how to read water meters (February 1977), maintaining a telephone hot line to answer questions on rationing (February 1977 through November 1977), distributing a booklet entitled, "Think About Water," to approximately 12,000 schoolchildren (February 1978), and implementing a six-part bill-insert series (November 1979 through October 1979).

Santa Barbara County Moving farther south brings us to Santa Barbara County, with Carpinteria, Summerland, Montecito, and Goleta forming the next group of communities. Even though these communities lie within a relatively small geographic area, their conservation programs differed considerably.

The Carpinteria County Water District recognized rather quickly the likely consequences from water supply overdrafts that occurred during the 1975–76 water year (July 1 through June 30). As part of its response, the district distributed two conservation brochures. During the summer of 1978, Carpinteria enacted a street banner exhorting its citizens to conserve. Educational literature included two conservation brochures, periodic newspaper advertisements encouraging conservation, and conservation reminders printed on customers' bills. The district also offered consumers additional information about conservation procedures, assistance in leak detection, and conservation kits for sale.

In response to the district's declaration of a water shortage emergency, Summerland initiated a moratorium on new water service in October 1974. During the drought, customers received a general conservation booklet with the April, May, or June 1976 billings. A flier promoting drip irrigation and explaining other conservation techniques was enclosed in the February, March, or April 1977 bills. Finally, a district representative contacted users who consumed water at an abnormally high rate to discuss and settle the matter.

The Montecito County Water District, also recognizing the need to address predrought water supply problems, declared a water shortage emergency in January 1973 and instituted a moratorium on new water hookups. Six months later the district incorporated a water rationing program into its long-term water management policy. Users were allotted a specific amount of water each fiscal year, with penalties for overconsumption assessed every six months. Complementing these actions were pamphlets promoting conservation. Every two months users also received water bulletins that contained both conservation tips and pertinent water use information. Finally, during 1977, district personnel gave a water conservation talk to fifth and sixth graders, and during the height of the drought they sent representatives to work individually with overusers.

Goleta instituted the most drastic conservation program in the Santa Barbara area. Its water supply problems resulted, in part, from rapid urbanization during the 1960s, forcing the Goleta County Water District (GCWD) to become a pioneer in water conservation. December 1972 marked the birth of Goleta's conservation program, at which time the district invoked a moratorium on new service connections. Still in effect today, this moratorium discourages further imbalances between water supply and demand. A new public concern about water supplies grew from this moratorium; perhaps as a consequence, voters mandated that GCWD review their water management policies. Goleta has subsequently been credited with establishing through local ordinances the most extensive regulation of water use in California (DWR 1976b).

Although regulating water use through local ordinances may be an expedient conservation method, the GCWD's general manager warned that such measures are ineffective unless integrated with a comprehensive, publicly accepted water conservation program (DWR 1976a). He cited three key elements for successful programs: public education, community communication, and personal commitment. Within this framework, ordinances can be used to meet immediate and measurable, as well as long-term, conservation objectives.

With this knowledge in mind, Goleta constructed ordinances based on the following six mechanisms for curtailing consumer demand (DWR 1976a):

1. connection prohibitions (moratorium);
2. waste-of-water prohibitions;
3. expansion of use limitations;

4. devices for saving water (ordinances supplementing the Uniform Plumbing Code);
5. provisions for mandatory rationing (setting priorities among user categories in the event of a drastic shortage; for example, first priority categories include domestic, fire protection, and sanitation users);
6. adoption of an equitable water rate structure (elimination of the declining block structure, which made the marginal cost of water less for large users).

Many other measures were undertaken by Goleta early in 1973 to encourage voluntary water conservation. For example, educational brochures on such topics as the installation of water conservation devices were printed and distributed. News releases provided information on other conservation practices and also detailed the water shortage. Billing records were used to monitor water use so that GCWD could provide feedback to those customers who consumed too much water. District staff provided customers with technical assistance in locating and repairing leaks. Finally, local restaurants served water only upon request.

As the drought worsened, further restrictions and prohibitions were built into water use ordinances. In July 1976 Goleta expanded the definition of "waste" to include excess water runoff, hard surface cleansing, routine system flushing, and neglected leakage; moreover outside watering was prohibited during specific hours. People who violated any of these ordinances could be charged with a misdemeanor.

In 1977 Goleta extended its conservation efforts to the schools and offered customers free conservation kits. Additionally, GCWD introduced a water conservation surcharge in June 1977, which was imposed upon users who exceeded their allotment. Agricultural users were subject to this surcharge from December 1977 until May 1978.

Ventura County The communities of Santa Paula, Port Hueneme, Oxnard, and Ventura belong to our Ventura County sample. As in Santa Barbara County, this group evidenced a potpourri of programs, despite the small geographic area they occupy. Santa Paula initiated a rather passive conservation campaign. During the peak of the drought: the district ran conservation advertisements in the local newspaper and provided water-saving kits upon request to about 25 percent of its customers.

Port Hueneme's conservation program was largely imported. Local officials seemed content to rely upon the media efforts of other locales, such as radio spots from neighboring Ventura and Oxnard, coupled with television and newspaper coverage from Los Angeles, sixty miles away. Port Hueneme's own efforts consisted merely of organizing a few public lectures during the drought and typing monthly conservation reminders on users' bills.

The city of Oxnard conducted its own publicity campaign throughout 1977. Conservation literature included two landscape magazines describing careful water use, a Department of Water Resources pamphlet, and a conservation flier written in Spanish. These efforts were complemented by two news articles published in the local newspaper and a city-sponsored conservation display at a local fair. In August 1977 Oxnard distributed water-saving kits to its customers, followed one month later by a questionnaire, which revealed that of the 63 percent who installed the devices, 86 percent were satisfied. An examination of billings after installation showed water savings of 10 to 15 percent.

Ventura initiated the most comprehensive and innovative program in this group, despite the fact that its water shortage was not severe. The city distributed and displayed a wide variety of materials, including bilingual literature, irrigation instructions, and many how-to-conserve pamphlets. Community participation was further encouraged through activities sponsored at a county fair in October 1975; a water conservation fair and poster contest held in November 1976 to promote careful water use; and the use of restaurant tents (self-standing cards) advocating conservation.

Educational efforts in Ventura have been intermittent since 1972, when the city held a lecture/film series about future growth and its implications for the water supply; the theme of conservation was germane to this series. Adult conservation education took place with the cooperation of civic organizations, such as the Lions Club. During the 1977 school year, water district personnel went to all of the elementary schools and worked with school staff in introducing the Captain Hydro and Water Play materials (coloring books and water problem sheets), which were furnished at the district's expense.

Ventura also used several conservation measures with economic underpinnings to influence old and new water users alike. First, the district initiated sewer charges for poor (nonrecyclable) effluent. Second, water consumption by large meters was monitored daily, and users were reminded that even losses from a system that is only 10 percent inefficient eventually add up. Third, not only did Ventura encourage the repair of meter malfunctions and general meter maintenance, they also enacted changes in the Uniform Plumbing Code in May 1976 requiring the installation of water conservation devices. Finally, wastewater reclamation was encouraged by offering free reclaimed water to large users (for example, construction sites and golf courses).

Ventura also attempted to reach large users, who were contacted individually and offered explicit conservation suggestions whenever possible. The district advised agricultural users, for example, to purchase a moisture-sensing device to measure the amount of water in the soil. Attached in sequence with a timer, the device activates a watering system only when necessary, thereby avoiding overwatering.

The Association of Water Agencies (AWA), to which Ventura belongs, launched a countywide conservation program in December 1978 and formed an agricultural task force; a public awareness task force; a legislative and regulatory task force; and an industrial, commercial, and governmental task force. Each designed conservation measures for its particular audience. In 1979 strategy teams were formed by AWA to implement the task force measures. During the spring and summer of that year, Ventura began a conservation program designed for apartment, condominium, and mobile home park residents.

Greater Los Angeles Pomona, Burbank, Los Angeles, and Alhambra comprise our sample of communities from the greater Los Angeles area. Conservation efforts in this group demonstrate statewide altruistic support for drought-stricken areas since these communities did not suffer from impending water shortages. All import substantial amounts of water from the Colorado River.

Pomona used the American Water Works Association booklet (see Figure 3.3) and supplemented its literature campaign with newspaper articles in June 1977. Moreover, a variety of educational measures was used. In April 1977 schools and parks were asked to reduce consumption by 25 percent. The following month, in cooperation with West End water agencies, the district sponsored a school poster contest and a water conservation week. These efforts resulted in a 30 percent reduction of school and park water consumption between April and June 1977. Schools also introduced the Captain Hydro program. Finally, the district made conservation booklets available at city hall and curtailed hydrant flushing.

The Burbank Public Service Department distributed several small conservation leaflets during the autumn of 1977. A Department of Water Resources flier containing water-saving hints and other conservation booklets rounded out this literature campaign. These materials could be obtained from the department office. Some voluntary educational projects evolved, and bumper stickers advocating conservation appeared on water trucks. In June 1977 a few electric signs displaying conservation messages were set up in public places. Finally, Burbank distributed approximately 1,000 bathroom kits in February 1977.

Alhambra relied upon Los Angeles' extensive campaign, and thus reported no measures of its own. Yet Alhambra did ask consumers for a voluntary 10 percent reduction in water use; between January and June 1977, a 22 percent reduction was reported.

The conservation program organized in Los Angeles demonstrates what an agency with strong financial support is able to do. Los Angeles began a predrought literature campaign during the summer of 1975, when the city's Department of Water and Power (DWP) sent bill enclosures asking customers to check for leaks and suggesting ways to reduce waste in outside water use. As the drought worsened throughout the state, Los Angeles faced the threat restrictions on supplies of imported water, and in March 1976 requests for voluntary conservation were stated with much more urgency. The DWP also began to send literature regularly with bills—bilingual mailers explaining an emergency conservation plan for the city, advice for apartment dwellers, and fliers on conservation lecture programs and movies. Other conservation paraphernalia, such as decals, bumper stickers, buttons, and posters, could be obtained at the DWP office. In 1976 Los Angeles brought conservation education into the school system by adopting the Captain Hydro program.

The efforts escalated throughout 1977, beginning with the formation of a conservation speakers' bureau in January and Mayor Bradley's request for a voluntary 10 percent cutback in water use to compensate for reduced supplies. Also in February the city learned that pumping of State Project water would be diverted to provide additional supplies for northern California. In response, the Los Angeles City Council adopted an emergency water conservation plan, which contained three sections: continuing education; prohibiting waste and regulating water use; a four-phase plan to reduce water use, contingent upon available supplies. Phase I, which regulated and restricted water use, was implemented in May 1977. A hot line was also established that month to provide water users with drought information. In June and July the courts authorized the pumping of additional water from other groundwater basins to increase supplies. Nevertheless, in July 1977 Phase II was put into effect, requiring a 10 percent reduction in water use by consumers and imposing a charge on overusers. Also during July, DWP distributed bathroom conservation kits.

As the drought eased in late 1977, Phase II (mandatory rationing) was rescinded, but DWP offered conservation consultation for commercial and industrial users. With the rains of 1978, Phase I of the water plan, which regulated and restricted water use, ended in April of that year.

The DWP has formulated a long-range conservation program, which currently contains eleven areas in which the department believes conservation can be practiced:

1. Metering.
2. Pricing: switch from a declining-rate block system to a uniform commodity charge.
3. New bill format: provides customers with historic consumption information so they can monitor use.
4. Water system operations: leak detection.

5. Public information: bill inserts, hotline, brochures.
6. Community contact: speakers' bureau service, water conservation presentations to various community groups, DWP conservation film, mobile trailer with conservation exhibits, drought-resistant plant display.
7. Local school program: Captain Hydro—adaptation, personnel training, and implementation.
8. Conservation devices: provided at no cost, retrofit study program with DWP employees.
9. Business and industry: Water Conservation for Industry program—brochures and information bulletins related to specific use (for example, beverage and food-processing industries); industry awards program to recognize companies that make special efforts to conserve; meters loaned to companies conducting in-plant water use surveys.
10. Residential irrigation program: information about outdoor water conservation; demonstration garden.
11. Cooperative programs with other organizations: participation in water conservation conferences and expositions.

These eleven points in Los Angeles' long-range program are the result of conservation policy addressing all aspects of water use. If its implementation is effective, the Los Angeles plan will be one of the most comprehensive in the state.

Greater San Diego Although it might initially seem surprising, our sample communities in San Diego County suffered little from the drought. Not only is the area habituated to smaller amounts of rainfall, but local consumers rely heavily on water imported from the Colorado River. Yet these communities did encourage conservation. Moving from the least to the most extensive programs, we mentioned earlier that San Diego enclosed a conservation leaflet with customers' July 1976 bills. Escondido supplied toilet flow restrictors, water displacement bottles, and conservation literature. Escondido also utilized the highly praised booklet, "Think About Water," to educate schoolchildren.

In Imperial Beach, a public relations person organized distribution of the "Think About Water" booklet, and also gave lectures at schools from March through July 1977. Additional literature was sent to customers in the form of monthly mailers (for example, "The Story of Water Supply"). Imperial Beach also distributed toilet flow restrictors at no charge.

Oceanside employed more innovative educational approaches. Besides furnishing booklets and posters at the billing office, Oceanside added previous year's consumption to customers' bills and requested a 10 percent reduction in water use. These procedures were used from

April 1977 to March 1978. Oceanside schools joined the statewide program, showing water conservation films, and the public library offered other films and conservation kits during November and December 1977. These efforts stand out as shining examples of interorganizational teamwork.

Desert Communities   El Centro, Blythe, Coachella, Indio, and Palm Springs constitute the final set of communities. With their dry climate and sandy soils, one would expect these desert communities to be particularly vulnerable to drought. Yet none ever faced severe shortages; in fact, El Centro did not initiate any conservation measures, since none were deemed necessary. Blythe was a bit more active. During 1977, general information on conservation was periodically sent to customers with bills, and meter readers delivered doorknob hangers listing conservation tips.

Both Coachella and Indio belong to the Coachella Valley County Water District (CVCWD), so they will be considered together. Beginning in fiscal 1975–76, films were available at the CVCWD office (for example, "Water Follies"). The educational campaign was expanded during the 1977 school year, when CVCWD's educational resource specialist visited schools to introduce a water awareness program, one part of which stressed conservation. In February 1977 CVCWD agreed to relinquish the district's 1977 entitlement of State Water Project water in order to augment supplies for communities in the drought-stricken North.

Palm Springs organized the most thorough conservation program among our desert communities with the city's Desert Water Agency (DWA) making appeals for conservation as early as 1972. At that time, greater emphasis was placed on conserving to avoid rate increases from increased pumping costs (which are incurred when water levels drop). Exterior lawn use and interior leaks were cited as the main causes of excessive use.

Palm Springs began working closely with large-volume users (for example, the Palm Springs School District) in 1974, teaching them conservation techniques and encouraging efficient water use. The goal was to eliminate what DWA saw as the three primary causes of wastefulness: defective water systems, misused water, and overwatering. It is easy to imagine how such focused efforts could result in substantial savings, since more than 50 percent of Palm Springs water was apparently used for landscaping purposes.

Turning its efforts toward residential consumers, in September 1975 DWA formulated a residential pilot conservation program based upon a general public information approach. In July 1976 the pilot program was activated. Additional guidelines for public information programs were adopted by the DWA board of directors in April 1976. Information disseminated to residential customers included suggestions for cutting both interior (particularly bathroom and kitchen) and exterior use, and leak detection hints.

DWA sponsored several other drought-related measures. The most notable was the decision to relinquish its 1977 entitlement of State Water Project water and permit a reallocation to northern California. The Desert Water Agency also operated a water booth at the city-sponsored annual Energy Fair, and during the drought the city's Welcome Wagon gave out approximately 200 pieces of literature per month. A media program was conducted from May 1977 through July 1978, with regular advertisements on one local TV station, on four local radio stations, and in one local newspaper.

Palm Springs still distributes information, gives talks at service clubs and schools, and provides direct help to large users, such as condominium complexes. The district has approval from the DWA board of directors to undertake new advertising campaigns when needed.

Summary and conclusions

It is readily apparent to anyone who takes a historical view that "the variability of California's weather seems to be its greatest consistency" (DWR 1978). Variation in weather is, of course, not the point, except to the degree that such patterns affect the impact of yearly cycles of precipitation. These cycles are the major natural sources of uncertainty facing water supply planners.

In this chapter we have reviewed the responses of local water agencies to a severe drought that was for all practical purposes impossible to predict. The enormous variation in drought effects and decentralized decison making resulted in a full range of conservation efforts. Agencies in northern California, accustomed to substantial annual rainfall, quickly depleted their reserves and, as the drought entered its second year, dramatically escalated conservation efforts, many of which were exemplary from the start. In contrast southern communities, which were able to rely on their local groundwater and supplies imported from the Colorado River, initiated much less aggressive conservation programs.

Our examination of the patterns of conservation program adoption over the predrought, drought, and postdrought periods demonstrated that some efforts were more closely linked to the drought than others. Metering, water recycling, plumbing code changes, and new service moratoriums did not appear to be linked to short-term water supply problems, whereas the wide variety of other interventions increased with the drought's onset and declined with its end. It is difficult to explain such differences. Perhaps the programs not directly linked to the drought were more difficult to implement quickly; one could certainly make this case for metering and water recycling, which require extensive physical alterations. Moreover, moratoriums on new service connections, which are likely to affect the long-term value of private real estate holdings, tend to be controversial and therefore perhaps slow to implement. Finally, the conservation efforts not directly linked to the drought may simply be habitually associated with long-term water management policies, while the other efforts may be viewed as extraordinary measures appropriate for periods of drought. Clearly, this is an area rich with future research possibilities.

It was also striking that despite the variety of programs instituted across the state, alterations in the price of water played a very small role in conservation. The only significant exception was the introduction in some areas of surcharges for excess use. It is surprising that across-the-board increases in the unit price of water were not common—particularly since water in California is substantially underpriced. Perhaps this reflects our earlier observation that water is rarely viewed as an economic good by policymakers and the public. Rather, access to adequate water is assumed to be a right, and pricing policies primarily reflect the revenue needs of local agencies. In any case, the failure to capitalize on the potential benefits of market mechanisms, even in periods of acute scarcity, seems to be a significant oversight in the conservation programs adopted.

Note also that residential consumers, while not the sole focus, were the primary targets of most conservation programs. This no doubt reflects in part the economic base of our sample communities; few were dominated by agricultural consumers, for example. When water is a factor in production, policymakers may feel that market considerations should determine the uses to which water is put and the amounts that are employed; that is, for nonresidential users, water may be viewed as an economic good. In addition, since nonresidential water use is linked to complicated, ongoing, and capital-intensive production processes, policymakers perhaps believe that rapid changes in consumption, even in response to acute shortages, are impossible to achieve and that public officials have no right to intervene when large costs are involved. Policymakers may also feel that they lack the technical expertise to advise (and pressure) nonresidential consumers. Whether or not these views are accurate, nonresidential users are typically among the largest consumers of water, both in aggregate terms and on an account-by-account basis. Thus, it is not at all obvious to us that nonresidential consumers should take a back seat when conservation programs are launched.

It is also interesting that with all of the emphasis on residential users, more effort was not devoted to making educational appeals to Spanish-speaking consumers. Some districts provided Spanish versions of certain printed materials, but the majority conducted their conservation campaigns almost exclusively in English. This oversight is striking, considering that in many of these communities studied Mexican Americans are well over 15 percent of the total population.

With respect to the reasons for conservation program adoption, both our case studies of local districts and our statistical analyses speak to the importance of at least two major causal factors: long-standing commitment to water conservation and local severity of the drought. There was also some evidence that districts with greater economic resources were able to respond more actively to the drought than those with fewer such resources. Although in retrospect none of these effects may be particularly surprising, hindsight should not be confused with accurate a priori expectations. Moreover, our multivariate regression analyses provided estimates of the size of causal effects, and these were certainly not available either from the case studies or from inspection of the patterns of program adoption. However, the detailed multivariate findings must be viewed cautiously because of specification errors.

We now have ample evidence that (1) there was a reasonably well-defined interval of two years in which a severe drought occurred; (2) during this time, conservation efforts were either increased or newly instituted; and (3) communities varied enormously in the intensity of their conservation efforts. Thus, it is apparent that substantial variation in conservation activities exists both over time and across locales. Clearly, such variation is required if we are to determine the impact of different programs on water consumption.

As we observed in Chapter One, there is already ample documentation that, in the aggregate, water consumption declined during the drought. In addition, aggregate postdrought analyses of statewide efforts suggest that those communities facing the most serious shortages often achieved the most dramatic reductions in water consumption (DWR 1978). Yet, for reasons detailed in our opening chapter, such analyses are at best incomplete. It is necessary, then, to implement the causal models proposed in Chapter Two and proceed with the statistical analyses.

4

What works: time series analyses of local water consumption

Introduction

As we argued in our opening chapter, a proper consideration of the impact of the water conservation programs introduced during the 1976–1977 drought requires the construction and estimation of multivariate causal models. In Chapter Two we provided a broad theoretical framework for such models, and in Chapter Three we examined the range of conservation activities undertaken by the communities in our sample. We are now ready to build on these foundations.

The statistical analyses that make up the bulk of this chapter will be undertaken separately for each geographic unit. Sometimes this unit will be a water district and sometimes a community within a water district. In each instance, however, we will work with the *least* aggregated unit. For ease of exposition, we will use the terms "community" and "water district" interchangeably (along with other words with similar meaning), unless it is important to be more precise.

Within each geographic unit, we will examine consumption patterns over time for several different kinds of water consumers (where such figures are available): residential, commercial, industrial, agricultural, and public users. Where breakdowns by consumer type are not available, we will use some larger aggregate, often simply total water sales.

All of the data will be arrayed over time by month for approximately an eight-year period, from January 1970 to June 1978, and each analysis will rest on approximately 100 observations, with variation in series length reflecting available data. Some areas did not have data for the entire period, in part because it often took over a year for local districts to transform information obtained through billing into summary figures for each month.

Longitudinal variation in water consumption for each kind of consumer (when available) will be examined as a function of three kinds of exogenous variables: measures of one or more conservation programs, an estimate of the "mean marginal price" of water, and several control variables. In this chapter our conservation program indicators are simple dummy variables coded "0" before the onset of a particular program and "1" thereafter. Changes *after* the drought will be captured in a summary fashion with a dummy variable coded "0" up to the end of the drought and "1" afterward. In the next chapter we will consider more sensitive ways to represent the effects of conservation programs. Our construction of mean marginal price is clearly imperfect, but it is an improvement over earlier work. Our control variables include monthly figures for local precipitation and temperature (to capture seasonal effects) and the number of accounts serviced by the particular geographic unit. The first two will be entered as legitimate exogenous variables, and the last will be used to standardize the monthly, aggregate consumption figures (that is, into consumption per service account).

One could no doubt quarrel with our implied model specification. Fortunately, the statistical procedures we will use often allow us to spot certain kinds of specification errors and make proper adjustments. For example, changes in water consumption per account that are not explained by our causal variables will often surface in recognizable ways, and they can be modeled as part of the error structure. To be more specific, we will be applying multivariate time series techniques in the Box-Jenkins tradition, and these are unusually powerful tools, despite the complications often involved when time-series data are used for causal modeling.

Variable construction

From the theoretical discussion in Chapter Two, it is apparent that ideally we would analyze data on individual water users—households, firms, farms, and the like. That is, our theoretical approach is derived from the optimizing decisions made by individual consuming units. However, individual data were not available from official sources, so our research design called for aggregate analyses of geographic areas. This causes several thorny theoretical complications that affect virtually all empirical work in which theory from one level of analysis is operationalized on another level. Fortunately, in our case serious distortions are not likely to result, with one possible exception that will be discussed later. Basically, we are proceeding on the assumption that aggregate patterns in individual-level variables are simply the sum of individual-level decisions.

Most purveyors of water keep aggregate records of their services and revenues. Such material, of course, is necessary for internal planning and to meet requests for information from outside agencies (for example, the State Department of Water Resources and the State Water Resources Control Board). Thus, water districts at least know the number of customers they serve, the rate structure(s) that applies, and the overall amount of water provided. What varies across agencies is the form in which the data are stored, the length of the official historical record, and the availability of less aggregated figures and supplementary information.

The statistical analyses that follow rest on a relatively small number of variables, both because the underlying theory is quite simple and because of the limitations in the date available. Since, as we argued earlier, water consumption should respond to climatic factors, we will use two: mean temperature per month and total monthly rainfall. These figures were available either from local water agencies or from other official sources. Note that variation in temperature and rainfall will capture not only certain direct climatic effects, but also other causal factors associated with seasonal patterns. For example, in the case of agricultural water users, temperature and rainfall will covary with such things as growing seasons. However, this confounding should present few critical problems because of the adjustments provided by ARIMA models of the error structure.

Table 4.1 presents some descriptive statistics for mean monthly temperature and total monthly rainfall. Note that the district is the unit of analysis; the figure for each district is the mean of approximately 100 monthly observations. The mean monthly rainfall for the sample is 1.65 inches. The standard deviation is .87 inches per month, the minimum rainfall is .17 inches, and the maximum rainfall is 4.24 inches. These data suggest substantial variation in monthly rainfall across the fifty-seven geographic areas. The mean temperature per month is 59.89 degrees. The standard deviation is 4.94, the minimum is 48.45, and the maximum is 72.69. Again, there is evidence of substantial variation across the sample.

The theoretical discussion in Chapter Two focused on the role of price as the crucial decision variable to which consumers respond. The conventional model of consumer demand assumes that the price of a good is independent of the amount consumed. This is clearly not always the case, however, for goods such as water and electricity, which are often priced according to a decreasing block schedule. For many of the communities considered in this study, the price of water varies at the margin according to a decreasing block schedule. Taylor (1975, 1980) proposes several solutions to the problems that decreasing block pricing systems introduce in the analysis of consumer demand.

The method adopted below rests on the marginal price of water for the average consumer. At each point in time we calculated the average consumption that identified the marginal block in the rate schedule, and it is this marginal block that is used in the analysis. We would

Table 4.1   Descriptive Statistics for Selected Variables Across Geographic Units

Variable [a]	N	Mean	Standard Deviation	Minimum	Maximum
Rainfall (inches/month)	57	1.65	0.87	0.17	4.24
Temperature (mean degrees/month)	57	59.89	4.94	48.45	72.69
Total Consumption (IICF/account/month)	9	27.03	13.45	12.42	46.45
Total Price (dollars/HCF)	13	0.17	0.09	0.00	0.32
Residential Consumption (HCF/account/month)	33	19.37	9.94	8.79	51.69
Residential Price (dollars/HCF)	33	0.19	0.07	0.07	0.41
Commercial Consumption (HCF/account/month)	32	58.02	25.93	17.73	130.19
Commercial Price (dollars/HCF)	32	0.18	0.06	0.08	0.35
Industrial Consumption (HCF/account/month)	30	2,121.98	5,864.86	12.33	31,121.20
Industrial Price (dollars/HCF)	30	0.16	0.05	0.08	0.34
Agricultural Consumption (HCF/account/month)	11	497.21	449.59	39.62	1,692.51
Agricultural Price (dollars/HCF)	11	0.13	0.06	0.02	0.23
Public Consumption (HCF/account/month)	33	234.30	181.88	34.71	940.47
Public Price (dollars/HCF)	33	0.17	0.05	0.08	0.31

[a] Consumption figures reflect the amount of water sold, not total water produced. Total consumption and total price refer to figures for all consumers in a district. The other variables pertain to particular kinds of consumers. Finally, sample sizes vary because of differences across districts in the data available.

have preferred to have the distributions of customers across the full rate schedule, but most water purveyors do not keep such detailed information. As a consequence, there is a minor misspecification involved in considering only the marginal price.

Consider a consumer who faces a block pricing scheme with three prices, $P^0 > P^1 > P^2$, that apply respectively to the consumption levels $0 < q \leq q^0$, $q^0 < q \leq q^1$, and $q^1 \leq q < \infty$. If the consumer purchases the level $q > q^1$, then the marginal price paid is P^2, but a "premium" has to be paid to reach that level of the marginal price. This intramarginal premium is the difference between what a consumer actually pays for water and what that consumer would have paid had he or she been able to purchase the entire quantity at the marginal price. In our example this is the difference $P^0q^0+P^1(q^1-q^0)+P^3(q^1-q)-P^3q$.

This intramarginal premium can be interpreted as an income effect and, strictly speaking, should be incorporated into the analysis. We will not do so for two reasons. First, since the time period for our analysis is relatively short and the rate structures and consumption patterns are relatively stable, the intramarginal premium shows little variation. Hence, the premium is largely absorbed. Second, since it can be interpreted as an income term, the actual impact of the premium is probably very slight. Indeed, since the income elasticity of water consumption is usually small, there are no a priori grounds for great concern.

We will also not include income in any of our equations, because income figures over time are simply not available at the community level of aggregation. This adds a second source of misspecification, but it is our firm belief (backed by a formal expression for the bias) that the combined effects at worst cause a slight attenuation in estimates of the price elasticity of demand. Furthermore, it is worth noting that our approach to the real marginal price of water is a substantial improvement over most past studies of water demand, which have determined the average price by dividing total revenues by total consumption (see, for example, Haver and Winter 1963, Gottlieb 1963). The problem with this procedure, of course, is that it amounts to including quantity on the right side of the equation.

Table 4.1 shows that real, mean marginal price varies across different kinds of water consumers. For example, agricultural users pay an average of 13 cents for each hundred cubic feet (HCF) of water consumed, while residential users pay an average of 19 cents per HCF. These are the lowest and highest prices, respectively. Other things being equal, the disparity suggests that residential consumers are subsidizing agricultural users. Average prices paid by commercial, industrial, and public users are closer to those paid by residential users. Note also that for each type of consumer, there is considerable variation across the 57 geographic areas. For example, residential prices range between 7 and 41 cents per HCF. Agricultural prices range between 2 and 23 cents per HCF. Much as in the case of variation in price across different kinds of users, variation across communities for particular kinds of users raises some important questions of equity that will be addressed later. Recall that many water districts draw heavily on water supply systems constructed with state and federal funds.

Given the enormous variation in the number and kinds of conservation programs undertaken across the state, developing measures of conservation efforts was fraught with difficulties. First, its was unclear how one would even in principle construct variables to capture within a common metric (or metrics) the content and intensity of conservation efforts. For example, even if cost data for particular conservation programs were available, money is at best an indirect indicator of intensity (and ignores content). Similarly, even if we had figures for the number of conservation leaflets distributed, the number of leaflets is at best only part of the story. In any case, such crude measures of intensity were typically not available. Second, many communities initiated several conservation programs in concert or on the heels of one another. Hence, the prospect of unraveling the unique impact of each was poor. Faced with these and other problems, we settled on constructing dummy variables coded "0" before the program and "1" thereafter. Programs introduced at about the same time were captured with a single dummy variable. The result was up to three dummy variables reflecting conservation efforts for each geographic area. Alternative approaches will be considered in the next chapter.

In addition to the impact of conservation programs undertaken during the drought, we were concerned with what happened afterward. More specifically, it was possible that, during the drought, habits were developed that facilitated water conservation, in which case postdrought water consumption might not increase. On the other hand, perhaps conservation efforts were closely linked to impending water shortages and were terminated once the drought had ended. Finally, the most plausible postdrought pattern a priori was that water consumption levels would gradually increase after the drought but would not reach predrought levels, in part because of technological changes (for example, installation of water-saving bathroom fixtures) and in part because of changes in attitudes. Moreover, the postdrought increase in consumption would occur only gradually as consumer practices reverted to earlier forms. In order to capture these sorts of effects, we constructed a dummy variable and coded it "0" up to the end of the drought and "1" thereafter. We will have more to say below about how this dummy variable was used to represent various kinds of postdrought patterns.

Turning to the construction of our dependent variables, we were able to obtain monthly consumption figures for most geographic areas. Different metrics (for example, gallons versus acre-feet) posed no particular problem, since conversions to units of 100 cubic feet were simple to make. However, variation across districts in meter-reading practices posed serious problems. Perhaps most troubling was the fact that some districts did not record consumption for all of their accounts each month. Often the meter reading was spread over a two-month interval, and it was typically impossible to determine which accounts were read during the first month and which were read during the second month. Generally, we could not even determine the proportion (or number) of accounts read during the first month compared to the second. If we were analyzing time series data with larger periods than one month (for example, six-month intervals), there would be no special cause for alarm. By collapsing "up," the variation in consumption as a function of meter-reading practices would disappear. However, for our monthly time series, meter-reading practices in the offending districts would be confounded with other month-to-month patterns. We could not simply adjust monthly figures to take account of which meters were read on which months, because we lacked the necessary information.

For those districts that read some of their meters one month and the rest the following month (none of our sample districts spread the collection of consumption data over more than two months), we settled on the practice of taking the consumption figures for the offending adjacent months, calculating the sum, and then attributing half of that sum to each month. While we will see later that this makes our statistical results a bit more complicated, serious distortions do not seem to have surfaced as a consequence. In effect, our worst sin was "smoothing" across adjacent months.

Aggregate monthly consumption figures are surely a function of the number of accounts served in a district: districts with a greater number of accounts should consume more water, other things being equal. Since water districts were routinely able to provide information on the number of accounts served each month, we simply divided the monthly consumption figures by the monthly number of accounts. The result was consumption per account in hundred cubic feet, and it is in this form that our dependent variables will be expressed.

While standardizing by the number of accounts removes the impact on consumption of the number of accounts served, it does not address changes in the size of the average account over time. Thus, the standardization procedure neglects an influx of larger industrial accounts or reductions in the average number of people living within a single household. If, for example, the size of the average household in a district is shrinking over time, the likely result is a longitudinal decline in our measure of water consumption.

In principle, failure to control for changes in the size of typical accounts over time could introduce serious difficulties in our analyses. However, several factors suggest that we need not be overly concerned. First, data on the average size of households year by year were available for some geographic areas, and there was little evidence that average household size was changing over time. Unfortunately, no such data were available for other kinds of consumers. Second, one of the advantages of having data for a large number of geographic areas and several kinds of consumers is that the results of different statistical analyses can be compared. If the overall story is similar across districts and kinds of consumers, there is no cause for alarm unless one is prepared to argue that all districts and all kinds of consumers are subject to the same sorts of distortions; in other words, all of the analyses are being distorted by parallel temporal trends, which seems unlikely. Third, the statistical procedures we will use can reveal the very trends and shifts that would be produced by changes in the average size of accounts and make proper adjustments. We will find, for example, that industrial consumption figures are especially suspect, but that reasonable results are typically obtained.

Table 4.1 indicates that monthly water consumption per account varies over water districts and over different kinds of water users. For example, in our 57 geographic areas, residential consumers use an average of 19.37 HCF per account during a single month, but some consume as little as 8.79 HCF, and others consume as much as 51.69. Agricultural consumers use an average of 497.21 HCF per account during a single month, but the figures range from 39.62 HCF to 1,692.51. Industrial consumers, on the average, are the largest and also the most variable users. Their mean is 2,121.98, with a low of 12.33 HCF and a high of 31,121.20 HCF.

We have now summarized the construction of all the variables used in analyses of geographic units and kinds of water consumers. While we have information on a large number of other variables, these are by and large aggregate measures of geographic areas, and hence are of no help in analyzing within-district effects. However, they will play a significant role in the next chapter when we compare geographic areas in terms of the effectiveness of price changes and their conservation programs. In short, our efforts to model water consumption for each area and each kind of user will be based on the variables just considered, and therefore some important causal factors are not directly represented. For example, we have no information on factors affecting the production of industrial goods or agricultural output. Again, we will try to capitalize on the power of a large number of replications and the strengths of time series statistical procedures. However, specification problems cannot be easily dismissed for at least some kinds of users, and we will address possible biases as they occur in the analyses.

Statistical procedures

At first blush it might seem as if the time series data for each locale and each kind of user could be analyzed using ordinary least squares (that is, multiple regression). However, the residuals are likely to be correlated, leading to inefficient estimates of the regression coefficients and inconsistent standard errors. Under such circumstances, it is common to employ generalized least squares with an error covariance matrix that assumes a simple autoregressive model for the correlated residuals (for example, see Kmenta 1971, pp. 269–297). In this study, however, we use more general specifications of the error process for two reasons.

First, there was no reason to assume that the usual AR1 model for the residuals was appropriate, especially given the likelihood of seasonal patterns and complications in the consumption figures caused by meter-reading practices. Should an AR1 model be used when another form is required, the generalized least squares adjustments are inadequate.

Second, the effects of initiating and/or terminating a conservation program may not be immediate, which suggests the possibility of using parameterizations implying lagged endogenous variables. For example, to model a gradual return to predrought consumption levels after the drought, current consumption must be regressed on consumption one or more months earlier (along with other variables). However, the usual generalized least squares procedures are inappropriate when one has both lagged endogenous variables and serially correlated residuals (Johnston 1972, pp. 303–320).

As an alternative to generalized least squares, we turned to time series techniques in the Box-Jenkins tradition (Box and Jenkins 1976). To be more specific, we formulated our models within a single-equation, multiple-transfer-function framework implying one-way causation. This framework is but one of many parameterizations of the general multiple time series model (Granger and Newbold 1977, pp. 215–267; Jenkins 1979, pp. 151–165), but it has the distinct advantage of permitting parameterizations that flow naturally from our causal theory. In effect, the single-equation, multiple-transfer-function framework allows a simple regression of water consumption (per account) on the conservation dummy variables, price and climatic factors.

While this approach is not new, some issues need airing. It is important to recall that in our theoretical models, formulated at the level of the individual decision maker, the amount of water consumed is the only endogenous variable. The onset of conservation programs, climatic factors, and price were assumed to be exogenous to consumption. In particular, we argued that price structures facing individual decision makers were determined by local policies, which were unaffected in the short run by the amount of water consumed by each *individual* consumer. However, we do not have data on individuals; instead, we have aggregate data for water districts or communities, and in the aggregate water consumption may affect the price structure determined by water district personnel. In other words, a theory based on the practices of water district policymakers and the aggregate consumption of the accounts served might make the price structure a function of consumption.

Nevertheless, the single equation approach is adequate for several reasons. First, since water is not viewed as an economic good, price is not considered to be a means to alter the demand for water. The price of water primarily reflects historical costs rather than demand. Therefore, one possible link between consumption and price is severed. In addition, price structures are not easily altered. Subject to extensive public hearings and approval by one or more regulatory agencies, proposed price changes must run the gauntlet of numerous political forces that inevitably delay and transform prospective alterations in pricing structures. Consequently, even if water district decision makers considered aggregate consumption figures in setting prices, there is certainly no guarantee that ultimate price structure alterations would reflect their concern. Finally, consistent with Box-Jenkins multivariate time series procedures, we routinely examined the cross-correlations between each of the model's residuals and all of our exogenous variables (at various lags). With the exception of occasional cross-correlations easily attributable to Type I errors, we found no evidence of feedback effects from consumption to price.

Second, we did not make routine use of prewhitening, which is primarily a device to assist in model specification (or model "identification" in time series parlance). If one has strong a priori theory or powerful external information to help in model specification, prewhitening may be superfluous. We had recourse to extensive theory from economics and social psychology coupled with a grounded knowledge (gained from fieldwork) of conservation programs.

Third, use of the Box-Jenkins specification strategy for single-equation models makes it unnecessary to prewhiten the endogenous variable (Box and Jenkins 1976; pp. 377–383) and inappropriate to prewhiten fixed regressors (Box and Tiao 1975). Among our regressors, only temperature and rainfall were considered to be stochastic. The conservation dummy variables are clearly binary and fixed, and, consistent with our view that price is also determined exogenously by the decisions of policymakers, price is treated as a fixed regressor.

Fourth, all of the results below are the end result of the usual interactive fitting process recommended for Box-Jenkins time series analyses. We employed the conventional variety of diagnostic devices (Box and Jenkins 1976, pp. 392–395) and also routinely plotted the predicted values from each equation on the same coordinates as the observed values. The plotting allowed us to gauge how well the predicted values "tracked" the observed values, thus providing another means to verify our model specifications. In other words, each and every equation was carefully scrutinized for possible specification errors in both the substantive, causal terms and within the noise model. By and large, the transfer function terms required the same parameters for all equations, while the noise models often varied. In the latter case there was a definite tendency for autoregressive terms to surface at lags of one and twelve months (as one might expect for monthly data). These were usually handled in a multiplicative form, but additional autoregressive or moving-average terms were frequently required, especially when particular districts did not read all of their meters each month.

Finally, while we relied heavily on the inductive procedures advocated for Box-Jenkins time series analysis, we also exercised a healthy dose of common sense, informed by what we knew about our sample of water districts. Following the advice of time series practitioners (Jenkins 1979, Granger and Newbold 1977), we did not allow ourselves to be blindly carried along by whatever the inductive procedures suggested. For example, the appearance of an occasional effect for rainfall lagged by five months, when no such effects were found for lags of three and four months, was dismissed as a Type I error.[1]

Results from six selected time series analyses

Given the large number of water districts (and communities) in our sample, coupled with data frequently available on several different kinds of water consumers, we estimated the parameters of nearly 200 separate time series models. We will summarize our findings, since it is clearly not feasible to discuss each model in detail. However, before presenting these summaries, it will perhaps prove instructive to consider a small set of results in some detail. At the very least, we will be able to report our overall results more swiftly once a few analyses are discussed in some depth. Consequently, we now turn to six models selected to represent typical results for different kinds of users.

Residential Water Use in Oceanside   Table 4.2 shows the time series results for residential consumers in Oceanside. Water consumption (HCF per-account per-month) is regressed on a single conservation "treatment" $(Tr1_t)$, mean monthly temperature (Te_t), monthly rainfall (R_t), and price (P_t). The conservation "treatment" involved conservation literature sent with water bills beginning in May of 1977, and the parameterization allows for rainfall to effect consumption in the same month and with a lagged impact of one month. However, the Oceanside time series was too short to allow for an estima-

Table 4.2   **Time Series Analysis of Residential Water Use for Oceanside (N = 101)**

$$RC_t = \mu + \omega_{0,1}Tr1_t + \omega_{0,5}Te_t + (\omega_{0,6} - \omega_{1}B_6)R_t + \omega_{0,7}P_t + N_t$$
$$N_t = (1 - \theta_1 B - \theta_2 B^6)(1 - \theta_3 B^{12})a_t$$

Parameter [a]	Estimated Coefficient	Elasticity	T-value
μ	22.55	—	69.38
$\omega_{0,1}$(dummy)	−2.65	—	3.19
$\omega_{0,5}$(degrees)	.55	—	7.19
$\omega_{0,6}$(inches)	−.40	—	2.32
$\omega_{1,6}$(inches)	−.65	—	3.84
$\omega_{0,7}$(dollars)	−33.06	−.33	3.96
$\theta_1(B)$	−.37	—	3.84
$\theta_2(B^6)$	.29	—	3.13
$\theta_3(B^{12})$	−.32	—	2.90

Residual standard error = 2.16
Chi-square   = 32.86 (P > .05, df = 32)
[a] When appropriate, signs have been changed to facilitate interpretation.

tion of postdrought effects. (In many other areas, we were able to consider postdrought effects.) That is, there were too few observations after the drought (N = 101).[2]

The causal model and the noise model are shown at the top of Table 4.2.[3] The mu represents the mean of the (centered) series. The omegas are causal parameters that can be interpreted like regression coefficients. Within the noise model (N_t), the thetas represent moving-average parameters, and in later models phis will be used to represent autoregressive parameters. The Bs are lag operators with superscripts indicating the length of the lag, and a_t symbolizes the white noise residuals.

When there is a single subscript associated with a parameter, the subscript indicates which parameter is involved. When there are two subscripts, the first denotes the lag and the second denotes the parameter. When, as in this instance, the parameter-indicator subscripts skip over one or more numbers in a sequence, it means that, for the given time series, the full array of treatment variables was not necessary. For example, in Oceanside there was only one conservation program, although we have allowed for up to three conservation programs and a "treatment" for the end of the drought. This subscripting procedure will facilitate our later discussion of results for many time series at once. By and large, our notational conventions follow directly from a number of popular expositions (for example, see Granger and Newbold 1977).

Starting at the bottom of the table, the chi-square is not statistically significant at the conventional .05 level, which means that one cannot reject the null hypothesis of white noise residuals. That is, the chi-square test on the first thirty-six serial correlations among the residuals indicates that we have an adequate fit. It will be our practice to report chi-square tests for the first thirty-six correlations, but in every case, chi-square tests for the first twelve and first twenty-four correlations also failed to reject the null hypothesis of white noise residuals. It is also important to keep in mind that for all the results reported, the model was judged to be adequate by the full range of diagnostic devices mentioned earlier. Finally, the residual standard error, here equal to 2.16, is a measure of how closely the residuals cluster around the "regression" hyperplane.

The parameter estimates are reported in the body of Table 4.2. These are produced through nonlinear least-squares procedures that minimize the error sum of squares. However, with the use of backcasting techniques, the parameter estimates very nearly approximate the results of unconditional-maximum-likelihood approaches (Box and Jenkins 1976, pp. 388–391). The associated *t*-values are produced from the last (linearized) iteration and are asymptotically valid.

Beginning with the mean (which is also the intercept of the centered equation), it is apparent that Oceanside residential consumers use an average of over 22 HCF of water per month in the typical household. Using this as a benchmark, the omega for Oceanside's literature campaign indicates that households used an average of 2.65 fewer HCF during the life of the program. Moreover, the decline is associated with a *t*-value of 3.19, which is statistically significant at the conventional .05 level, for a two-tail test. (We shall use two-tail tests and the .05 level in the analyses to follow.)[4]

The climatic control variables behave as expected, and all have statistically significant *t*-values. Each additional degree in mean monthly temperature leads to an increase of .55 HCF in water consumption. Given about a fifteen-degree seasonal temperature variation, effects as large as plus or minus 8 HCF can be anticipated. Perhaps more interesting, the effect of temperature provides one metric for the impact of Oceanside's conservation program, which has an effect about equal to a 5-degree decrease in mean monthly temperature.

For most of the areas sampled, the cross-correlations suggested that rainfall had both a simultaneous effect and an effect lagged by one month. Oceanside is no exception, and, for both effects, each 1-inch increase in monthly rainfall leads to a reduction in water consumption of about .50 HCF. Given a monthly variation in rainfall as large as 5 inches, water consumption is affected by as much as about 5 HCF (taking both lags into account). Finally, if the impact of rainfall is used as a metric, Oceanside's conservation campaign has effects roughly equal to a 2-inch increase in monthly rainfall.

The last omega in Table 4.2 indicates that price also has its predicted effects. The *t*-value is statistically significant, and the omega indicates that for every dollar increase in price, water consumption drops by 33 HCF. Of course, the price of water is typically under 20 cents per HCF, so that a more reasonable interpretation is that a 10-cent increase in price yields a reduction of over 3 HCF in the average household. Thus, a 10-cent increase in price has approximately the same impact as Oceanside's conservation program. In more familiar terms, the elasticity (at the mean) of water consumption with respect to price is −.33.

At this point, it may be worth stressing that the results for Oceanside passed all of the usual diagnostics. This means, for example, that the impact of actual changes in price was felt immediately (prospective price changes are announced well in advance) and that there was no need for additional parameters to capture lagged effects. That is, there was nothing in the analysis of the cross-correlations suggesting the need for either more omega parameters at longer lags or delta parameters to represent dynamic effects (that is, gradual price effects). The same holds for Oceanside's conservation program and all the other variables in Table 4.2.

The noise model parameters are shown near the bottom of the table. Analysis of the autocorrelations and partial autocorrelations among the residuals suggested that three moving-average parameters were required at lags of one, six, and twelve months. Given monthly data, such lags seem reasonable, although, following usual practice, the noise model will be given no substantive interpretation.

To summarize, the findings for Oceanside are typical of our findings for residential consumers. The climatic variables function as expected, and both price and conservation efforts have their anticipated effects. In short, both price and conservation programs "work," and their impacts are clearly nontrivial. The Oceanside conservation campaign produced over a 10 percent reduction in water consumption, and price increases on the order of 10 cents per HCF would yield similar results.

Agricultural Water Use in Montecito While available data permitted us to estimate models for residential use that were reasonably consistent with our theory, there was good reason a priori to be uneasy with our specifications for agricultural water consumption. In particular, we were forced to neglect several variables likely to affect the production of agricultural goods and therefore the amount of water consumed by agricultural users (primarily for irrigation). Nevertheless, Table 4.3 indicates that our analysis produced sensible and expected results.

There are three "treatment" variables. First, in January 1973 Mon-

Table 4.3 Time Series Analysis of Agricultural Water Use in Montecito (N = 114)

$$IRC_t = \mu + \omega_{0,1}Tr1_t + \omega_{0,2}Tr2_t + \omega_{0,3}Tr3_t + \omega_{0,5}Te_t + (\omega_{0,6} - \omega_{1,6}B)R_t + \omega_{0,7}P_t + N_t$$
$$N_t = (1 - \theta_1 B - \theta_2 B^{12})a_t$$

Parameter [a]	Estimated Coefficient	Elasticity	T-value
μ	440.06	—	27.78
$\omega_{0,1}$(dummy)	−188.24	—	34.75
$\omega_{0,2}$(dummy)	−171.51	—	3.90
$\omega_{0,3}$(dummy)	110.63	—	2.24
$\omega_{0,5}$(degrees)	23.44	—	7.05
$\omega_{0,6}$(inches)	−8.16	—	1.61
$\omega_{1,6}$ (inches)	−21.71	—	4.58
$\omega_{0,7}$ (dollars)	−3554.07	−.87	5.41
θ_1 (B)	−.25	—	2.76
θ_2 (B^{12})	−.32	—	3.57

Residual standard error = 109.49
Chi-square   = 41.7 (P > .05, df = 33)
[a] When appropriate, signs have been changed to facilitate interpretation.

tecito introduced a moratorium on new service hookups in response to concern about overdrafts of existing groundwater. While one might anticipate no impact for such a program (since customers already being served are unaffected), water consumption in fact dropped by 188 HCF. The *t*-value is easily significant at the .05 level. One possible interpretation is that the moratorium served in part as an educational device; it was introduced with a great deal of public discussion and controversy. Recall that across the state, moratoriums on new service hookups were rare, perhaps because of the serious economic implications.

Second, in September 1976 Montecito introduced a variety of conservation activities in response to the drought. A reduction of 171 HCF followed, which is also statistically significant. In other words, on top of an initial reduction of 188 HCF, a second reduction of nearly equal magnitude followed. Clearly, agricultural users in Montecito were very responsive to local conservation programs.

Finally, Table 4.3 indicates that postdrought water use increased by 110 HCF. This statistically significant effect means that consumption returned to about two-thirds of earlier (preconservation) levels. Our use of April 1978 as the date for the end of the drought is somewhat arbitrary, because heavy rains began to fall in December 1977, but official declarations that the drought was over were not made until early spring. Moreover, there was no precise termination date for drought-related conservation programs. Therefore, our selection of April 1978 reflects an inductive use of cross-correlational analyses. That is, it was reasonable to fix the end of the drought sometime during the winter or early spring of 1978. Within this interval, however, we relied on patterns in the data.

To be more precise, early in the study we examined cross-correlations between water consumption and a dummy variable for the end of the drought and, in addition, estimated models for water consumption using several different dates. We also tried a number of different causal formulations, including delta parameters, to capture gradual transitions from the drought to the postdrought period. All evidence pointed to a single omega parameter with effects beginning in the early spring. Of course, we might well have gotten a better reading with a larger number of postdrought observations (there were typically about ten), and perhaps the need for delta parameters would have been apparent. Indeed, for a large number of communities virtually no postdrought observations were available. However, we settled on April 1978 as the point at which (on the average) the largest effects were found, and we used that date for all water districts and communities, reasoning that the end of the drought was a statewide occurrence. We found that the results were almost identical for several months before and after April.

What all this means is that our estimates of postdrought changes in consumption should be treated cautiously. More important than the somewhat arbitrary date set for the end of the drought is the relatively short series of postdrought observations in those communities for which postdrought consumption figures were available. Perhaps with more data a different parameterization would have surfaced and/or different estimates of the amount of backsliding would have been found. In short, Table 4.3 presents evidence of nontrivial increases in water consumption with the end of the drought, but the precise magnitude should not be taken too seriously.

Turning to the climatic variables in Table 4.3, we find that for each degree increase in mean monthly temperature, agricultural water consumption increases by 23 HCF. The t-value is statistically significant at the .05 level. If these effects are used as a metric, the impacts of Montecito's conservation programs were each roughly equivalent to an 8-degree decrease in temperature. From this perspective, Montecito's conservation programs had a somewhat larger impact on agricultural water consumption than Oceanside's conservation programs had on residential consumption. Alternatively, if the means of the two consumption series are taken into account, the impacts are similar.

While both omega coefficients for rainfall have effects in the predicted direction, only the coefficient for a lag of one month is statistically significant. Since the climatic variables are included primarily for control purposes, this should be no cause for alarm. Part of the problem is that the two rainfall omega coefficients are highly correlated (as one would expect), making statistical significance more difficult to achieve.

The effect of price is in the predicted direction, large and statistically significant at the .05 level. A 10-cent increase in price yields a reduction of 355 HCF in agricultural consumption. This means that a 10-cent increase in price produces a little less than the combined effects of Montecito's two conservation programs. Yet the elasticity of consumption with respect to price is $-.87$, well over twice as large as the elasticity for Oceanside's residential consumers. Thus, in Montecito at least, agricultural consumers are not only more responsive to water conservation programs, but also more responsive to changes in price. Recall that we predicted agricultural users would be more sensitive to price changes in part because of the large amount of water used in irrigation.

Finally, the noise model required two moving-average parameters at lags of one and twelve months, formulated in additive terms. Again, the lags make sense given monthly data.

Commercial Water Use in Burbank   A priori, we were even less confident about our model specifications for commercial consumers than for agricultural consumers. Perhaps most important, commercial establishments use water in many different ways, sometimes as a vital part of their operations (for example, in the case of restaurants) and sometimes peripherally (e.g., for clothing stores). Yet we had no variables to capture such variation. A second problem was the small number of commercial accounts in some communities, where one or two large consumers were predominant. If these large commercial users consumed widely differing amounts of water from month to month (or season to season) as a function of neglected causal variables, our models would be in considerable trouble. At the extreme, should a large user go out of business or a new large user appear on the scene, water consumption would be significantly altered (even in per-account form), but not as a function of the included exogenous variables. In short, we anticipated weaker results in two forms: less compelling effects for our causal variables and more complicated noise models.

Table 4.4 shows that our fears were sometimes warranted. While all of the omega parameters are in the predicted directions, only the coefficients for mean monthly temperature and the simultaneous effect of rainfall are statistically significant at the .05 level for a two-tail test. Under a one-tail test, the effect of price is statistically significant at the .05 level. In September 1976 Burbank circulated conservation kits and literature, which apparently had little effect on commercial consump-

Table 4.4   Time Series Analysis of Commercial Water Use in Burbank (N – 102)

$$CC_t = \mu + \omega_{0,1}Tr1_t + \omega_{0,2}Tr2_t + \omega_{0,5}Te_t + (\omega_{0,6} - \omega_{1,6}B)R_t + \omega_{0,7}P_t + N_t$$
$$N_t = [(1 - \theta_1 B^5 - \theta_2 B^7)/(1 - \phi_1 B^1 - \phi_2 B^4)]a_t$$

Parameter [a]	Estimated Coefficient	Elasticity	T-value
μ	69.53	—	69.51
$\omega_{0,1}$(dummy)	−1.21	—	.44
$\omega_{0,2}$(dummy)	3.75	—	1.07
$\omega_{0,5}$(degrees)	.61	—	9.49
$\omega_{0,6}$(inches)	−.30	—	1.96
$\omega_{1,6}$(inches)	−.19	—	1.39
$\omega_{0,7}$(dollars)	−66.46	−.17	1.67
$\theta_1(B^5)$	.44	—	5.09
$\theta_2(B^7)$	.24	—	2.54
$\phi_1(B^1)$	.60	—	8.08
$\phi_2(B^4)$	.46	—	5.52

Residual standard error= 3.31
Chi-square   = 35.3 (P > .05, df = 31)
[a]When appropriate, signs have been changed to facilitate interpretation.

tion. Similarly, the end of the drought in April 1978 did not appear to make a notable difference. Finally, the noise model is the most complicated we have seen so far: two moving-average and two autoregressive parameters coupled with somewhat surprising lags in at least two cases.

The analysis of commercial water use in Burbank is typical of our experience with commercial consumers; by and large the signs are in the predicted direction, but the results are somewhat weaker than for residential and agricultural accounts. However, it is important to keep in mind that we have the prospect of drawing on a rather large number of replications across different locales that, at the very least, should provide a great deal more information. Weak results for individual analyses may appear stronger if they surface in a number of settings. We will return to this issue shortly.

Industrial Water Use in San Diego   Just as there were grounds for concern about our model specifications in the case of commercial water consumption, there are grounds for concern about our specifications for industrial consumption. Coupled with the prospect of missing variables was the even more severe problem of small sample sizes for each community. In some cases consumption figures were based on fewer than twenty accounts. In such situations, the opening

Table 4.5 Time Series Analysis for Industrial Water Use in San Diego (N = 101)

$$IC_t = \mu + \omega_{0,1}Tr1_t + \omega_{0,5}Te_t + (\omega_{0,6} - \omega_{1,6}B)R_t + \omega_{0,7}P_t + N_t$$
$$N_t = (1 - \theta_1 B^8 - \theta_2 B^{11} - \theta_3 B^{12})a_t$$

Parameter [a]	Estimated Coefficient	Elasticity	T-value
μ	1085.00	—	18.83
$\omega_{0,1}$(dummy)	−153.73	—	1.33
$\omega_{0,5}$(degrees)	1.20	—	.13
$\omega_{0,6}$(inches)	13.19	—	.44
$\omega_{1,6}$(inches)	−25.28	—	.85
$\omega_{0,7}$(dollars)	−1663.40	−.35	.98
$\theta_1(B^8)$	−.14	—	1.38
$\theta_2(B^{11})$	−.18	—	1.69
$\theta_3(B^{12})$	−.36	—	3.27

Residual standard error = 341.85
Chi-square   = 39.0 (P > .05, df = 32)
[a] When appropriate, signs have been changed to facilitate interpretation.

or closing of a single large plant might significantly alter consumption patterns and, hence, shift the consumption time series, thereby distorting our statistical results.

Table 4.5 shows that, once again, our fears had some basis in fact. Not a single omega managed to attain the .05 level of statistical significance, although four of the five are in the predicted direction. For example, in July 1976 San Diego sent conservation literature with its customer bills. The relevant omega suggests a reduction in water use of 153 HCF, but the *t*-value is only 1.33. When the drought ended, consumption increased by 1.2 HCF, but the *t*-value is virtually zero. Similarly, the impact of price looks promising until the *t*-value of .98 is taken into account. Finally, the noise model requires three moving-average parameters at unusual lags.

As we noted in the case of commercial consumption in Burbank, however, these are the results from a single area. A great deal more information is available when the effects across a number of locales are considered. We will turn to these other districts shortly.

Public Authority Water Use in Berkeley   Recall that in Chapter Two we questioned our ability to formulate a complete causal model for the amount of water consumed by public consumers (for example, schools). When this consideration is added to the likely specification errors and small samples of public consumers in given areas, there is once again substantial grounds for concern.

Table 4.6   Time Series Analysis for Public Authority Water Use in Berkeley (N = 114)

$$PAC_t = \mu + \omega_{0,1}Tr1_t + \omega_{0,2}Tr2_t + \omega_{0,3}Tr3_t + \omega_{0,4}Tr4_t + \omega_{0,5}Te_t +$$
$$(\omega_{0,6} - \omega_{1,6}B)R_t + \omega_{0,7}P_t + N_t$$
$$N_t = a_t/[(1 - \phi_1 B)(1 - \phi_2 B^2 - \phi_3 B^4 - \phi_4 B^6)]$$

Parameter [a]	Estimated Coefficient	Elasticity	T-value
μ	296.84	—	85.48
$\omega_{0,1}$(dummy)	17.71	—	1.28
$\omega_{0,2}$(dummy)	−72.28	—	5.27
$\omega_{0,3}$(dummy)	−37.90	—	1.37
$\omega_{0,4}$(dummy)	43.87	—	2.81
$\omega_{0,5}$(degrees)	2.73	—	2.23
$\omega_{0,6}$(inches)	−3.78	—	2.21
$\omega_{1,6}$(inches)	−3.58	—	2.24
$\omega_{0,7}$(dollars)	−1178.65	−.64	3.58
$\phi_1(B)$	.49	—	4.90
$\phi_2(B^2)$	−.32	—	3.24
$\phi_3(B^4)$	−.25	—	2.57
$\phi_4(B^6)$	−.51	—	5.45

Residual standard error = 39.10
Chi-square   = 40.2   (P > .05, df = 31)
[a] When appropriate, signs have been changed to facilitate interpretation.

Yet Table 4.6 indicates that something of interest is going on: the majority of omegas have statistically significant effects. In November 1972 Berkeley developed a water conservation plan. At the very least, this generated considerable publicity about water conservation. However, the omega is in the wrong direction and the *t*-value is only 1.28, suggesting that the introduction of the water plan had no impact. In March 1974 Berkeley launched a program to find and stop leaks, which apparently led to a statistically significant reduction of 72 HCF in water consumption by public users. Then in March 1977, during the height of the drought, a water rationing program was initiated. While a reduction in water consumption of 38 HCF appears to have resulted, the *t*-value is only 1.37. Finally, with the end of the drought in April 1978, water consumption increased a statistically significant 44 HCF. In short, two of the four policy interventions had statistically significant effects as expected, and one of the remaining two shifted water consumption in the predicted direction.

All of the climatic variables had the anticipated effects beyond chance levels. More important, each 10-cent increase in the price of water for public consumers reduced water use by 118 HCF. The reduction is statistically significant at the .05 level, and the elasticity is −.64.

Thus, despite the fact that public users *may* have less need to respond to changes in the price of water, they do respond to prices. In fact, the elasticity of water consumption with respect to price is among the largest we have seen so far.

Finally, for public users, in Berkeley at least, the noise model is rather complicated. Four autoregressive parameters are required, all with lags of six months or less, and three of the four have negative signs.

In summary, our time series analysis for public consumers in Berkeley performs rather well, despite our anxieties. However, the results of the time series analysis for all public users remain to be seen.

Total Water Production in Watsonville We were able to obtain breakdowns for up to five different kinds of water consumers for the majority of locales in our sample, but a few could not provide data in that form. In these cases, consumption data were aggregated in terms of either the total amount of water produced or the total amount of water sold. The difference results from leaks in the supply system, faulty meters, and the like. For communities in which breakdowns by consumer type were not available, we analyzed one or both of these aggregate consumption series.

Given the aggregation of all kinds of consumers, the possibilities for specification errors are numerous. Nevertheless, we proceeded with the same sort of formulation that we used for specific kinds of consumers, primarily because we had no choice.

Table 4.7 shows that, at least for Watsonville, our analysis of total water produced leads to reasonable results. In October 1976 Watsonville circulated water conservation kits and literature. The omega indicates that water use declined by 1.53 HCF, but the t-value of 1.78 is not statistically significant at the .05 level for a two-tail test (a one-tail test would be statistically significant). The climatic variables, in contrast, are all statistically significant in the predicted directions. Most important, every 10-cent increase in price leads to a reduction of 2.17 HCF in water produced and the t-value is 2.05. The elasticity is $-.19$. Finally, the noise model requires two autoregressive parameters at reasonable lags of one and twelve months.

In summary, the findings for total water production in Watsonville are consistent with our expectations, despite several possible problems. Price appears to be an effective conservation device, and the impact of Watsonville's conservation program is at least in the predicted direction. But, as before, more general conclusions will have to await analysis of data for a larger number of locales.

Summary Having now reviewed time series analyses for six kinds of users in six different communities selected to represent

Table 4.7   Time Series Analysis for Water Use Based on Total Production in Watsonville (N = 101)

$$TPC_t = \mu + \omega_{0,1}Tr1_t + \omega_{0,5}Te_t + (\omega_{0,6} - \omega_{1,6}B)R_t + \omega_{0,7}P_t + N_t$$
$$N_t = a_t/[(1 - \phi_1 B)(1 - \phi_2 B^{12})]$$

Parameter [a]	Estimated Coefficient	Elasticity	T-value
μ	21.04	—	19.36
$\omega_{0,1}$(dummy)	−1.53	—	1.78
$\omega_{0,5}$(degrees)	.65	—	7.18
$\omega_{0,6}$(inches)	−.36	—	3.07
$\omega_{1,6}$(inches)	−.20	—	1.64
$\omega_{0,7}$(dollars)	−21.66	−.19	2.05
$\phi_1(B)$	.26	—	2.33
$\phi_2(B^{12})$	.55	—	6.97

Residual standard error = 2.07
Chi-square   = 29.91 (P > .05, df = 33)
[a]When appropriate, signs have been changed to facilitate interpretation.

typical results, it is apparent that a sensible story is emerging. The climatic control variables are behaving as expected, while both price and conservation programs appear to have the impact anticipated. There is also a hint that post drought water consumption returned at least part of the way to predrought levels. In short, despite several potential problems, our initial theoretical expectations are broadly confirmed.

However, findings from six analyses are hardly the whole story, and rather than draw conclusions from the results so far, we must consider the findings from the larger data set. We turn to those findings now.

Summary of the results of our time series analyses

The full array of time series results is presented in Appendix B. Even a brief glance at the tables indicates that not every analysis conforms to our expectations, and in a few instances large coefficients are in the opposite of predicted directions. While in some cases counterintuitive results can be explained by severe data problems (for example, a very small number of accounts from which to calculate monthly consumption), there is no simple or truly defensible way to discard some of the data and keep the rest. In any case, it is difficult to draw many overall conclusions from the tables alone.

The obvious solution is to employ some means to reduce the tables to manageable proportions, and we shall proceed with the following rationale. On descriptive grounds alone, it makes sense to calculate the means for the causal coefficients (for example, for price) over all of the communities for a particular kind of water consumer (for example, residential consumers). However, although a perfectly good measure of central tendency under usual circumstances, the mean is known to be vulnerable to outliers. And in some instances a few large outliers exist. By "large" we mean estimates of parameters an order of magnitude bigger or smaller than the rest. Consequently, in addition to reporting means, we will also report medians. Moreover, we will rely far more heavily on the medians of coefficient estimates to avoid distortions from outliers.

If one is prepared to assume that the coefficient estimates for a given parameter over a single kind of user (for example, the impact of temperature for all commercial consumers) are drawn at random from a single population with a normal distribution, we can do even better; we can employ confidence intervals to provide a sense of the likely range of variation in a large number of replications. That is, we can report the confidence interval for the mean of the coefficients that reflects the proportion of times in a large number of replications (for a given sample size, here the number of communities) that the true mean of the coefficients would fall within a particular confidence interval. We will report the 95 percent confidence interval to be consistent with our earlier use of the .05 level of statistical significance.

However, given the existence of large outliers, it is unlikely that the coefficients come from a single, normal distribution. Indeed, tests of the normality assumption were routinely rejected. Therefore, we will also report the 95 percent confidence interval for the median based on the binomial distribution. This nonparametric approach will eliminate the problem of outliers (Marascuillo and McSweeney 1977, pp. 39–62) and the need to rely on the normal distribution.

The use of a confidence interval assumes that whatever the underlying distribution of the coefficients across the different communities (for a particular kind of water consumer), all coefficients come from that distribution. In effect, this means that each given population parameter is constant across all communities. For example, it is necessary to assume that the impact of conservation programs in Marin County is really the same as in San Diego. Whether or not we should be concerned about this premise is a question to which we will return in the next chapter. Suffice to say that our confidence intervals are tentative and perhaps should not be taken too seriously.

Table 4.8   Summary of Time Series Results for Residential Users

Parameter Values	Mean	95% Confidence Interval [a]		Median	95% Confidence Interval [b]		N
Mean	19.38	15.88 to	22.84	16.59	13.7 to	19.76	33
Conservation programs [c]	−5.50	−7.35 to	−3.65	−4.01	−6.61 to	−2.65	33
Temperature	0.25	0.17 to	0.33	0.17	0.08 to	0.28	33
Rain (lag = 0)	−0.13	−0.23 to	−0.03	−0.06	−0.14 to	0.02	33
Rain (lag = 1)	−0.32	−0.56 to	−0.09	−0.15	−0.23 to	−0.07	33
Price	−50.23	−89.95 to	−10.51	−18.77	−32.52 to	−7.50	33
Elasticity	−0.38	−0.59 to	−0.17	−0.23	−0.46 to	−0.06	33
End of drought	5.12	2.08 to	8.16	2.66	0.44 to	4.45	26 [d]

[a] Based on *t*-distribution (*t*-test).
[b] Based on binominal distribution (sign test).
[c] The sum of all the omega coefficients for conservation programs.
[d] Seven communities had time series that did not include a sufficient number of postdrought observations.

Summary Results for Residential Users   Table 4.8 reports the means, medians, and their respective 95 percent confidence intervals for the causal effects found for residential consumers. Thirty-three districts or communities were able to provide data specifically on residential consumers. Since locales varied in the number of conservation programs launched (and hence there were different numbers of conservation parameter estimates), in order to summarize the impacts of conservation programs, we have summed the relevant coefficients. In other words, the mean for "conservation programs" is the mean across the thirty-three areas after first summing all of the causal coefficients related to conservation programs. The summing process provides an estimate of the total impact of a community's conservation program. Finally, for some locales, we did not have a sufficient number of post drought observations to estimate the degree to which consumption levels changed after the drought. Thus, the sample size will routinely be smaller for the means and medians calculated on the end-of-drought coefficient. We lost seven communities in this manner.

It is apparent that the signs of the medians are all in the predicted direction for residential water consumers. Moreover, the 95 percent confidence interval for the median indicates that, with the exception of the median for rainfall at a lag of zero, we can perhaps reject the hypothesis that the true parameter values are zero. In short, we seem to be on the right track.

The median for the mu parameter estimates (the mean of each series) is 16.59 HCF per account. Since all of the time series were centered before analysis (for each exogenous variable, the mean was subtracted from the observations), the figure of 16.59 also serves as an

intercept in the usual regression terms. With this as a baseline, conservation programs on the average reduced water consumption for residential users by a little over 4 HCF, or about 25 percent relative to the
mean. Perhaps a better way of thinking about the impact of the conservation programs is to observe that the total impact is about equal
to the effects of a 23-degree drop in mean monthly temperature or a
19-inch increase in monthly rainfall. Thus, for residential consumers,
the aggregate reductions associated with water conservation programs
are large, at least in relative terms; the reductions are far in excess of
the effects of the usual month-to-month variation in temperature and
rainfall, and are a bit larger than the effects of typical winter-to-sum-
mer variation in temperature and rainfall.

It is also apparent that the impact of price is important. The median
price effect for residential consumers indicates that for every 10-cent
increase in price, water use declines by 1.88 per account. This figure
is a little over 10 percent of the mean and translates into an elasticity
of −.23. The effect of a 10-cent increase in price is roughly equivalent
to an 11-degree decrease in mean monthly temperature or nine additional inches of rain in a given month. However, 10-cent increases in
price were rare (most increases were much smaller) so that probably
the best standardized indicator for the impact of price is its elasticity.

Finally, with the end of the drought, water consumption per account increased by 2.66 HCF. This increment is over 16 percent of the
mean and 66 percent of the reduction associated with the conservation
programs. In other words, over the short postdrought period for
which we have data, consumption returned to a point about one-third
below normal levels. Perhaps the backsliding will continue, but we
suspect that postdrought consumption levels will stabilize a bit below
earlier consumption levels. Recall that some of the conservation efforts
involved alterations in water use technology (for example, leak repairs
and water-saving bathroom fixtures), the reductions that resulted from
these measures should carry over. What may be lost are the reductions
based on consumer behavioral changes.

Results for Agricultural Users   Table 4.9 shows the aggregate results for agricultural consumers. Again, all of the medians
for the parameter estimates are in the predicted direction. However,
only the confidence intervals for the mean and for the impact of temperature do not include zero. While this may be a cause for concern,
it is important to keep in mind that in order to make the confidence
intervals interpretable, one must assume that all of the coefficients for
a given exogenous variable are drawn from the *same* underlying distribution. We will explore this assumption in the next chapter. In addition, only eleven communities were able to provide consumption
data for agricultural users alone. Thus, our statistical power is very

Table 4.9 Summary of Time Series Results for Agricultural Users

Parameter Values	Mean	95% Confidence Interval [a]		Median	95% Confidence Interval [b]		N
Mean	497.21	226.09 to	768.31	381.34	179.62 to	829.91	11
Conservation programs [c]	−114.20	−229.92 to	1.52	−83.32	−354.42 to	32.45	11
Temperature	20.25	3.91 to	36.59	11.66	0.78 to	41.55	11
Rain (lag = 0)	−22.63	−51.89 to	6.63	−4.61	−72.64 to	2.61	11
Rain (lag = 1)	−18.38	−37.50 to	0.74	−5.38	−50.11 to	0.15	11
Price	5074.42	−8806.48 to	18,955.32	−1380.89	−3554.07 to	1270.40	11
Elasticity	−0.43	−0.85 to	−0.01	−0.65	−1.05 to	0.22	11
End of drought	−6.24	−64.13 to	51.67	78.76	−101.19 to	110.63	8 [d]

[a] Based on t-distribution (t-test).
[b] Based on binomial distribution (sign test).
[c] The sum of all the omega coefficients for conservation programs.
[d] Three communities had time series that did not include a sufficient number of post-drought observations.

low, and it is extremely difficult to reject the null hypothesis of no effect. With these two constraints in mind, it probably makes sense to interpret the medians, although with a bit more caution.

The overall mean (mu) for water consumption among agricultural users is 381.34 HCF per account. This figure is about twenty times larger than the mean for residential consumers. In this context, the impact of the conservation programs is also larger; water consumption declined by over 83 HCF as a function of local water conservation programs. While we will have more to say about the relative effectiveness of conservation programs for different kinds of users later, it is interesting to note that the reduction is about 22 percent of the mean. Recall that the impact of water conservation programs for residential users was approximately 25 percent of the mean. Put another way the reduction associated with conservation efforts is roughly equivalent to the effect of a 7-degree decrease in mean monthly temperature or an 8-inch increase in monthly rainfall. In short, by almost any metric, the impact of conservation programs is nontrivial.

The impact of price is even more striking. Each 10-cent increase in the price of water yields a reduction in consumption of 138 HCF per account. This is broadly equal to the effect of a 12-degree decrease in mean monthly temperature or nearly a 14-inch increase in rainfall in a given month. Most telling, the elasticity of water consumption with respect to price is −.65, nearly three times the elasticity found for residential consumers. Recall that this is fully consistent with our theoretical perspective.

With the end of the drought, argricultural consumption increased substantially: over 78 HCF per account. Thus, over 90 percent of the

Table 4.10 Summary of Time Series Results for Commercial Users

Parameter Values	Mean	95% Confidence Interval [a]		Median	95% Confidence Interval [b]		N
Mean	58.02	48.93 to	67.18	51.53	40.15 to	65.34	32
Conservation programs [c]	−3.73	−10.35 to	2.90	−7.68	−11.87 to	−2.19	32
Temperature	0.62	0.40 to	0.84	0.43	0.22 to	0.81	32
Rain (lag = 0)	−1.06	−2.26 to	0.14	−0.41	−0.68 to	−0.20	32
Rain (lag = 1)	−0.77	−1.17 to	−0.37	−0.50	−0.79 to	−0.19	32
Price	−307.28	−489.84 to	−124.72	−181.86	−323.94 to	−96.22	32
Elasticity	−0.87	−1.18 to	−0.56	−0.62	−1.04 to	−0.28	32
End of drought	11.91	6.97 to	16.85	11.15	5.31 to	22.1	23 [d]

[a] Based on t-distribution (t-test).
[b] Based on binomial distribution (sign test).
[c] The sum of all the omega coefficients for conservation programs.
[d] Nine communities had time series that did not include a sufficient number of postdrought observations.

reduction associated with conservation programs was lost in the post-drought period. If one takes this conclusion seriously, it raises the question of why such significant backsliding occurred. After all, agricultural consumption is certainly a function of the technology employed, and there is powerful conservation technology available (for example, drip irrigation). If such technology was introduced during the drought, the backsliding should be less dramatic. We suspect, however, that the drought period was too brief to generate major changes in agricultural technology. Instead, farmers turned temporarily to less water-intensive crops, took smaller yields, or drew from wells. When the drought ended, it was business as usual.

Results for Commercial Users Table 4.10 shows the results for commercial consumers. The medians indicate that, once again, all of the signs are in the predicted direction. Moreover, in every instance, the confidence intervals do not include zero. That is, if we are prepared to undertake statistical inference for the parameter estimates, we can universally reject the null hypothesis of no effect.

As a group, water conservation programs reduced water consumption by nearly 8 HCF per commercial account. This figure represents a decline of about 16 percent relative to the mean, which is roughly equal to the effect of an 18-degree decrease in mean monthly temperature or a 9-inch increase in rainfall in a particular month. Clearly, conservation works for commercial users, as well as for residential and agricultural users.

The impact of price is also substantial. Each 10-cent increase in price yields a decline in water consumption of over 18 HCF. This is

Table 4.11   Summary of Time Series Results for Industrial Users

Parameter Values	Mean	95% Confidence Interval [a]		Median	95% Confidence Interval [b]		N
Mean	2121.98	−19.56 to	4263.52	428.84	319.72 to 737.95		30
Conservation programs [c]	−527.36	−2757.54 to	1702.87	−35.81	−88.85 to	32.63	30
Temperature	3.15	−2.49 to	8.79	8.20	0.57 to	5.77	30
Rain (lag = 0)	4.08	−19.20 to	27.36	−0.35	−4.22 to	0.08	30
Rain (lag = 1)	−4.80	−11.10 to	1.50	−1.81	−3.09 to	−0.01	30
Price	1718.28	−14,103.32 to 17,538.88		−806.25	−1663.40 to	−39.59	30
Elasticity	−0.39	−1.17 to	0.39	−0.32	−0.88 to	−0.01	30
End of drought	156.04	−0.60 to	312.64	7.28	−16.65 to 103.95		21 [d]

[a] Based on *t*-distribution (*t*-test).
[b] Based on binomial distribution (sign test).
[c] Sum of all the omega coefficients for conservation programs.
[d] Nine communities had time series that did not include a sufficient number of post-drought observations.

broadly equivalent to the effect of a 41-degree drop in mean monthly temperature or a 20-inch increase in rain in a given month! Consistent with these large comparative effects is the elasticity of −.62. Thus, it appears that commercial users are nearly as responsive to changes in price as agricultural users, which is what we predicted.

Finally, there is again some evidence of backsliding. With the end of the drought, consumption increased by over 11 HCF. Keeping in mind the short postdrought series and the reduced sample size for estimates of postdrought effects, the consumption increase at the end of the drought is larger than the sum of the effects of local conservation efforts. While we could easily invent a number of post hoc explanations for such large postdrought gains, we are inclined to think that we are being victimized by data problems.

Results for Industrial Users   Table 4.11 reports the aggregate results for industrial consumers. As before, all of the signs of the medians are in the predicted direction. However, if one takes the confidence intervals seriously, one cannot reject the null hypothesis of no effect for the impacts of the conservation programs, rainfall with a lag of zero, and the end of the drought. On the other hand, given the issues raised earlier about the underlying assumptions for such tests, we will proceed as if all of the effects were real. It should also be noted in passing that there are large differences between the means and medians for industrial users, primarily because of several particularly large outliers.

Industrial consumers use an average of 428 HCF of water per account. Using this median as a baseline, the decrease in consumption

Table 4.12 Summary of Time Series Results for Public Authority Users

Parameter Values	Mean	95% Confidence Interval [a]		Median	95% Confidence Interval [b]		N
Mean	234.30	170.92 to	297.62	179.28	137.77 to	231.46	33
Conservation programs [c]	−70.99	−122.89 to	−19.09	−57.68	−92.47 to	−26.03	33
Temperature	5.62	1.96 to	9.28	2.78	1.81 to	4.38	33
Rain (lag = 0)	−2.13	−4.19 to	−0.07	−1.16	−3.78 to	−0.41	33
Rain (lag = 1)	−2.72	−4.66 to	−0.78	−2.56	−3.50 to	−1.27	33
Price	−854.95	−1252.63 to	−457.26	−576.41	−1215.10 to	−269.12	33
Elasticity	−0.73	−0.74 to	−0.72	−0.47	−0.92 to	−0.31	33
End of drought	41.55	14.97 to	68.13	37.03	7.40 to	62.58	23 [d]

[a] Based on *t*-distribution (*t*-test).
[b] Based on binomial distribution (sign test).
[c] Sum of all the omega coefficients for conservation programs.
[d] Ten communities had time series that did not include a sufficient number of post-drought observations.

of about 36 HCF associated with water conservation efforts translates into only an 8 percent reduction—the smallest relative effect for conservation programs we have seen so far. This reduction is roughly equal to the effects of a 4-degree decrease in mean monthly temperature or a 17-inch increase in rainfall in a given month. In short, conservation "works" for industrial users, but in a less dramatic fashion.

The price effects are also more modest. Every 10-cent increase in price results in about 81 fewer HCF of water consumed, 19 percent of mean use. In other terms, the 10-cent increase is about equal to the effects of a 10-degree decrease in temperature or a 38-inch increase in rain. (Note that while the last comparison suggests large relative effects, the impact of rainfall for commercial consumers is small.) Probably the best indicator of modest price effects is found in the relatively small elasticity of −.32. Only for residential consumers is the elasticity smaller.

Turning to postdrought effects, the amount of backsliding is quite small. The increase in consumption of over 7 HCF is only about 2 percent of the mean and only 20 percent of the water savings stemming from conservation programs. What this seems to suggest is that industrial users are somewhat less responsive overall to manipulable variables; conservation effects, price effects, and postdrought effects are by and large smaller than for the other kinds of consumers examined so far. We will return to these issues shortly.

Results for Public Authority Users Table 4.12 shows the aggregate results for public water users. Once again, all of the median signs are in the expected direction, and for these users, as for most of the others, none of the confidence intervals include zero. Therefore, if one wants to take significance tests seriously for these data, it is possible to reject the null hypothesis of no effect.

Given a mean consumption of 179 HCF over all public users, the introduction of conservation programs reduced water consumption by about 58 HCF, or about 30 percent of mean consumption. This amount of reduction is roughly the same as the effects of a 21-degree decrease in mean monthly temperature or a 16-inch increase in rainfall in a particular month. Public users are clearly responsive to conservation programs.

Every 10-cent increase in price yields a drop of 58 HCF in water consumption, representing about the same relative effects found for conservation programs. The elasticity of $-.47$ is also substantial, but not as large as that found for agricultural or commercial consumers.

Finally, with the end of the drought, water use among public users increased by 37 HCF. This increment represents about two-thirds of the savings resulting from conservation programs, which is about the same amount of backsliding as that found for residential consumers. Of course, the short postdrought series and the smaller sample make such observations somewhat suspect.

Results for Combined User Categories   For eleven communities we were able to obtain consumption figures only in terms of the total water produced per month; for six communities we were able to obtain consumption figures only for total sales; and for five communities, commercial and residential users were combined. There seems to be no substantive reason for reporting the results from these breakdowns in any detail, and the small sample sizes make it difficult to draw conclusions from aggregate results. To make matters worse, in seven of the communities for which total production figures were available, consumers paid a fixed price at the beginning of each month to obtain access to water but incurred no additional costs according to the amount of water used. Once the fee was paid, the next unit of water was free, and the marginal price was zero. This means that marginal price is a constant and cannot be analyzed.

Despite these and other difficulties, it may be comforting to know that, by and large, our earlier results are replicated. Using medians across communities for the 5 communities in which commercial and residential consumption data were combined, average consumption was 19.7 HCF. Using this as a benchmark, conservation programs reduced water use about 4 HCF, and the median elasticity was $-.28$. For the 6 communities in which consumption figures were in terms of total sales, average water consumption was 18.02 HCF. Water consumption was reduced about 2 HCF by conservation efforts, and the median elasticity was −.09. Finally, for the 11 communities in which totals were for production (not sales), average consumption was 43.5 HCF. Water conservation programs reduced water consumption by about 6 HCF. While estimates of the elasticity with respect to price could be obtained only for 4 locales, the median elasticity was −.14. In short, the results seem quite reasonable.

Conclusions

Despite a number of potential statistical problems, our overall findings are clear. On the average, water consumption responds in a meaningful way to both conservation programs and price. This conclusion applies to the full array of users. Whether the consumption figures reflect the actions of residential, agricultural, commercial, industrial, public, or even combined categories of users, policymakers have at least two vehicles with which to alter water consumption.

Over and above the broad similarity of average results for different kinds of users, the relative effectiveness of conservation programs and price varies; that is, some types of users seem to respond better than others to conservation programs, price, or both.

There are a number of possible reasons for differential responsiveness to conservation efforts and price. First, each set of analyses for a particular kind of consumer may be subject to its own specification errors. Consequently, what we take to be differences in responsiveness may just be distortions caused by the poor fit between the models estimated and the underlying causal mechanisms.

Second, even focusing on the median coefficients for different kinds of users, comparisons across consumer types are vulnerable to sampling error. In other words, apparent differences may simply be the result of chance variation.

Third, the differences across users may be "real" differences in the means for consumer types. It stands to reason that, in response to exogenous factors, large users can alter their water consumption by greater absolute amounts than can small users. For example, compare a farmer whose major use of water is to irrigate 100 acres of land with a homeowner whose major use of water is to "irrigate" a 2-acre yard. If price is increased by 5 cents per HCF, then, ceteris paribus, the total reduction in water use is almost certainly going to be larger for the farmer's account.

Finally, there may be real differences in responsiveness across consumer types, but these differences may reflect disparate demand

Table 4.13   Median of Causal Coefficients as a Proportion of the Median
             Mean of the Series

	Residential	Agricultural	Commercial	Industrial	Public	Total Production
Conservation programs	−0.24	−0.21	−0.15	−0.08	−0.32	−0.14
Temperature	0.01	0.03	0.01	0.02	0.02	0.03
Rain (lag = 0)	−0.00+	−0.01	−0.01	−0.00+	−0.01	−0.03
Rain (lag = 1)	−0.01	−0.01	−0.01	−0.00+	−0.01	−0.01
Price	−1.13	−3.62	−3.53	−1.88	−3.22	0.34[a]
End of drought	0.16	0.21	0.22	0.02	0.21	no data

[a] This reflects the practices of only four communities.

curves. In essence, because the uses of water and its importance vary, different users may have different elasticities of demand. Recall that we made precisely these arguments in Chapter Two.

We can do little at this point to provide alternative specifications or formally address the role of sampling error. In the case of the former, we have exhausted our list of plausible causal variables, and in the case of the latter, comparisons across user types are complicated by the fact that often different subsets of communities are involved. Also, if statistical inference was suspect for the one sample of confidence intervals used earlier, it is at least as problematic for two or more sample tests across disparate user types.

However, we can gain a better sense of the substantive issues. Table 4.13 shows each of the median coefficients for different kinds of users standardized by the median mu of each consumption series; that is, each median coefficient is expressed as a proportion of average consumption (mu). In effect, this controls for variation in the average size of accounts across categories of consumers. If differences in responsiveness remain, they reflect differences in the determinants of demand for the various types of users, as we discussed in Chapter Two.

Public users seem to be most responsive to water conservation programs, followed by residential and agricultural users; industrial users appear to be the least responsive; and total production and commercial users fall in between. Thus, responses to conservation programs do vary by the type of user, even when adjustments are made for the average size of accounts. On the other hand, it is not necessarily apparent why such variation occurs. Since public users are often subject to the same political and organizational forces that influence local water agencies, one might expect public consumers to be especially sensitive to conservation appeals. Once local governments decided to reduce water use, they made a special effort to control those uses over which they had some control—water conservation begins at home. The high level of responsiveness by residential users may reflect the fact that these consumers were typically the targets of conservation programs. In Chapter Three we observed that residential consumers were singled out for special attention.

At the other extreme, commercial and especially industrial users, who were not nearly as central in conservation programs, may view water as an economic good subject to market forces. That is, conservation appeals may be somewhat irrelevant. Of course, this leaves the relatively high level of responsiveness by agricultural users unexplained; one might speculate that since they depend on water for irrigation, agricultural users may be particularly sensitive to impending shortages. Recall that many agricultural users are dependent on water drawn from local wells, and these supplies are often threatened by periods of severe drought. Finally, the low level of responsiveness by combined users is difficult to disentangle, because we have no way of determining the relative contributions of different kinds of consumers.

There is also considerable variation in the size of climatic effects when adjustments are made for average consumption. The fact that the standardized median coefficients are small should not be allowed to obscure their comparative magnitudes. Ignoring the figures for total consumption for the reasons cited above, we see that agricultural users are unusually responsive to variation in temperature and at least as responsive as other consumer types to variation in rainfall. This makes sense given the central role of climatic factors in agricultural production. At the other extreme, industrial users are unresponsive to variation in rainfall, as one might expect. In contrast to agricultural consumers, they make no direct use of rainfall in the production process. Beyond these comparisons, however, it is difficult to arrive at any overall conclusions. Part of the problem, no doubt, is that our climatic variables are capturing the impact not only of rainfall and temperature, but also of more general seasonal patterns. For example, commercial users may be responding to seasonal variation in demand for their goods and services, and restaurants located near major highways may serve a larger number of customers in the summer, when highway travel increases.

The patterns across user types broadly correspond to the different elasticities discussed earlier (as they should). As we predicted in our theoretical discussion, residential consumers are the least responsive to changes in price, and agricultural consumers are the most responsive, followed closely by commercial and public consumers. Without additional information on how water is used in the production of goods and services, however, it is difficult to make much more of these patterns. For example, we cannot explain why industrial users show little responsiveness to changes in the price of water.

Just as industrial users were the least responsive to conservation programs in their communities, their behavior changed the least in the postdrought period. Perhaps we are again witnessing what occurs when water is treated primarily as an economic good, but this does not explain why such large relative increases in postdrought water use are found for commercial and agricultural consumers. Possibly the answer lies in the degree to which the amount of water used is fixed in the production process in the short run. Agricultural and commercial users may have considerably more discretion; for example, farmers can plant less water-intensive crops, and restaurants can serve water to customers only upon request. In contrast, manufacturing technology may require specific and predetermined amounts of water (for example, to brew beer or cool machinery), leaving little room for discretion. This may also explain the relatively small effect of price on industrial use. Of course, disaggregated data are required for an empirical consideration of such differences.

Where does this leave us? Beyond the observation that water consumption broadly responds to conservation programs and pricing as our a priori models predicted, it appears that differential effects across consumer types are partly a function of differences in the average amount of water used per account and partly a function of differences in the determinants of demand. The latter implies that if future studies are to explain variation across consumer types, it will be critical to formulate the production functions associated with different kinds of users, to collect measures on the relevant factors affecting production, and to collect disaggregated data.

5

What works better in some communities than others: differential effects across communities

Introduction

In general terms, it is apparent that water consumption responds both to conservation programs and variation in the per-unit price of water. It also seems that these conclusions hold on the average across the full array of users we have considered, although there is some evidence that some consumer types are typically more responsive than others to one or both variables. Recall that public and residential users, for example, responded especially well to conservation programs, while agricultural and commercial users responded especially well to price. In short, it appears that policy-relevant variables are differentially important depending on the kind of decision maker.

Just as one can ask about differential effectiveness over a variety of consumer types, one can also ask about differential effectiveness over different locales for each type of consumer. For example, perhaps residential users in communities with higher average consumption levels are more responsive to conservation programs. Or perhaps the responsiveness of residential users has as much to do with the number of conservation programs introduced during the drought; other things being equal, the greater the local conservation efforts, the less water consumed. Similar questions could be asked about all of our consumer categories.

An examination of differential effects across locales (for each user type) may be important for several reasons. First, in the last chapter we applied confidence intervals based on the somewhat suspect assumption that all coefficients for a particular variable were drawn from the same underlying sampling distribution. If this assumption is untenable, the confidence intervals have little inferential meaning. One way to consider the premise of a single underlying distribution is to examine whether variation in the estimated coefficients for a given variable(s) can be explained by exogenous factors (for example, population, median income, the number of conservation programs introduced during the drought, and median education). If a sufficient amount of variance beyond chance levels can be explained, then we must reject the assumption that the coefficients come from a single distribution.

Second, the question of differential effectiveness is important from the policy perspective. Policymakers are not satisfied by generalities, such as our conclusion that, broadly speaking, conservation works. Since they must make day-to-day decisions in a particular locale, policymakers seek information about what is likely to be effective in *their* community. In this respect, information about differential responsiveness as a function of measurable variables can be quite instructive. While such insights are clearly no substitute for detailed findings on the geographic area in question, they are useful in their own right and certainly complement local results. For example, local officials can develop water management policy based on results from communities "just like" theirs.

Third, to this point we have examined the impact of conservation programs in an all-or-nothing manner, with conservation programs represented by dummy variables that obviously neglect the intensity of local conservation efforts. This flies in the face of our rich discussion of conservation programs in Chapter Three and, in addition, raises at least two critical questions: if some investment in conservation programs is good, is a greater investment better? If so, is there some point at which declining marginal returns begin to materialize? These issues speak to differential effectiveness and to a variety of possible functional relationships between the intensity of conservation efforts and actual reduction in water use. Note also that both theoretical and policy issues are involved.

Fourth, what is the relationship between the effectiveness of conservation programs and the effectivenesss of price? Simply put, are these two approaches to water reduction competitive, complementary, or synergistic? When one looks across communities at the effectiveness of local conservation programs compared to the effectiveness of changes in price, what sorts of patterns surface? Do communities with especially potent conservation programs show disappointing results from price changes? Do communities that appear to respond particularly well to price pay little heed to conservation appeals? Do communities with successful conservation efforts also respond well to price? Are there some communities in which effects from both conservation programs and price are unusually dramatic? Again, both theoretical and policy issues are involved.

With these four issues as background, we turn now to a consideration of the differential impact of both local conservation programs and alterations in the price of water. In other words, we will address whether there is a substantial variation in the impact of these policy variables across communities that may at least in part be attributed to exogenous forces. In principle, one could ask a similar question of changes in water consumption after the drought (that is, differential backsliding), but the number of communities is already very small and up to a third (depending on the kind of consumer) had too few post-drought observations to make any estimation of postdrought effects feasible. In addition, even when such data were available, the number of postdrought observations from which to gauge the amount and time path of local backsliding was hardly generous (typically under ten). At some point, discretion becomes the better part of valor, and that point is reached with a consideration of differential postdrought effects.

It is one thing to propose examining variation in conservation and price effects and quite another to formulate an appropriate causal model. To begin with, we must think in terms of interaction effects: given the fact that conservation programs and price increases reduce water consumption in general, what sorts of factors should affect that reduction? In addition, the formulation of such interaction effects must take different kinds of consumers into account. One might antic-ipate, for example, that for residential users the median income of a community will affect responsiveness to changes in the price of water. Similarly, median educational level might alter the effectiveness of lo-cal conservation appeals. But what should be the role of these and other variables for public or commercial consumers?

There are also practical constraints. Besides the relatively small sam-ple size, the kinds of variables available at the community level are hardly exhaustive. Again, the data limitations become all the more problematic when we attempt to construct different models for different kinds of consumers. Finally, as we pointed out in Chapter Three, many of the possible causal variables are highly correlated, so that the spectre of multicollinearity hangs over the analysis.

Having considered these other difficulties, we will use the follow-ing exogenous variables (which we also used in the analyses in Chap-ter Three):

1. mean water consumption (in HCF);
2. population (in 100,000s);
3. median income (in 1,000s of dollars);
4. minimum annual runoff (in inches);
5. maximum annual average evaporation (in inches);
6. groundwater available (in millions of acre-feet);
7. percentage shortfall in 1976 precipitation;
8. number of conservation programs introduced during the drought;
9. median years of schooling completed.

Analyses will be undertaken separately for three kinds of users: res-idential, commercial, and public. An analysis of agricultural users is omitted because agricultural breakdowns were available for only eleven communities. Industrial users will also be ignored because of enormous difficulties with outliers.[1] For about a third of the thirty-three locales in which data on industrial consumers were available, conservation and price effects were either extremely large and negative or extremely large and *positive*. Recall that this was one of the primary reasons for resorting to medians in the last set of analyses, when we summarized average effects. Moreover, preliminary analyses for industrial consumers indicate that the impact of outliers could not be overcome, even if "robust regression" procedures were applied (more on those shortly). Finally, we do not analyze communities with data only for aggregate distribution, aggregate sales, or unusual combinations of consumers (for example, commercial and residential) because the sample sizes are too small.

Differential effects for residential users

Faced with a small sample of thirty-three communities for which residential breakdowns were available and collinearity among prospective causal variables, we opted for "lean" specifications. That is, we initially specified models for differential program and price effects in which only exogenous variables with clear justifications were included. To analyze conservation program effects, measured as the sum of the omega coefficients for conservation programs from the time series analyses, we began with three exogenous variables: mean water consumption (per account) in a community, median years of schooling completed, and number of conservation programs introduced during the drought. As we argued earlier, communities with larger mean consumption have the capacity to respond more dramatically to conservation programs. Median years of schooling completed can be used to indicate an aggregate ability to understand and assimilate conservation information and perhaps a general sympathy for conservation. Few would dispute that, to date, the environmental movement has been a middle class affair. Finally, the number of conservation programs introduced during the drought can be used as an indication of local investment in conservation. While the number of conservation programs is hardly a perfect measure, we did see in Chapter Three that, as a "gain score," it responded as one would expect. For example, the East Bay Municipal Utility District, which is widely known for its involvement in conservation, was especially likely to introduce a large number of conservation programs during the drought.

Developing a model for price is much more difficult. Again, it seems reasonable to expect that communities with large average consumption per account will be more responsive to change in price than communities with small consumption. However, the role of other exogenous variables is far less clear. Should large-consumption communities or those with smaller stores of groundwater be more responsive to price? It is important to keep in mind that, by and large, price increases were not part of local conservation efforts but were introduced for other reasons (for example, to achieve equity or increase revenues).

Given these complications, we initially settled on a single additional regressor: median income. On the one hand, in communities with greater median income, we may well find that residential users occupy a discretionary part of the demand curve; in other words, much of the residential consumption is accounted for by watering large lawns, filling swimming pools, and the like. Such communities should be particularly responsive to price increases. On the other hand, with higher median income comes a greater ability to pay for price increases in the sense that water bills have a much smaller impact on a household's monthly expenses. Following this reasoning, communities with higher median income should be less responsive to price increases. Thus, while reasonable arguments can be made that median income has an important effect, it is difficult to predict the direction of this effect.

We have two separate equations, and if one is prepared to assume that the *residuals* from each equation are drawn from a single (normal) distribution, it seems appropriate to proceed using ordinary least squares (OLS). However, we are once again facing the prospect of cross-sectional correlations among the residuals, since some communities fall within a single water district. Unfortunately, for reasons discussed in Chapter Three, we will have to ignore the possible difficulties that can result, and readers should keep in mind that our significance tests may be biased.

A more troubling difficulty is the serious distortion that can result from outliers. If outliers were a problem (for the coefficients) in the previous chapter, why not here? In fact, least-squares procedures necessarily give disproportional weight to more deviant observations (relative to the mean) and therefore may produce misleading results when outliers are present. As an alternative to least squares, one can employ a technique that minimizes the sum of the absolute values of the residuals. As one form of robust regression, "least absolute residual" (LAR) procedures markedly reduce the impact of outliers (Madalla 1977, pp. 308–317). Unfortunately, the sampling distributions of the resulting estimates are unknown, so we cannot undertake significance tests or construct confidence intervals. Thus, we will use LAR procedures to check the least-squares results. If the patterns of coefficients from the two approaches are similar, the OLS results are perhaps not

Table 5.1   Analysis of Program Adoption (number of programs introduced during the drought)

Variable	Regression Coefficients		
	Residential	Public	Commercial [a]
Constant	10.16**	9.80**	10.81**
EBMUD (dummy)	1.22**	1.41**	0.87
Population (100,000s)	−0.29*	−0.21	−0.34*
Median income (1000s of dollars)	−0.12	−0.06	−0.12
Minimum annual runoff (inches)	0.04	−0.00+	−0.02
Maximum annual average evaporation (inches)	0.01	−0.01	0.02
Groundwater available (millions of acre-feet)	−0.03**	−0.03*	−0.03**
Percentage shortfall in 1976 precipitation	−0.06**	−0.05**	−0.07**
$\bar{R}^2$ =	.72	.68	.65
F =	12.39	10.57	9.88
P =	<.05	<.05	<.05
N =	33	33	30

[a] Three outliers were dropped.
* $1.64 <$ t-value < 1.96.
** t-value ≥ 1.96.

seriously distorted by outliers. If the patterns differ, the LAR estimates are probably superior.

Another complication is introduced by the fact that the number of conservation programs introduced during the drought is used as a regressor in the equation predicting differential conservation effects. In Chapter Three we argued that unless adjustments are made for the fact that some communities launched more conservation activities during the drought than others, the estimated impact of the number of programs on the amount of water savings may be biased and inconsistent. The same reasoning pertains to these analyses: if residuals from an equation predicting the number of programs introduced are correlated with the residuals from an equation (using the number of programs as a regressor) predicting differential reductions in consumption, biased and inconsistent regression coefficients will result in the second equation. Consequently, even in the face of small sample sizes, we will employ instrumental variable techniques (formally justified in large samples only), and consistent estimates will result. Instruments will be constructed for both the least-squares and LAR procedures.

Building on the results from Chapter Three, Table 5.1 shows the equations for three kinds of consumers when efforts are made to predict the number of conservation programs introduced during the

Table 5.2 Analysis of Differential Effects for Residential Users

| | Program Effects (in HCF) | | | Price Effects (in HCF/cent) | | |
| | OLS | | LAR | OLS | | LAR |
Variable	Coefficient	t-value	Coefficient	Coefficient	t-value	Coefficient
Constant	45.46	4.48	41.19	1.45	1.70	0.24
Mean consumption (HCF)	−0.26	−3.32	−0.21	−0.06	−3.39	−0.01
Median years of school completed	−2.91	−3.77	−2.76	—	—	—
Gain in number of programs during drought[a]	−1.71	−4.82	−1.48	—	—	—
Median income (1000s of dollars)	—	—	—	−0.07	−1.09	−0.03
$\bar{R}^2$ =	.53		.37[b]	.23		.04[b]
F =	12.92		—	5.96		—
P =	<.05		—	<.05		—
N =	33		33	33		33
	Cross-correlation = −.13					

[a] An instrumental variable.
[b] The ratio of the adjusted regression absolute sum of residuals to the total absolute sum of residuals.

drought. Recall that in Chapter Three we worked with the full sample of fifty-seven communities, whereas in Table 5.1 the results rest on smaller samples for which breakdowns by kind of consumer were available. Nevertheless, the results are much the same, which is not surprising since the specifications are identical. The only new insight is that communities with greater supplies of groundwater instituted fewer conservation programs during the drought. While this makes sense and is fully consistent with our original justifications for including the amount of groundwater as a variable, the main purpose of the equations in Table 5.1 is to construct instruments for the number of programs introduced. That is, from each equation one instrumental variable will be constructed by the usual procedures (Hanushek and Jackson 1977, pp. 234–236). The large adjusted R^2's indicate that instruments with high "leverage" are forthcoming. The instrument for the residential equation will be used immediately below.

Table 5.2 shows the results for residential users when program and price effects are used as endogenous variables. In the case of conservation effects, all three regressors have statistically significant coefficients. Communities with greater average consumption per account, larger median years of schooling completed, and a greater number of drought-related conservation programs experience greater water savings. Each additional HCF in average consumption leads to an additional savings of .26 HCF. Given a standard deviation of nearly 10 HCF in average water consumption, variation in savings of plus or minus 2.6 HCF was apparently quite common. Since median savings as a result of local conservation programs was about 4 HCF, this translates into a savings of plus or minus 65 percent. Clearly, average consumption per account matters in the effectiveness of local conservation programs.

Each additional year of schooling increases the effectiveness of conservation programs introduced during the drought by 2.91 HCF. Given a standard deviation in median education of .81, variation in water savings of plus or minus 2.36 HCF was common. Again, this translates into a variation of plus or minus 65 percent.

Finally, with each additional conservation program introduced during the drought, water savings increased by 1.71 HCF. Moreover, an examination of the scatter plot indicates that the relationship is roughly linear over the range of variation found in our sample of 33 communities. Thus, there is no evidence of declining marginal returns for our sample. More is consistently better than less, and each new program is about as effective as the last. Given a standard deviation of 2.47 in the number of programs introduced, variation in savings of plus or minus 4.2 HCF occurred with some regularity. This translates into a variation of plus or minus 105 percent in the effectiveness of local conservation efforts!

We do not have to be concerned about the LAR coefficients, which are rather similar to the least-squares coefficients. In order words, there is no evidence that the least-squares results are being distorted by outliers. A scan of the relevant scatter plots confirmed this conclusion.

Given the results of the lean model shown in Table 5.2, we experimented with additional exogenous variables among those listed earlier. Not a single additional variable (or set of variables) was statistically significant or added substantially to the adjusted R^2. The only consequence was to inflate the standard errors of the significant variables in Table 5.2, so that eventually some significant effects disappeared. That is, the only contribution of the variables introduced was to increase the multicollinearity.

In contrast to our success in explaining the differential effectiveness of local conservation programs, the results for differential price effects were somewhat disappointing. The least-squares results suggest that communities with greater average consumption per account experienced greater declines in consumption with price increases. Each additional HCF of average consumption (per account) led to an enhancement of .06 HCF/penny in the impact of price. Given a standard deviation of nearly 10 HCF in average consumption, variation in price effects of plus or minus .60 HCF/penny were common. With a mean price effect of −.50, this translates into a variation of over plus or minus 100 percent. If the median price effect is used as a benchmark instead, the percentage of variation in impact is over twice as large!

Unfortunately, the LAR coefficient for price is much reduced, from −.06 to −.01. Moreover, an examination of the relevant scatter plots suggests that the large impact of mean consumption is primarily a function of only 5 of the 33 communities. The impact of mean consumption is much smaller for the remaining 28. Consequently, while there is clearly an overall tendency for communities with greater average water use per account to be more responsive to changes in price, the least-squares estimate is probably too large.

The impact of median income on differential price effects is negative, but the *t*-value is only 1.09, and the LAR effect is even smaller. Thus, there is no evidence that communities with higher median income are more responsive to price.

Faced with these disappointing results, we again introduced variables from the earlier list, both alone and in sets, but nothing of interest surfaced. As a last gasp, we examined zero-order correlations between a much larger set of potential regressors and the impact of price. Most of the correlations hovered around zero, and we could extract nothing to guide further model specifications. Thus, while mean consumption may well affect the impact of price changes, little else does.

To sum up, there is evidence that the effects of local conservation programs vary across community partly in a systematic manner. The omega coefficients for these effects do not appear to come from a single, underlying distribution. However, the omega coefficients for price effects may come from a single underlying distribution. When we paid attention only to the equation for differential program effects, our exogenous variables performed as expected. In particular, more programs are better than less, and there is no evidence for declining marginal returns. It also appears that communities with greater average consumption and with higher educational levels are more responsive to conservation efforts. Finally, the cross-correlation of −.13 between the residuals of the two least-squares equations (shown at the bottom of Table 5.2) indicates that when the effects of our regressors are taken into account, the impact of local conservation programs is virtually independent of the impact of price. This means that price increases and conservation programs are, for residential consumers, complementary and *not* competing ways to reduce water use. Thus, policymakers can introduce price changes with no concern about their effect on conservation programs and vice versa. If the zero-order correlation of .33 between price effects and program effects is used instead of the correlation between residuals, there is apparently a modest tendency for communities that respond better to conservation programs *also* to respond better to price. However, this results primarily from the impact of mean consumption on both.

Differential effects for commercial users

Turning to differential effects for commercial consumers, we have good reason to anticipate problems. To begin with, many variables implied by our theoretical framework for commercial consumption are unavailable in the aggregate data to which we are limited. And if the data are flawed for analysis of consumption, they are at least as suspect for analysis of the differential effects on consumption. Equally important, most of our variables describe attributes of the general population: median income, median years of schooling completed, and the like. The role of such variables in the differential impact of local conservation programs and price is typically obscure for *commercial* users. What might be the role of the size of an area's population or the average number of people per household? Should commercial users in large cities, for instance, be especially responsive or unresponsive to changes in price?

Faced with these and other difficulties, we settled on the following strategy. First, for commercial users we initially employed exactly the same lean specification developed for residential consumers. We speculated that individuals in communities with higher educational levels might be more aware of and involved in environmental issues, and commercial establishments in such communities might feel greater pressure to conserve. For example, for the sake of public relations, local restaurants might decide to refrain from serving water except upon request. Therefore, the role of schooling was justified post hoc as a general indicator of local support for conservation. In addition, commercial users in higher income communities might be less responsive to price increases if they can pass along the increased costs to their more affluent customers. For this reason, the inclusion of median income was also justified post hoc. The other two exogenous variables have the same justifications as before.

Second, after estimating the lean models, we experimented with other possible regressors from the list discussed earlier. After discounting for Type I errors, we hoped to find some additional predictors.

Finally, we examined the zero-order correlations between the two endogenous variables and a much larger number of possible regres-

Table 5.3   Analysis of Differential Effects for Commercial Users

| Variable | Program Effects (in HCF) | | | Price Effects (in HCF/cent) | | |
	OLS Coefficient	t-value	LAR Coefficient	OLS Coefficient	t-value	LAR Coefficient
Constant	−11.40	−0.36	−49.85	−1.46	−0.90	−0.41
Mean consumption (HCF)	−0.19	−2.07	−0.10	−0.01	−0.41	−0.01
Median years of school completed	2.38	1.08	4.86	—	—	—
Gain in number of programs during drought[a]	−2.85	−2.38	−2.65	—	—	—
Median income (1000s of dollars)	—	—	—	−0.01	−0.12	−0.04
$\bar{R}^2$ =	.16		.28[b]	.00		.02[b]
F =	2.87		—	.08		—
P =	>.05		—	>.05		—
N[c] =	29		29	29		29
		Cross-correlation = .14				

[a] An instrumental variable.
[b] The ratio of the adjusted regression absolute sum of residuals to the total absolute sum of residuals.
[c] Three outliers were dropped.

sors. The idea, of course, was to see if other potential regressors could be found. More generally, we viewed all of our efforts as highly exploratory, given the problems discussed above.

Table 5.3 shows the results for commercial users. With respect to the differential effectiveness of conservation programs, two regressors have statistically significant *t*-values under the least-squares procedures. As before, conservation efforts are more effective in communities with higher average consumption per account and in communities that introduced a larger number of conservation programs during the drought. Schooling appears to have no effect, at least for the least-squares results. So much for post hoc theory development.

Each additional HCF of average water consumption leads to a .19 HCF improvement in the effects of local conservation programs. Given a standard deviation of about 20 HCF in average water consumption, variation in program effects of plus or minus 4 HCF is relatively common. And considering a mean reduction in consumption of about 4 HCF, this translates into a variation of plus or minus 100 percent. If the median for water savings is used as a benchmark instead, the variation is plus or minus about 60 percent. If anything, therefore, the impact of mean consumption on the effectiveness of conservation programs appears to be even larger for commercial consumers than for residential consumers. However, it is also important to note that the LAR coefficient is about half the size of the least-squares coefficient, so that the impact of average consumption is somewhat suspect. Perhaps a more reasonable conclusion is that while average consumption may well be important for commercial consumers, it is less important than for residential consumers.

Each additional conservation program introduced during the drought leads to an additional water savings of 2.85 HCF. Given a standard deviation of about 2.5 in the number of drought-related conservation programs, a variation of plus or minus 7 HCF is hardly unusual. This translates into a variation of plus or minus 175 percent when the mean reduction is used as a yardstick, and plus or minus 100 percent when the median reduction is used as a yardstick. Thus, if anything, the differential effects from the number of programs introduced are larger for commercial than for residential consumers. Note also that the LAR coefficient is comparable to the least-squares coefficient. [2]

In summary, the differential conservation effects across communities are in two of the three cases rather similar to those found for residential consumers. The main disparity is the null finding for schooling, and, if anything, the LAR coefficient in Table 5.3 indicates that higher educational levels lead to *smaller* reductions. It may also be important to notice that we are able to explain far less variation in differential conservation effects for commercial than for residential consumers.

The model predicting differential price effects for commercial consumers is a total failure. There is little to discuss; the causal coefficients are small under both least-squares and LAR procedures, the t-values are less than 1.0, and virtually no variation is explained. Thus, we do even worse than we did for residential consumers.

For both dependent variables, we "fished" through our list of potential exogenous variables and came up empty. An examination of a large set of zero correlations also proved fruitless. In short, given the data on hand, the results presented in Table 5.3 are about as good as one is likely to obtain. Finally, the cross-correlation (at the bottom of Table 5.3) indicates that, once our causal variables are taken into account, variation in the impact of conservation programs is nearly independent of variation in the impact of price. Much as in the case for residential consumers, reduced consumption resulting from conservation programs and reduced consumption resulting from price increases appear to be unrelated. Thus, both can be implemented with little concern for their effects on each other.

Differential effects
for public users

The difficulties in formulating appropriate models for differential effects among public users are at least as severe as the difficulties in formulating models for differential effects among commercial users. We are hindered not only by an absence of theory, but also by problems with the variables on hand and potential specification errors from neglected variables. Thus, we will proceed much as before; the main difference will be in the post hoc justification for the inclusion of schooling and median income in our causal models.

In the case of median years of schooling completed, perhaps (again) communities with higher levels of education are likely to provide more fertile settings for the introduction of conservation programs. Administrators, teachers, and students in public schools, for instance, may already have substantial environmental concerns that potentiate water conservation efforts.

The argument for using median income follows the same logic employed for residential consumers. On the one hand, public institutions in wealthy communities may have a stronger financial base, thanks to greater per capita tax revenues. Thus, they may be at a more discretionary part of their demand curve. Public parks, for example, may make special efforts to keep baseball diamonds in good shape. As a result, there may be larger water savings associated with price increases. On the other hand, given their stronger financial foundation, public institutions in wealthy communities may consider their water bills to be a relatively small fraction of their monthly costs, or they may feel that they can go back to the public for more money to meet price increases. Therefore, there may be smaller water savings associated with price increases. In short, median income may well be important, but we have no a priori expectations for the direction of possible effects.

Table 5.4 shows the results for public users. For differential effects from conservation programs, only mean consumption per account appears to make a difference. With each additional HCF in average consumption, conservation programs result in a reduction of .54 HCF. Given a standard deviation of about 181 HCF, variation of plus or minus 100 HCF is common. Using median reductions of 60 HCF as a benchmark, this translates into plus or minus 160 percent, the biggest effect for mean consumption so far. Even if the smaller LAR coefficient is used, the impact of mean consumption is substantial.

Perhaps the null finding for schooling is to be expected, but the

Table 5.4 Analysis of Differential Effects for Public Users

Variable	Program Effects (in HCF)			Price Effects (in HCF/cent)		
	OLS Coefficient	t-value	LAR Coefficient	OLS Coefficient	t-value	LAR Coefficient
Constant	43.12	0.14	7.69	−2.12	0.22	8.07
Mean consumption (HCF)	−0.54	−4.47	−0.25	−0.01	−1.27	−0.02
Median years of school completed	1.79	0.07	1.90	—	—	—
Gain in number of programs during drought[a]	−1.97	−0.20	−8.50	—	—	—
Median income (1000s of dollars)	—	—	—	−0.28	−0.36	−0.95
$\bar{R}^2$ =	.37		.11[b]	.00		.07[b]
F =	7.42		—	0.82		—
P =	<.05		—	>.05		—
N =	33		33	33		33
		Cross-correlation = −.01				

[a] An instrumental variable.
[b] The ratio of the adjusted regression absolute sum of residuals to the total absolute sum of residuals.

null finding for the number of conservation programs is somewhat surprising. The sign of the least-squares coefficient is in the correct direction, and the LAR coefficient looks promising. However, even if one uses the LAR coefficient in conjunction with the standard error from the least-squares procedures, the *t*-value does not exceed 1.0. While this is hardly a rigorous test, it indicates how far from statistical significance the least-squares effect really is.

The disappointing effect of the number of conservation programs can perhaps be explained by the nature of organizational relationships between public institutions. There is often an explicit chain of command, so that once the city council, for example, endorses local conservation efforts, it simply requires that all agencies under its auspices fall into line. Alternatively, cooperation may be obtained horizontally across local agencies through friendship networks, exchange of favors, or elite peer pressure. One could imagine, for instance, a local water manager calling a friend who happens to be the official in charge of parks and recreation and asking for cooperation in community water conservation efforts. In short, convincing the general public or commercial consumers to conserve requires that individuals be converted one by one; under such circumstances, the greater the investment in local conservation programs the better. However, to the degree that one can capitalize on the power of political elites and formal hierarchies both within and between agencies, the number of conservation programs may be beside the point. The trick is to gain cooperation from a few key officials, and there is no reason to believe that the conservation program is particularly relevant to this end.

Consistent with the pattern for commercial users, Table 5.4 shows that we are unable to explain more than trivial amounts of variation in cross-community price effects. The adjusted R^2 is zero and the proportion of variation explained under the LAR procedures is .07. Perhaps more important, the two t-values are very small, and there is no evidence from the LAR coefficients that our null findings result from outliers.

For both equations we again introduced a number of single variables and sets of variables with nothing of interest surfacing. Similar results followed from a culling of a large correlation matrix. In short, given the data on hand, we do not seem to be missing anything. Finally, it is again apparent from the correlation between the residuals of the two equations that the differential effects of conservation programs are unrelated to the differential effects of price. The conclusion is the same as before: both conservation programs and price increases can be introduced with no concern about their effects on one another.

Summary and conclusions

With the possible exception of residential consumers, variation across communities in responsiveness to change in the price of water cannot be explained with the data on hand. We drew complete blanks for commercial and public users, while the apparent impact of mean consumption for residential consumers turned out to be a likely consequence of outliers. Therefore, our best guess at this point is that the coefficients for the earlier time series analyses representing the causal impact of price on water consumption come from the same underlying distribution.[3]

Variation in the impact of local conservation programs across communities is a much more interesting story. For residential consumers, conservation efforts are more effective in communities with greater average water consumption (per account), in communities with higher educational levels, and when a greater number of conservation programs is launched. For commercial users, conservation efforts are more effective in communities with greater average water consumption (per account), and when a greater number of conservation programs is launched. Finally, for public users, the only important variable is mean consumption per account: the greater the mean consumption, the greater the impact of local conservation efforts.

The relative success of our model for residential consumers can perhaps be explained by the validity of our original theoretical justifications. We were also able to capitalize on the fact that our important exogenous variables reflected attributes of the general public, the very group whose behavior was the subject of study. Conversely, the greater problems we had with our equations for commercial consumers probably derive from weaker theoretical foundations and the absence of any direct measures of commercial consumers. Finally, the somewhat disappointing findings for public users perhaps stem not only from weak theoretical foundations and an absence of direct measures of public consumers, but also from the central role of local public officials in getting conservation off the ground.

Whatever the merits of our cross-community analyses, there is no evidence that when the correlations among the residuals are considered, program and price effects are substantially related. Thus, public officials can introduce conservation programs with little risk of undermining the impact of price increases, and vice versa. In principle, therefore, both programs and pricing can serve as instruments of water conservation to be used in isolation or in concert.

Finally, by combining the results from Table 5.1 with the results from the other tables, we can clarify the role of drought severity. Other things being equal, communities with greater precipitation shortfalls launched a greater number of conservation programs. Then residential and commercial users in communities with a greater number of programs achieved larger water savings. However, there is no *direct* relationship between drought severity and program effectiveness. Rather, the role of drought severity is funneled through the number of programs initiated.

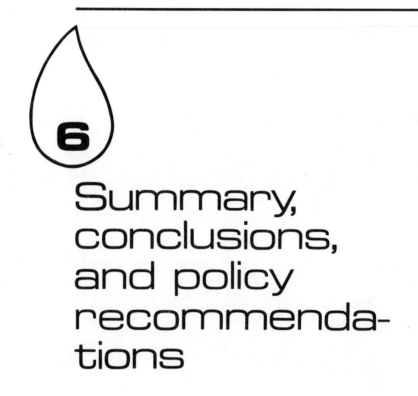

6

Summary, conclusions, and policy recommenda-tions

Introduction

Water shortages associated with the caprice of regional weather patterns are usually experienced as a highly localized and temporary phenomenon. Marin County's problem in 1977 becomes North Dakota's problem in 1980. As with floods, tornados, earthquakes, and other natural disasters, it is all too easy to believe that somehow droughts affect "other people" and that, whatever the short-term consequences, better times are just over the horizon. Moreover, since it is often only farmers and ranchers who appear to be severely victimized, broad public concern is often difficult to mobilize.

There are several reasons why water resources must not be taken for granted. First, while it is certainly true that farmers and ranchers suffer the most direct and visible costs, the economic consequences of droughts are far-reaching. Coupled with higher prices for farm products are net losses to regional economies and the suffering that comes from unemployment and geographic dislocation.

Second, long-term efforts to moderate the impact of droughts are extremely costly. In order to guarantee sufficient water supplies, taxpayers are asked to shoulder the enormous construction and maintenance costs of dams, reservoirs, aqueducts, and pumping stations. While public works of this nature serve a variety of economic needs, a substantial portion of their capacity is designed to dampen the impact of dramatic variation in annual precipitation.

Third, it is not as if a drought's immediate consequences leave nonagricultural users untouched. As communities respond to the expectation of genuine shortages, water consumers are asked to bear a variety of costs: the installation of water-saving technology, repairs on faulty plumbing, changes in habitual water use, reduction of water-intensive activities, and the like.

Finally, public agencies responsible for local water supplies have their energies and budgets diverted in unanticipated ways when business as usual can no longer be maintained. Supply systems must be repaired, emergency plans for water provision developed, and con-

143

sumer educational campaigns launched. Agency personnel are routinely embroiled in time-consuming political controversies about how best to proceed. Ultimately, of course, the general public foots the bill.

In addition to water shortages brought about by droughts, we argued that water supplies more generally are being increasingly jeopardized by a combination of growing demand and serious threats to water quality. In the Southwest, for example, economic development is creating new demands for water supplied by the Colorado River at a time when virtually all of its capacity has been allocated. Recent proposals to extract oil from western coal and oil-bearing shale, with technology requiring enormous amounts of water, will only make matters worse. Moreover, as the Colorado River flows southward, it carries along increasing amounts of dissolved mineral compounds, which at the very least reduce the productivity of irrigated land.

One has only to scan the front pages of local newspapers to realize that the difficulties concerning water supplied by the Colorado River are hardly unique. For example, many regions depend on wells drawing on deep aquifers that are not rapidly replenished by natural means. In these areas water (like fossil fuels) virtually becomes a nonrenewable natural resource; recall the case of the Ogallala aquifer serving states from Texas to South Dakota. Equally important, pollutants from a variety of sources are fouling local water supplies. The Love Canal tragedy is but one instance of a burgeoning problem documented in thousands of sites across the country by the Environmental Protection Agency.

In short, it may not be alarmist to assert that the energy crisis of the 1980s will be combined with the water crisis of the 1990s. We must find ways to increase water supplies from natural sources, to reduce unnecessary losses from supply systems, and to expand the use of recycled water. At the same time, however, we must reduce demand. And there are many ways to do this: educational campaigns, water-saving technology, mandatory rationing schemes, management of local economic development, and an enormous range of water-pricing strategies.

In the preceding chapters we have examined local responses to the severe drought experienced by California in 1976 and 1977 to determine whether local public policies had their intended effects. In essence, therefore, we were addressing efforts by California communities to reduce the demand for water in a period of acute scarcity. However, keep in mind that while our data came from a single state, in a particular historical period, and under an unusual set of climatic circumstances, the discussion has far more general relevance. The 1976–1977 drought set in motion an enormous natural experiment with important implications well beyond the 1970s and well beyond California's borders.

Defining a water shortage

Virtually all of the conservation efforts launched during the 1976–1977 drought were justified by claims that serious water shortages were in the offing. While there were sometimes heated disputes in particular areas about whether water resources were really inadequate, most parties neglected to define a water shortage. Such a definition is anything but obvious, and there are several subtle definitional issues that need to be clearly understood if public policy is to proceed in a rational manner and if demagoguery is to be avoided.

As we noted in Chapter One, California experiences wide variation in precipitation from year to year and from region to region. Some areas enjoy large annual rainfall while others must obtain most of their water from other sources. Some years are characterized by almost steady rain or snow for months at a time, while in other years only an occasional Pacific storm provides precipitation. In this context, a "drought" is but a single point on a precipitation distribution that requires the imposition of some subjective label. That is, droughts are not defined on the basis of hydrologic principles alone, but in concert with a range of social consequences, which in turn rest heavily on judgment calls about the adequacy of local water resources.

Local water supplies are affected by several factors besides precipitation: water inflows from other areas, water outflows to other areas, losses through transpiration and evaporation, increases or decreases in the amount of water stored, and the degree to which local water can be recycled. Some of these factors are routinely subject to human manipulation (for example, the amount of water stored), while others are not (for example, transpiration). Moreover, some of the manipulatable factors can be affected in the short run (for example, increasing the extraction of groundwater), while others cannot (for example, building new storage facilities).

In this context, large reductions in the usual amounts of precipitation tax existing resources by making "new water" less available, but create potential problems only when compensatory resources cannot be obtained through other means. For example, if greater amounts of water cannot be imported, supplies may become inadequate. The problem with "droughts," therefore, is that they require a large and relatively rapid provision of additional water. Local water districts are sometimes unable to meet this challenge.

If the demand for water remains constant in the face of diminishing supplies, a water shortage results. It cannot be overemphasized that water shortages reflect a failure of supply to match demand and that if demand is reduced commensurate with the decline in supply, *there is no water shortage.* Consequently, for a warning of impending "water shortages" to be more than rhetoric, it should rest on a reasonable expectation that if demand remains *at existing levels,* the short-run means to meet existing demand for water will prove inadequate.

The California drought ended late in 1977, and we will never (fortunately) be able to determine which communities were really facing severe water shortages, but in one sense the accuracy of local claims is beside the point. What matters is that, in response to assertions of impending shortages, communities throughout the state introduced a variety of measures to reduce demand. These can serve as a meaningful starting point for an analysis of "what works." Moreover, even if we were analyzing the social and political processes used to launch local conservation efforts, more important than the "true facts" are the "social facts" on the basis of which local actors operated; what individuals believed to be true was most immediately relevant.

In another sense, however, the accuracy of local claims does matter, in part because there are several policy lessons to be learned. First, while there is no doubt that some communities in California faced real water shortages, in too many communities local data were not up to such assessments. At the very least, water districts must have current data on available water resources and consumer demand. As we pointed out in Chapter One, many districts lacked the means (and perhaps the motivation) to monitor their operations closely. In addition, if assessments of possible water shortages are to be useful for policy formation, they must be projections about future circumstances. This is a *forecasting* problem requiring historical data and, quite commonly, the application of sophisticated statistical techniques. Even if appropriate data are available, the statistical technology is likely to be beyond the skills of local water district personnel. Thus, if public policy is to respond accurately to the prospect of water shortages, water districts must upgrade their forecasting procedures. To do so, they will need additional resources and technical expertise or routine access to appropriate outside agencies (for example, universities or consulting firms).

A second policy lesson is that assertions of impending shortages must integrate what is known about the factors affecting consumer demand. Virtually all kinds of water consumers respond to price, and when projections of future demand are made, the impact or price *must* be considered.[1] Thus, if a drought materializes during a period in which the price of water is changing (or is expected to change), projections of demand must be altered accordingly. Until more complete empirical analyses are undertaken, the results reported in Chapters Four and Five can be used for this purpose.

A final policy implication is that public claims about water shortages must make clear that a water shortage is a mismatch between supply and demand at existing prices. Too often the demand side is ignored, and a water shortage is viewed only as a gross shortfall in supplies. This fosters a special kind of crisis mentality in which blame is initially directed at the uncertainties of nature and solutions are sought primarily by increasing supply. In the long run, this often results in construction of new public works to moderate the impact of future droughts. If the implications of demand are considered, it may turn out that there is really no water shortage or that the shortage is much less severe than originally thought. Moreover, given the enormous costs that are typically incurred by efforts to increase existing supply systems, we suspect that it might be sounder public policy to consider ways to reduce demand first. Indeed, if the demand side is ignored and expensive public works are undertaken, taxpayers may well be saddled with excess capacity. Recall that the real costs of new supply systems are likely to be increasing (because "cheap" water is exploited first); should these costs be passed on to consumers, the demand for water will fall.[2]

Toward causal models of water consumption

In Chapter One we summarized a variety of aggregate statistics collected by the California Department of Water Resources. They indicated that in many communities water consumption declined dramatically during the drought. These reductions were officially attributed to local conservation efforts. However, we also argued at some length that reductions revealed through such aggregate data may be misleading and certainly neglect several important questions. Without developing formal models of water consumption and estimating the parameters associated with these models, one cannot be confident that all of the reductions were real (not attributable to chance) or that conservation programs should receive the credit. It is important to keep in mind that water consumption normally varies substantially from month to month, season to season, and year to year. Moreover, it is possible that many factors other than local conservation programs affect water consumption.

In Chapter Two we turned to theory from microeconomics and social psychology to develop causal models of water consumption. Microeconomic theory provided the basic framework and important insights into the impacts of different pricing structures on the quantity of water demanded. Theory from social psychology was used to suggest the kinds of conservation appeals that might alter the shift of the demand curve. We turn now to several general issues drawn from our theoretical discussion.

Given the practical difficulties of instituting marginal cost pricing,[3] water consumption in periods of acute scarcity can be placed within the larger context of a "commons dilemma,": short-run individual interests conflict with long-run public welfare so that, ultimately, no one's self-interest is really served. To take a recent example, the prospect of continued overdrafting of the Ogallala aquifer has apparently prompted individual farmers to extract the maximum amount of water their crops can effectively utilize (Frazier and Schlender 1980). From the perspective of each *individual* farmer, this is the best way to ensure the greatest short-run profits. With water supplies diminishing in the near future, farmers will eventually be forced to accept smaller yields from water-intensive crops and/or smaller profits from crops requiring less irrigation. In the meantime, it pays for each farmer to use as much of the declining stocks as possible. Unfortunately, this strategy is almost certainly suboptimal (especially in the long run) from the perspective of farmers as a group. Furthermore, individual farmers will ultimately be worse off than if the welfare of all farmers had been taken into account. Similar problems can result from drought-related shortages. They can be avoided only if the behavior of individuals is altered so that self-interest and group welfare correspond more closely.

When water is the commodity in short supply, conservation programs may be used to solve the commons dilemma. Under normal circumstances, each individual's effort to conserve makes so small a contribution to aggregate savings that there is little motivation to reduce water consumption. Therefore, conservation programs seek to alter individual perceptions so that consumers understand their place in the larger picture. In microeconomic terms, preferences ("tastes") are modified, and the demand curve is shifted.

We were able to extract from a number of social psychological studies the following general conclusions that implicitly guided many local conservation efforts and may be used to design more effective conservation programs in the future:

1. Conservation programs will be more effective when consumers can be convinced that a genuine shortage exists and that it constitutes a problem for a group(s) with which consumers identify.
2. Conservation programs will be more effective when appeals are made to moral principles, stressing the need to make a "fair" contribution to group welfare.
3. Conservation programs will be more effective when consumers are convinced that their individual efforts can make a difference for collective welfare.
4. Conservation programs will be more effective when consumers can be convinced that the individual costs and inconveniences

stemming from their conservation efforts will not be great (assuming this is true).

5. Conservation programs will be more effective when consumers are convinced that all members of the relevant group(s) are also making sincere efforts to conserve.

All of these findings can be integrated into local conservation programs. For example, one could imagine enclosing in consumer bills literature asking consumers to do their fair share and stressing the ease with which conservation activities can be implemented, and also enclosing a community "scorecard" reporting *aggregate* water savings for the previous month.

One of the critical conclusions from our review of the relevant microeconomic theory is that water is significantly *underpriced*. This results in part from the fact that, in the long run, water production is subject to increasing costs, and therefore the marginal cost curve is typically above the average cost curve. Since water districts generally base their prices on average costs, water becomes too cheap. In addition, water supply systems are often heavily subsidized by state and federal funds that are not reflected in consumer bills. Finally, a host of externalities are routinely neglected, regardless of whether average or marginal costs are considered. To illustrate, agricultural and recreational users in Goleta, California, currently pay $72 per acre-foot of water consumed. Yet according to an estimate, reported in Cooley and LaCivita (1979, p. 219), if water supplies are increased by importing "state water," the real marginal cost of the next acre-foot will be $1,466!

Given the degree to which water is underpriced, it follows that *too much water is consumed*. Moreover, when these inflated consumption figures are used to project future demand, the need to expand existing supply systems is greatly exaggerated. We are hardly alone in these observations; the unfortunate consequences of current pricing practices have been emphasized by several economists (for example, Hirshleifer, DeHaven, and Milliman 1969). If current water management policies in California are typical, these pricing practices will not change, and the construction of costly supply systems will continue. Indeed, as we were in the final states of this study, the state legislature, with the governor's full approval, initiated a massive program of public works construction with a price tag of $5.1 billion. While this is not the place to consider the likely costs and benefits, it appears that the effort would have been unnecessary if water were sold at a price close to its marginal cost (Moore, Graubard, and Shishko 1978).

Under marginal cost pricing, droughts are not qualitatively different from periods of more normal precipitation. With reduced stocks of water, the cost of the next unit consumed will typically be higher. If such costs are passed along to consumers, market mechanisms will yield the desired water savings. To take an extreme example, if local water resources are being dramatically outstripped, water may be trucked in from outside. Presumably, the per-unit cost of such water will be significantly higher than the per-unit cost of water consumed before, and if users are required to pay these marginal costs, demand will fall substantially. In short, if marginal cost pricing were routinely used by water agencies, there might be no need to introduce special water management policies when precipitation shortfalls occurred.

One possible criticism of marginal cost pricing during severe droughts is that, at some point, further reductions in water consumption create extreme hardship and disruptive discontinuities in local economies. For example, if it were necessary to irrigate large farms with water trucked in over long distances, and if the costs of such water were borne by farmers, local crops would cease to be competitive. Should this condition persist for several years, many farms would go out of business, local enterprises depending on agriculture would close down, and large segments of the population would move away.

However, if the drought reflects a long-term change in prevailing weather conditions, one might be prepared to live with such consequences. Presumably, greater efficiencies will follow if farm production is relocated to areas more richly endowed with cheap water (other things being equal). Despite the problem of short-term human suffering (for which there are a variety of possible remedies), it is not at all clear that subsidies should be provided to sustain an agricultural economy when it ceases to be competitive.

One might counter that droughts rarely last more than a few years, and considering the substantial costs of closing down local economies only to resurrect them shortly thereafter, a case can be made for subsidizing drought-stricken areas in the short run (for example, by declaring the locale a "disaster area"). In other words, reliance on marginal cost pricing may create costly discontinuities that are not in the best interest of long-term public policy. Under these circumstances, it may make sense to provide government grants or low-interest loans.[4]

Yet it is important to stress that, at least in California, massive supply systems exist that significantly dampen the impact of droughts. Moreover, if water were sold at its marginal cost (or a close approximation of its marginal cost) in times of plenty, consumers would be more highly motivated to introduce water-saving technology and use water more efficiently. Thus, water districts would enter periods of drought with lower demand, and the moderating effects of extant supply systems would be dramatically enhanced. In other words, the need to subsidize local economies during periods of drought would be significantly reduced. In this context, one should keep in mind that the 1976–1977 drought was the worst that California experienced in this century, yet even with prevailing inefficiencies, few areas were on the brink of running out of water.

To summarize, if economic efficiency is used as the primary criterion, a strong case remains for marginal cost pricing, *even in periods of drought*. Given the low probability that an even more severe drought will occur in the foreseeable future, the extensive supply systems already in place, and the enormous potential for more efficient use of existing water resources, marginal cost pricing incurs few risks and promises substantial benefits.

There remains the practical problem that since water in California is *not* sold at its marginal cost, other pricing options during droughts need to be considered. That is, we need to examine "second best" alternatives. There are a wide range of possibilities resting as much on distributional and normative principles as on economic efficiency. While it probably makes sense to increase the *per-unit* cost of water sold, the exact form of the price increase is far less clear.

To begin with, in establishing the uses of water that are excessive, public policy should consider both the purpose of water use (for example, sanitation versus landscaping) and the amount of water involved. Communities may decide that providing water to car washes is less important than providing water to hospitals or that public swimming pools should be sacrificed to the needs of the local zoo. Similarly, there may be an agreement that households should not be penalized for water use up to fifty gallons a day, but that the price of additional water should be increased significantly.

Once these priorities are established (which is no mean feat), water agencies need to examine the differential costs of policing their decisions. Again, the issues are complicated, since the costs reflect not only the direct burden on agency budgets and personnel, but also the impact of enforcement on the perceived legitimacy of agency efforts. Strong-arm tactics, for example, may substantially undermine popular cooperation, making water use priorities virtually impossible to enforce. It is one thing to impose large surcharges for excessive use and quite another to disconnect people on fixed incomes who are unable to pay for large across-the-board price increases.

Equally important is the question of distributional consequences. While it might seem equitable to increase the price paid by all residential consumers, every household requires some nontrivial amount of water to survive, and low-income households may be severely penalized. One obvious solution is to establish a two-tiered pricing structure in which households are allotted a maximum amount of water at the usual price (to cover necessities) and are charged a higher price for water used in excess of the initial allotment. Of course, establishing the amount of water required for necessities across different kinds of households is not a simple procedure.[5]

Finally, if prices are increased in response to impending shortages, water agencies may collect "surplus" revenues. Since typical pricing practices are designed to cover historical costs, water agencies may incur a "profit," and it is not clear what should be done with the extra money. One possibility is that excess revenues may be redistributed to low-income households to alleviate any perverse distributional effects. However, *even in the absence of marginal cost pricing,* the excess revenues should be distributed either in the form of lump sum payments (that is, money) or perhaps in the form of a fixed maximum (and modest) amount of free water, which is less than the household would consume at the existing price. While water consumption will probably increase as a result of income effects, the increase should be small. That is, households will be able to use their "windfall" in a variety of ways, not just to support greater water consumption. In contrast, declaring a moratorium on water charges for one or more months is likely to produce a dramatic increase in water use, since the marginal price of water over that period is zero. In other words, small income effects will be combined with large substitution effects.

The final issue raised in Chapter Two concerns the differential responsiveness across consumer types to changes in price. In particular, the demand associated with residential consumers should be less elastic, while the demand associated with agricultural, commercial, and industrial consumers should be more elastic. Given the problems of constructing a model for public consumers, however, it is unclear what the nature of their elasticity should be. Note that differential elasticities are of more than academic concern. By linking percentage changes in price to percentage changes in consumption, elasticities provide a vital tool for public policy. Presumably, it is important to know which kinds of consumers will be more or less responsive to price increases (or decreases) when price changes are contemplated. This knowledge is relevant whether price is being used consciously to reduce demand or to adjust water district revenues.

What did communities do during the drought?

Theoretical models of water consumption can be valuable, especially when they are based on concepts and causal relationships that have proved important in earlier work. If nothing else, applied theory forces one toward conceptual clarity, which in turn may improve the ways in which public policy is formulated. However, at some point theories must be moved from the chalkboard to the field, and we began that process in Chapter Three by examining the kinds of local water conservation efforts undertaken in California. Conservation programs were implicitly defined as conscious efforts to reduce water consumption in the face of an impending water shortage, although the shortage did not have to be a result of the drought, and price increases in the service of conservation were included.

The data base included fifty-seven geographic areas, either urban water districts or communities within urban districts. These areas were selected to reflect variation across the state in climate, economic base, and size. Districts were included from the Bay Area, greater Los Angeles, and San Diego, as well as from smaller communities in the central and northern coast, the central valley, the Sierras, and the southern deserts. Teams of research assistants visited these areas to collect data covering the eight years from the middle of 1970 to the middle of 1978.

In order to examine conservation programs that were introduced in response to the drought, we had to consider what communities were doing before the 1976–1977 period. That is, we needed to determine which programs reflected long-standing conservation concerns and which were direct reactions to the drought. In the process, we discovered that many communities, particularly in the Bay Area, were heavily involved in water conservation well before the drought, and that local efforts rested on an enormous variety of conservation strategies and tactics.

Conservation programs were organized under three broad headings, speaking to the organizational and implementation process involved: voluntary conservation by individual consumers; institutional conservation by public agencies; and proscriptive conservation imposed by statute, ordinance, or regulation. Specific conservation programs could, in principle, fall under more than one heading. Increases in the price of water, for example, could be implemented through an administrative decision by a local water purveyor or through a city ordinance imposing surcharges for excessive consumption. With this conceptual framework in hand, we then turned to the data, and the following empirical results emerged.

First, we found enormous variation in the number and kind of conservation programs introduced by the communities in our sample. At one extreme, the Marin Municipal Water District introduced a wide variety of conservation activities as part of a broad water management plan, including educational campaigns, a moratorium on new service connections, mandatory rationing, penalty charges for excessive water use, and distribution of water-saving devices to residential consumers. At the other extreme, San Diego's conservation program consisted of no more than the circulation of a single informational leaflet.

Second, although the greatest amount of conservation activity occurred during the drought, several communities had aggressive conservation efforts underway before 1976, and many activities begun during the drought remained in place thereafter (although our post-drought period is very short). In other words, while the drought stimulated a great deal of conservation activity, other factors were also involved.

Third, some kinds of conservation programs were more closely linked to the drought than others. In particular, metering, water recycling, plumbing code changes, and new service moratoriums seemed to be rather insensitive to shortages created by the drought. We offered several reasons why such efforts were unlikely to respond to the drought, including the large number of obstacles impeding rapid implementation. In contrast, other conservation approaches increased dramatically in popularity with the onset of the drought and were less salient when the drought was over: educational leaflets, surcharges, rationing, advertisements in local papers, informational programs for schoolchildren, and the like.

Fourth, the characteristics of programs actually launched revealed some important gaps between targets and procedures. To begin with, most conservation programs were aimed primarily at residential users. While in the aggregate, residential use often dominated local water consumption figures (for our sample of communities), agricultural, commercial, industrial, and public users were hardly unimportant. We suggested that the emphasis on residential accounts could result from a number of factors, including a hesitancy on the part of water district personnel to intervene where they lacked the expertise, but also stressed that nonresidential consumption should not be neglected. In addition, the kinds of programs that were introduced neglected price as an instrument of public policy. That is, it was relatively unusual to find price increases used to reduce consumption, which we attributed in part to the common belief that water should not be considered an economic good. Finally, we observed that despite large Spanish-speaking populations in many of our sample communities, few districts provided Spanish versions of educational materials.

Fifth, even though we lacked sufficient data on the implementation process, we explored why some communities made greater conservation efforts than others. In particular, we examined the number of programs introduced before, during, and after the drought, along with the change in the number of programs over time as a function of several aggregate characteristics of water districts or communities. Predictors included median income, population, available groundwater, and the severity of the drought's local impact. Three explanatory factors emerged: a long-standing commitment to conservation, the local impact of the drought, and (less important) the economic resources of the local water agency. All were positively related to conservation activity.

What works?

Our analysis of the kinds of conservation programs that were initiated set the stage for an examination of whether these efforts were successful in reducing water consumption. It was clear that the type and intensity of conservation activities varied enormously both over time and across locales. Now the question was whether such variation could be used to explain variation in water consumption.

To estimate program effects, we had to specify causal models of water consumption for five kinds of users: residential, agricultural, commercial, industrial, and public. For these models we drew heavily on the theoretical material discussed in Chapter Two. As we proceeded, it was apparent that the a priori specification for residential users was relatively sound, but that there were grounds for concern when the models for other users were considered. In particular, our exogenous variables probably did not account for several important causal factors. Nevertheless, we argued that sensible results might follow, thanks to our ability to capitalize on a large number of replications across user types and communities, and the special properties of the statistical procedures we planned to employ.

For each community and each kind of user for which breakdowns were available, the data were organized by month and arrayed over the eight-year period bracketing the drought. That is, each analysis rested on monthly time series data including approximately 100 longitudinal observations. In each case, the endogenous variable was aggregate water consumption divided by the number of water accounts being served. In other words, we were attempting to explain variation over time in water used by particular kinds of consumers in particular communities, standardized for the number of service connections (that is, water consumption per account). Our exogenous variables included one or more dummy variables to capture the introduction of various conservation programs, a dummy variable reflecting the end of the drought, a measure of "mean marginal price," total rainfall in each month, and average temperature in each month. We worried about possible specification errors, including whether price should really be treated as exogenous. Typically, we were able to provide a number of arguments supporting our specification decisions, so that, as we approached the data, there were some grounds for optimism.

For a variety of reasons, the statistical analysis was undertaken using time series procedures within the Box-Jenkins tradition. However, we used a parameterization of the general multivariate time series model that was particularly well suited to causal modeling and that could be interpreted much like multiple regression. Nearly 200 separate time series analyses were undertaken and then summarized.

By and large, our models performed as expected, especially when aggregate results across communities were examined. First, while we were not particularly interested in the precise parameter estimates for the impact of temperature and rainfall (since they were control variables capturing a range of causal processes), we found that, typically, water consumption rose in months with higher temperatures and fell in months with greater precipitation. We would have been quite concerned had such reasonable effects not surfaced.

Second, conservation programs generally worked, in the sense that water use declined after the programs were launched. The reductions were often large in both absolute and relative terms. Using mean consumption as a benchmark, for example, reductions of 30 percent were common. We also found that some kinds of consumers were more responsive than others to water conservation programs. Residential and public users were the most responsive, while industrial users were the least responsive; agricultural and commercial users fell in between these extremes. We argued that the special responsiveness of residential consumers resulted in part from the residential emphasis of most local conservation programs (as we noted above). We argued that the special responsiveness of public users resulted in part from the organizational links between public institutions in particular communities. Once a city manager, for example, makes a commitment to water conservation, he or she can simply order local institutions to comply. In contrast, private sector institutions were more likely to govern their water use through production technology (which is often difficult to change in the short run) and market forces. These users perhaps had less reason to respond to conservation appeals, even when they were directed at private sector institutions.

Third, price worked as well. Price elasticities for residential consumers were typically in the $-.30$ range, while price elasticities for other consumer types were two to three times as large. Having expected larger elasticities for commercial, industrial, and agricultural users, the large price effect for public users caught us by surprise. Public water consumers are perhaps more cost-conscious than some people have argued.

Fourth, our effort to estimate postdrought changes in water consumption was severely hindered by the small number of postdrought observations overall (around ten months), and the lack of any postdrought data for about a third of our communities. Nevertheless, considerable backsliding was evident after the drought. Using water savings from conservation programs during the drought as a yardstick, we found postdrought gains of up to 60 percent or more of predrought consumption. However, because of inadequate data, we were

Table 6.1   Equivalences Between the Effects of Conservation Programs and the Effects of Price

Residential Users (N = 33)

Median reduction from conservation programs (−4.01 HCF) =
a 21.3-cent increase in price =
a 112% increase in price

Agricultural Users (N = 11)

Median reduction from conservation programs (−83.32 HCF) =
a 6.0-cent increase in price =
a 46% increase in price

Commercial Users (N = 32)

Median reduction from conservation programs (−7.68 HCF) =
a 4.2-cent increase in price =
a 23% increase in price

Industrial Users (N = 30)

Median reduction from conservation programs (−35.81 HCF) =
a 4.4-cent increase in price =
a 28% increase in price

Public Users (N = 33)

Median reduction from conservation programs (−57.68 HCF) =
a 10-cent increase in price =
a 59% increase in price

unable to determine if postdrought water consumption had stabilized at somewhat lower levels or whether further backsliding was in the offing. We speculated that, thanks to water-saving technology introduced during the drought, at least part of the water savings achieved during the drought would be retained afterward.

In summary, despite many theoretical and practical difficulties, our causal analyses of water consumption produced several useful and sensible findings. It is clear that both conservation programs and price work, and that both are viable instruments for water management policy. However, the question of relative effectiveness remains, and we have constructed Table 6.1 to address that question.

For each kind of water consumer for which breakdowns are routinely available (note the sample sizes), we have provided two equivalences for median reduction in water consumption resulting from local water conservation programs. That is, for the median reduction (summed across all programs introduced in particular communities), we have calculated the price increase that would produce identical savings and the proportional price increase that is implied.

The median reduction for residential consumers was −4.01 HCF, which is equivalent to the effect of a 21.3-cent increase in the per-unit price of water or a 112-percent price increase. In other words, on the average one would have to roughly double the price of water to obtain the same reductions that were achieved from drought-related conservation programs. Clearly, large price increases are implied, and this raises some important issues concerning water management policy. On the one hand, inducing water savings through price increases has the distinct asset of yielding reasonably predictable effects with low administrative overhead. In the context of current practice, price increases may also be more efficient economically, moving water prices closer to real marginal costs. In contrast, conservation programs require substantial investments of agency time and money, and the success of such efforts will depend on a variety of factors that are difficult to anticipate. For example, it is not at all clear how severe a drought must be before consumers are likely to take conservation appeals seriously. Recall that these conservation programs were put in place during the worst California drought in this century. On the other hand, doubling the price of water is almost certain to incur significant political costs; indeed, it may be politically impossible to double the price of water. Moreover, dramatic price increases raise a number of important distributional problems, some of which we discussed earlier. Doubling the price of water may, for example, impose serious hardships on low-income families. Thus, one might want to develop a method to redistribute any agency profits resulting from a price increase, perhaps in the manner we described briefly above.

For agricultural users, Table 6.1 indicates that the median reduction of −83.32 HCF obtained from conservation programs is equivalent to a 6-cent price increase, which in turn represents a 46-percent increment in price. Compared to residential consumers, a smaller price increase is implied, yet the same practical issues arise. Indeed, the political costs may be even higher. Both state and local agricultural lobbies in California are extremely powerful. Also, considering the tradition of de facto subsidization of agricultural water consumption through tax revenues, it is difficult to imagine that agricultural interests would accept a 46 percent increase in water prices.

For commercial users, the median water savings of −7.68 HCF from water conservation programs is equal to the impact of a 4.2-cent increase in the price of water, which translates into only a 23-percent increment. A similar pattern is found for industrial consumers: the median water reduction of −35.81 HCF from conservation programs can be obtained through a 4.4-cent price increase, or a 28-percent increment. Perhaps it is more feasible in political terms to use price as a conservation mechanism for commercial and industrial consumers. However, this will depend in part on how important water is in the production of particular goods and services. Retail stores might well acquiesce, but food processors would probably object.

Finally, a median water savings of −57.68 HCF for public users is equivalent to the impact of a 10-cent price increase, or an increment of 59 percent. Again, the political feasibility of such an increase will probably vary depending on the kind of public consumer involved. Water bills may not figure significantly in the costs of running a hospital, for example, but the cost of maintaining public parks (especially those with swimming pools) depends heavily on the price of water. Perhaps this is an instance in which excess revenues collected through price increases can be carefully redistributed to support particularly important public services.

In summary, the good news is that water savings can be achieved either through conservation programs or through price increases. Moreover, these savings can be substantial in absolute and relative terms. The bad news is that political and administrative considerations will probably intervene, so that even an optimal strategy may not be viable. One possible solution is to combine conservation programs with more modest price increases, but that raises some empirical questions to which we will now turn. In particular, we need to determine if the impacts of conservation programs and price increases are related to one another.

Where do things work better?

While the central tendencies from the many time series analyses reported in Chapter Four are clear, we found wide variation in effects across different communities. In some locales, for example, conservation programs led to water savings of over 60 percent, while in others virtually no savings were achieved. Similar differences surfaced for price, and when coupled with data quality problems in a few communities, large *positive* elasticities were sometimes found.

Variation in the effects of conservation programs and changes in price are of interest for several reasons. First, water management decision makers need to know not only the probable outcome of their efforts (an expected value), but also the distribution of possible effects. Can they be confident, for instance, that conservation programs will at least not make things worse? Better still, can they attach probability estimates to different ranges of outcomes? Equally important, policymakers need to have some sense of whether the effectiveness of local conservation depends primarily on the luck of the draw, or whether there is something about their area that enhances or inhibits the impact of conservation activities. Should communities in which average water consumption per household is higher, for example, anticipate greater water savings from increases in price? Finally, it is important to know whether variation across communities in program and price effects is subject to manipulation. Communities with larger populations, for instance, may be more responsive to conservation programs, but population is not a manipulable variable. In contrast, perhaps it pays for communities to introduce many conservation programs, because each new program yields additional water savings; more is better than less.

Near the end of Chapter Four and especially in Chapter Five, we addressed differential effects across communities. Using the community as the unit of analysis, we examined the distributions of the parameter estimates from the time series analyses and considered explanatory factors that might help us to understand the sources of that variation. On a descriptive level, we examined the full array of user types: residential, agricultural, commercial, industrial, public, and various aggregated categories (for example, total production). Then we turned to causal modeling and focused on only those consumer types for which there were adequate sample sizes (that is, the number of communities), and reasonably continuous distributions of coefficients (that is, little evidence of outliers). Thus, for example, agricultural users were dropped, because agricultural breakdowns were available in only eleven communities, and we abandoned causal analyses of industrial users because of serious difficulties with outliers.

Our first conclusion was that most of the 95 percent confidence intervals across different parameters and user types did *not* include zero. The confidence intervals were based on nonparametric procedures that are robust to outliers, and if one is prepared to assume that in each instance the coefficients were drawn from the same underlying distribution, conservation programs or price increases will probably not make things worse.

To determine whether the parameter estimates for program and price effects were drawn from the same underlying distribution (given a particular user type), we then turned to a causal analysis of the observed distributions. Two estimation procedures were employed: least squares and least absolute residual. The latter had the distinct advantage of reducing the impact of outliers, although significance tests could not be undertaken. In both cases, we regressed conservation program effects and price effects on a variety of exogenous variables, including a community's median income, median years of schooling completed, mean water consumption level (per account), and number of conservation programs introduced.

These analyses led to a second conclusion: by and large, we could not explain variation in the impact of price increases across communities, regardless of which consumer type was considered. On the other hand, the null findings were not especially surprising, given our earlier observation that, with one exception, there was little reason to expect *systematic* differences in price effects across communities. Our expectation that communities with larger mean consumption levels would be more responsive to price increases was not confirmed by the data. We uncovered little to reject the assumption that price effects across communities for particular consumer types were drawn from a single underlying distribution. However, the presence of enormous outliers for price effects among industrial users prevented an appropriate causal analysis, and the existence of outliers itself suggests that something other than a single underlying distribution is involved. While it is likely that our difficulties with industrial consumers derived from problems with the data (very small numbers of industrial accounts in many of our communities), variation in price effects for industrial accounts may well have important systematic components.

In contrast, we had considerable success explaining variation across communities in the impact of local conservation programs. Thus, our third conclusion was that conservation effects for particular consumer types were not drawn from the same underlying distribution. In particular, for residential users, conservative programs were more effective in communities with greater average water consumption per account, higher levels of education, and a greater number of conservation programs. The impact of education, for example, we attributed in part to a greater ability to process the information contained in conservation appeals and greater involvement in environmental issues among the better educated.

For commercial users, conservation efforts were more effective in communities with greater average consumption (per account) and a larger number of conservation programs. No effects were found for aggregate levels of schooling. In retrospect this is not surprising, since educational level speaks to characteristics of the general public, not to characteristics of commercial establishments. What we needed (but did not have) were direct measures of commercial enterprises (for example, size, clientele served, goods and services sold).

For public users, the sole predictor was mean water consumption per account: conservation programs were more effective in communities in which average consumption was higher. The lack of effect for education can be explained, as before, by the fact that this variable does not directly tap characteristics of public agencies. The null finding for the number of conservation programs we attributed to the structure of public agencies within communities and the ways in which political elites orchestrate public policy. In essence, once one or more individuals (or organizations) in authority decide that public agencies should conserve water, conservation programs are largely beside the point. "Education" and "persuasion" have already been accomplished.

We found no evidence for declining marginal returns from the number of conservation programs initiated. A greater number of conservation programs led to greater savings (for residential and commercial users), and the impact of each additional program was about the same. Of course, this conclusion holds only for our sample. It is virtually certain that a point could be reached when the next program has less impact than the last; indeed one could even imagine situations in which the next program actually increases water consumption. In other words, declining marginal returns must eventually materialize, although that point was not reached in our sample of communities. Obviously, certain minimum amounts of water are required for necessities, and as this minimum is approached, additional conservation programs will yield smaller and smaller marginal savings.

Finally, our sample offered no evidence of trade-offs between the impact of conservation programs and the impact of price. Program and price effects were unrelated, especially once the causal effects of community characteristics were taken into account (in our causal models). The zero-order correlations between the impact of local conservation activities and the impact of changes in the price of water were small (about .15), and the correlation among the residuals from the equations predicting program and price effects hovered around zero. Our finding that conservation activities and price increases are unrelated is extremely important, suggesting that, at least during droughts, they can be mixed and matched at will. We have found that both conservation programs and price increases are important vehicles for water savings, and now we know that water savings from one does not compete with water savings from the other.

Some important unanswered questions

No piece of research is ever fully satisfying, and ours is certainly no exception. Flaws exist throughout, partly as a function of our own limitations and partly as a function of practical and technical constraints beyond our control. Thus, while a number of conclusions and policy recommendations can be put forward with some confidence, important questions remain.

First, it is critical to keep in mind that, by and large, the effects we have found for conservation programs reflect reductions in water consumption that occurred during the worst drought that California experienced in this century. Some communities introduced conservation programs before the onset of the drought, typically in response to long-term water management concerns, but most local conservation efforts began in 1976 and 1977. For this reason, it is probably risky to generalize our findings for the effects of conservation programs to periods enjoying more normal levels of precipitation. What we have demonstrated is that in situations of acute scarcity (or perceived acute scarcity), conservation programs work. Whether they work at other times remains to be seen. In contrast, recall that the price of water varied over the entire eight-year period, and price was rarely used as a conscious vehicle for conservation. Consequently, our conclusions about price effects have far greater external validity.

Second, we were unable to integrate sensitive measures of the content and intensity of particular conservation efforts into our causal analyses. We do not know, for example, whether literature campaigns are more effective than talks at public schools, or whether it is better to enclose conservation appeals in consumer water bills or send literature under separate cover. Perhaps the major obstacle was that many communities launched their programs in concert, making it virtually impossible to unravel the unique effects of each conservation activity.[6] Therefore, we cannot identify the kinds of conservation programs that are likely to be most effective.

Third, the data available on water consumption after the drought are not up to the task of accurately estimating postdrought effects. The time series is simply too short, even for communities that were able to provide postdrought observations. Consequently, we have only the most general notions about how much backsliding really occurred and what the time path for the backsliding might be. Among other things, this means that we can provide few insights into the long-term effects of conservation programs undertaken during the drought.

Fourth, it cannot be overemphasized that for some of our consumer types, important causal variables were unavailable. While this does not seem to have produced anomalous results, especially in the aggregate, more accurate estimates of conservation program effects and price elasticities would no doubt follow from more properly specified models. At the very least, statistical efficiency would be improved. In addition, however, one would be able to feel more confident about the results for individual communities. Recall that most of our general conclusions about program and price effects were derived from median coefficient estimates over many locales; we were basically betting that, in the aggregate, specification errors not handled within Box-Jenkins techniques would cancel out. Even if this is reasonable, it still ignores possible distortions when individual time series analyses are examined. Readers who consult Appendix 3 for the results for particular communities should keep this in mind.

Fifth, aggregate data for each community obscured important variation for particular kinds of households, commercial establishments, factories, and the like. Thus, we are necessarily silent on differences in the impact of conservation programs, except for the rather broad consumer types that the data allowed us to investigate. We cannot speak to such questions as whether home owners are more responsive than renters to conservation appeals, or whether restaurants are more concerned than gas stations about saving water.

Sixth, efforts to alter water consumption, whether through conservation programs or changes in price, have several economic consequences. Conservation programs incur administrative costs, for example, while price changes affect the revenues water agencies collect. These are important outcomes over and above reductions in water consumption, and we have no data with which we can investigate such matters. We cannot provide even a rough benefit-cost analysis of different conservation strategies, although such analyses can and probably should be done. Indeed, some economists would argue that they are essential in the absence of marginal cost pricing.[7]

Finally, we have proceeded in a manner that leaves day-to-day water use unexamined. Neither our theory nor our data directly address how water is used within households, factories, businesses, schools, or farms. In effect, the underlying mechanisms and processes through which conservation programs and price have their impacts have not been explored. For example, we are totally ignorant about how households alter their activities when water becomes more expensive. Similarly, we have little to offer on what happens in public schools when children are asked to conserve.

Fortunately, none of these shortcomings appear to invalidate our overall findings or undermine our policy recommendations. Moreover, each of the questions that we raised can be explored well within the boundaries of existing social science theory and analytic methodology. The major constraint is the funding available for such research. If we are correct in assuming that serious water management problems will be with us for some time to come, adequate research funding is essential.

APPENDIX 1
Data collection instrument

DATA COLLECTION FROM CALIFORNIA WATER AGENCIES

NAME_____

WATER AGENCY_____

ADDRESS_____

TELEPHONE_____   CONTACT(S)_____

_____   _____

1. Obtain the water agency's total revenue per year since 1965.

1965_____	1973_____
1966_____	1974_____
1967_____	1975_____
1968_____	1976_____
1969_____	1977_____
1970_____	1978_____
1971_____	1979_____
1972_____	

2. How does the water agency obtain its revenue? Check all that apply.

        [ ]   Charges for water
        [ ]   Taxes
        [ ]   Bonds
        [ ]   Other (describe)_____

        _____

3. From 1965 to the present, obtain the percentage of the agency's total revenue coming from each of the above mentioned sources of revenue.

1965_____	1973_____
1966_____	1974_____
1967_____	1975_____
1968_____	1976_____
1969_____	1977_____
1970_____	1978_____
1971_____	1979_____
1972_____	

DATA COLLECTION

4. What is the political organization of the water agency?

          [ ]   Public supplier of water
          [ ]   Private supplier of water

   a. If public, how is it organized? (Appointed officials? Elected officials

_____

_____

   b. If private, how is it organized? (Stockholders?)

_____

_____

5. Where does the water agency get its water? Check all that apply. Indicate what percentage of total water production is obtained from each of the follow ing sources of water:

<u>Source of Water:</u>   <u>% of Total Production</u>

[ ] Wells (give names)

     a_____   a_____
     b_____   b_____
     c_____   c_____
     d_____   d_____
     e_____   e_____

[ ] Local reservoirs (give names)

     a_____   a_____
     b_____   b_____
     c_____   c_____
     d_____   d_____
     e_____   e_____

[ ] Water from rivers (give names)

     a_____   a_____
     b_____   b_____
     c_____   c_____
     d_____   d_____
     e_____   e_____

[ ] Water purchased from other
     agencies (give names)

     a_____   a_____
     b_____   b_____
     c_____   c_____

DATA COLLECTION

[ ]   Other (describe)_____

_____

a_____   a_____
b_____   b_____
c_____   c_____

6. How does the water agency charge accounts for the water they use?

a. Are accounts metered? [ ] Yes   [ ] No

b. If yes, what are the different kinds of meters?_____

_____

c. How often are accounts metered?_____

_____

d. What is the present charge structure?_____

_____

e. Since January 1965, how often has there been a rate change?

Date_____   Description of change_____

_____

Date_____   Description of change_____

_____

Date_____   Description of change_____

_____

7. What is the total number of accounts served by this water agency annually?

1965_____   1973_____

1966_____   1974_____

1967_____   1975_____

1968_____   1976_____

1969_____   1977_____

1970_____   1978_____

1971_____   1979_____

1972_____

DATA COLLECTION

8. What is the total annual number of accounts broken down by <u>type</u> of consumer?

1965: Type and Number_____

_____

_____

1966: Type and Number_____

_____

_____

1967: Type and Number_____

_____

_____

1968: Type and Number_____

_____

_____

1969: Type and Number_____

_____

_____

1970: Type and Number_____

_____

_____

1971: Type and Number_____

_____

_____

1972: Type and Number_____

_____

_____

1973: Type and Number_____

_____

_____

DATA COLLECTION

1974: Type and Number_____

_____

_____

1975: Type and Number_____

_____

_____

1976: Type and Number_____

_____

_____

1977: Type and Number_____

_____

_____

1978: Type and Number_____

_____

_____

1979: Type and Number_____

_____

_____

9. What is the total annual number of accounts broken down by each meter size?

1965: Size and Number_____

_____

_____

1966: Size and Number_____

_____

_____

1967: Size and Number_____

_____

_____

DATA COLLECTION

1968:   Size and Number_____

_____

_____

1969:   Size and Number_____

_____

_____

1970:   Size and Number_____

_____

_____

1971:   Size and Number_____

_____

_____

1972:   Size and Number_____

_____

_____

1973:   Size and Number_____

_____

_____

1974:   Size and Number_____

_____

_____

1975:   Size and Number_____

_____

_____

1976:   Size and Number_____

_____

_____

DATA COLLECTION

1977: Size and Number_____

_____

_____

1978: Size and Number_____

_____

_____

1979: Size and Number_____

_____

_____

.0. Have there been changes in the rate structure (e.g. moving from a declining
rate structure to a flat rate structure)?

               [ ] Yes   [ ] No

Fully describe these changes, how often they occurred, and the dates of their
initiation/termination.

_____

_____

_____

_____

_____

_____

_____

1. If the water agency has operated on more than one type of rate structure at
the same time (e.g. within the city limits operating on a flat rate structure
while outside the city limits operating on a declining rate structure), obtain the annual number of accounts for each type of rate structure.

1965: Rate structure and number_____

_____

_____

DATA COLLECTION

1966:   Rate structure and number_____

_____

_____

1967:   Rate structure and number_____

_____

_____

1968:   Rate structure and number_____

_____

_____

1969:   Rate structure and number_____

_____

_____

1970:   Rate structure and number_____

_____

_____

1971:   Rate structure and number_____

_____

_____

1972:   Rate structure and number_____

_____

_____

1973:   Rate structure and number_____

_____

_____

1974:   Rate structure and number_____

_____

_____

DATA COLLECTION

1975:   Structure rate and number_____

_____

_____

1976:   Structure rate and number_____

_____

_____

1977:   Structure rate and number_____

_____

_____

1978:   Structure rate and number_____

_____

_____

1979:   Structure rate and number_____

_____

_____

12.   Does this water agency have any plans to increase the supply of water?

                    [ ] Yes   [ ] No

      a.   What is their position of Feather River water?_____

_____

_____

      b.   Are they digging more wells?_____

_____

_____

      c.   Are they building new reservoirs?_____

_____

_____

DATA COLLECTION

    d.   Other measures (describe)_____

_____

_____

    e.   How are the above measures financed?_____

_____

_____

    f.   What have been/will be the effects of Proposition 13?_____

_____

_____

_____

_____

_____

_____

13. Are there any programs that could affect this area's water use and growth?

               [ ] Yes   [ ] No

    Describe the programs and the dates they were instituted and/or ended_____

_____

_____

_____

_____

_____

_____

_____

_____

_____

DATA COLLECTION

14. On a monthly basis, obtain production figures. Be sure and note how the agency measures its units of water (by acre-feet, cubic feet, millions of gallons,
etc.)

1965_____

1966_____

1967_____

1968_____

1969_____

1970_____

1971_____

1972_____

1973_____

1974_____

1975_____

1976_____

1977_____

1978_____

1979_____

15. On a monthly basis, obtain (a) total sales figures, and (b) sales figures
broken down by type of consumer. Chart these out and attach to this questionnaire.

16. Include definitions of what constitutes each consumer category_____

_____

_____

_____

_____

_____

_____

_____

_____

DATA COLLECTION

17. Does the water agency keep population figures for its district?

        [ ] Yes   [ ] No

If yes, how are the figures obtained? Record all population figures from January 1965 to the present_____

_____

_____

_____

_____

_____

18. Did the water agency sponsor any educational programs concerning water conservation?

        [ ] Yes   [ ] No

Describe these programs and the dates they were initiated and/or ended_____

_____

_____

_____

_____

_____

19. Did this water agency send literature to its consumers encouraging water conservation?

        [ ] Yes   [ ] No

Obtain copies of the literature (and/or description of the literature) and
the dates they were sent_____

_____

_____

_____

_____

_____

DATA COLLECTION

20. Was there any form of moratorium by this water agency?

        [ ] Yes   [ ] No

    What was the nature of the moratorium?_____

    _____

    _____

    _____

    _____

21. Did this agency initiate any water rationing programs?

        [ ] Yes   [ ] No

    Describe any such programs and the dates of their initiation and/or termina-
    tion_____

    _____

    _____

    _____

    _____

22. Describe any other water conservation programs sponsored by this water
    agency and the dates of initiation and/or termination of these programs_____

    _____

    _____

    _____

    _____

    _____

23. What is this agency's nearest National Weather Service Station?_____

    _____

24. Will we be able to obtain access to:

    a. Billing accounts: [ ] Yes   [ ] No
    b. Names and addresses of customers? [ ] Yes   [ ] No
    c. Copies of individuals' billing
        histories?   [ ] Yes   [ ] No

25. Be sure to obtain a detailed map of the area served by this water agency.

APPENDIX 2
Some theoretical considerations in water pricing[1]

It is a basic principle of economics that the most efficient allocation of resources in a market occurs when the price of marginal purchases is equal to
the marginal cost of last unit produced, with all consumers paying the same
price. To apply this concept to the water industry we must deal with the following problems.[2] First, the water industry is not competitive. Like other utilities, it is a "natural" monopoly. Second, the marginal cost of delivering water
may be different for different classes of consumers. Third, three different marginal costs are involved: commodity, customer, and capacity. Fourth, the
water industry, like other utilities, must deal with the peak load problem. We
will elaborate on these points below.

It is usually necessary to regulate natural monopolies to force them to set
price equal to marginal cost. In the decreasing-cost case, marginal cost pricing
leads to losses that must be subsidized, while in the increasing-cost case, it
leads to profits that must be distributed. Utilities are usually considered decreasing-cost industries. We will demonstrate shortly that while this may be
true for the water industry in the short run, in the long run it is an increasing-
cost industry. This implies that at any given point in time some water agencies will be incurring losses, while others will be earning profits. In the long
run, however, they will all earn profits. This raises three questions: how
should losses be subsidized, how should profits be distributed, and should
price be set equal to short-run or long-run marginal cost?

By their nature, water systems require large initial investments but have
relatively small variable costs at outputs up to full capacity. This suggests that
marginal costs are small relative to fixed costs and relatively constant until the
system is near full capacity. As capacity is approached, marginal costs begin
to rise rapidly, and once capacity is reached, they become very large. When
the system is in the vicinity of full capacity, plans are made for another investment to increase capacity. Since the most readily available water sources
are developed first, however, new sources are usually more costly to develop.
The short-run cost curves for a system with three different capacities are
shown in Figure A-1. Note that the minimum average cost increases with size
of the system, reflecting the addition of more costly sources of water. Adding
the long-run curves for the system in Figure A-2, we see that the system is
characterized by increasing costs in the long run.

As noted above, at any given point in time some water agencies will be
operating in an area of decreasing costs and incurring a loss that must be
subsidized. A common method for financing such a loss is through government subsidy. For federal water projects, this subsidy comes from income
taxes. On the state and local levels, the most common form of subsidy is the
property tax.[3] As long as price is equal to marginal cost, neither of these taxes

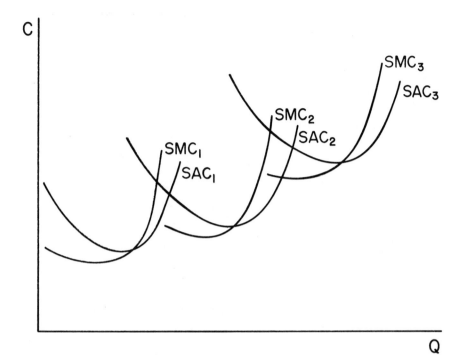

Figure A.1 Short-Run Cost Curves for Water Supply

will affect economic efficiency, but there are distributional effects involved with both.

Other methods of subsidization attempt to capture some or all of the consumers' surplus to raise the additional revenue. The first of these methods is to establish a per-unit rate, which is a declining function of the quantity used. The rates are structured such that all consumers still pay a price equal to the marginal cost for the last unit purchased. While this method has theoretical appeal because it is economically efficient, it is difficult to administer because the correct rate schedule must be established through trial and error. Moreover, it has adverse distributional effects. The second method is to assess a lump sum charge on each consumer, based on the intensity of demand of the different consumer classes. Although this charge is easier to apply than the declining per-unit charge, the lump-sum method is not as theoretically appealing, since it may introduce some inefficiency in the case of very small users (Hirshleifer et al. 1969, p. 92).

For those water agencies operating in the region of increasing costs, the relevant question is how to distribute the profits. Again this is a distributional question, which does not affect efficiency as long as the solution does not involve an allowance of "free" water to dispose of the profits.

It is interesting to note the pattern of water prices that results from short-run marginal cost pricing. In Figure A-3 demand curves have been added to the cost curves of Figure A-2. Assume that a community's present water system is represented by the cost curves SAC_1 and SMC_1, and that the relevant

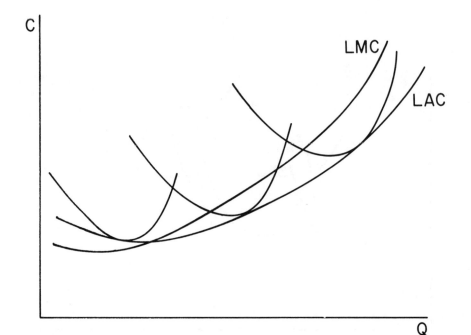

Figure A.2   Short-Run And Long-Run Cost Curves For Water Supply

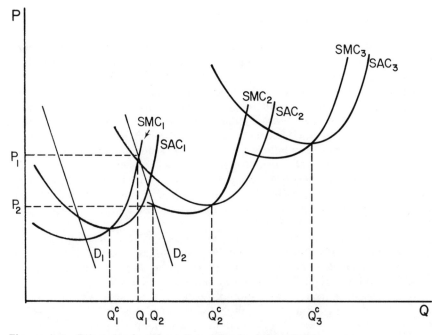

Figure A.3   Prices Under Short-Run Marginal Cost Pricing

demand curve is D_1. As the community grows, the demand for water increases, shifting D_1 to the right. As D_1 nears system capacity at Q_1^c, marginal cost (and price) begin to rise. Suppose D_1 shifts to D_2 before new sources of water are developed. Then price is P_1, and quantity demanded is Q_1. When the new sources of water are added to the system, capacity is increased to Q_2^c, and SAC_2 and SMC_2 are the relevant cost curves. Price will now drop to P_2. As the community continues to grow, D_2 will shift to the right and the process will be repeated. Thus, price will fluctuate systematically under short-run marginal cost pricing.

This discussion leads to the question of whether short-run or long-run marginal cost pricing is more efficient. While both methods result in the same price in long-run equilibrium, most water agencies are not in equilibrium, as evidenced by the numerous proposals for expanding water supplies. In answer to this question, Hirshleifer et al. argue that "the normal sale of water is in the nature of a short-run agreement; a purchase of water at this minute does not bind the customer to take more water at any later date" (1969, p. 97). Therefore, the pricing of water is a short-run problem, and price should be equated with short-run marginal cost.

Grima (1972) objects on several grounds. First of all, the systematic price fluctuation of short-run marginal cost pricing means that the water system will require subsidization in early years, while profits will have to be distributed in later years. Second, "changing marginal prices every few years would also create some confusion in the minds of consumers; it may also be inconvenient for a family to buy a dishwasher . . . when the marginal price of water is low . . . and find out a few years later that it is now too expensive to use" (1972, p. 148). Third, long-run marginal-cost pricing is "simpler to administer." Once long-run marginal cost has been determined, price will be constant. Moreover, since average cost is increasing in the long run, the system will always generate profits, which can be distributed. Finally, Grima argues that "the contract between the water supply enterprise and *the residential consumers as a whole* is in the nature of a long-term contract. Once service is connected it is reasonable to suppose that water will be on tap for the foreseeable future" (1972, pp. 148–149, author's emphasis). Although long-run marginal cost pricing may be simpler to administer, several factors suggest that Grima's objections may not be valid. First, long-run marginal cost pricing requires forecasts of both long-run marginal cost and the long-run demand curve. If these forecasts are not accurate, prices may have to be changed after all.[4]

Second, Grima's argument that consumer investments in durable goods (dishwashers, and so forth) may be adversely affected by changing prices assumes that consumers consider only the present price of water in their investment decisions. Since water rates have changed very little in many areas, this may be loosely true. However, if consumers know that the price will change in future years, there is no reason why they cannot incorporate this knowledge into their investment decisions. Furthermore, this price information can be made available by the water agency.

Third, since this price information can be made available, there is no reason why changing prices should "confuse" consumers. Moreover, as Hirshleifer et al. point out, "no buyer has any good reason to expect that prices will remain fixed while conditions of supply and demand change" (1969, p. 98).

Finally, and perhaps most important, Grima is confused about the nature of the water contract. The confusion results from his focus on the number of water hookups installed rather than the quantity of water demanded. Although a hookup to the system is necessary to receive water, the existence of the hookup does not obligate the consumer to purchase any water. The water contract is not made until the consumer opens his or her tap. Furthermore, even if it is reasonable to assume that since the hookup exists it will be used in the future, there is no reason to believe that it will be used to demand the same quantity of water. For example, if every toilet in a community is fitted with a water-saving device, then, ceteris paribus, the quantity of water demanded by consumers individually and *as a whole* will decline. Since the water contract thus seems to be short run in nature, equating short-run marginal cost with price will result in the most efficient allocation of resources.

As we noted at the outset of this discussion, water utilities incur marginal costs associated with three different categories of cost: commodity, customer, and capacity. Commodity costs are those costs incurred in making the actual delivery of water, that is, to meet the average demand. Marginal commodity cost, then, is the cost of delivering one more unit of water, with capacity and the number of customers fixed. It is this marginal cost that should be used to determine the marginal price of water. One problem here is that the marginal cost of delivering water may differ for various customers. However, these costs are approximately the same for customers receiving the same type of service, thus, the solution is to charge a price equal to the marginal cost of delivering water to each consumer class.

Customer costs are those costs associated with the number of customers served, for example, meter installation and meter reading. Marginal customer cost is the cost of adding one more customer to the system, with capacity and deliveries constant. Since these costs are not marginal to water deliveries, they should not be included in the marginal price. Instead, those marginal customer costs that are one-time events (meter installation) should be paid at the time they are incurred; those that are recurring events (meter reading) should be recovered as a fixed charge each month.

Capacity costs are those associated with the size of the plant. Marginal capacity cost is the cost of adding one unit of capacity, with deliveries and customers constant. To determine the role of marginal capacity cost in pricing, we must again consider the nature of the water contract. Because the water supplier must deliver water on demand, the water system must have the capacity to deliver an adequate supply during those times when demand is highest. Maximum demands is called peak demand, and it usually occurs during hot, dry spells in the summer. Since the system must be designed to meet both peak and average demand, it operates at levels much lower than its designed capacity in off-peak periods, particularly in winter. This suggests that marginal capacity costs in the summer are higher than those in the winter. When marginal capacity costs are added to marginal commodity costs, the result is a marginal price structure with higher rates in the summer.[5]

APPENDIX 3
Time series results for the full sample

RESIDENTIAL

Santa Barbara County

Community	Mean Est. Coeff.	Mean t-Value	T1 Code	T1 Est. Coeff.	T1 t-Value	T2 Code	T2 Est. Coeff.	T2 t-Value	T3 Code	T3 Est. Coeff.	T3 t-Value	T4 Code	T4 Est. Coeff.	T4 t-Value	Temp. Est. Coeff.	Temp. t-Value	Rain Est. Coeff.	Rain t-Value	Rain t-1 Est. Coeff.	Rain t-1 t-Value	Price Est. Coeff.	Price t-Value	Elasticity	Noise MA	Noise AR
Carpinteria	15.63	(46.27)	B	-3.41	(3.80)	K	.44	(.47)							.19	(3.51)	-.11	(2.09)	.19	(3.61)	-32.52	(2.26)	.36	--	(1)(6,12)
Greater Los Angeles																									
Burbank		DF(1)	C	-7.25	(2.00)	K	2.89	(.68)							.46	(4.08)	-.15	(1.29)	.37	(3.22)	-49.11	(.98)	.23	--	--
Greater San Diego																									
San Diego	16.50	(4.21)	A	.57	(.58)										-.004	(.05)	.24	(2.10)	.26	(2.23)	-4.72	(.33)	-.06	(1)	(1)(12)
Oceanside	22.55	(69.38)	C	-2.65	(3.19)	K	.99	(.12)							.55	(7.19)	-.40	(2.32)	.65	(3.84)	-33.06	(3.96)	-.33	(1,6)(12)	--
Escondido	43.24	(10.79)	B	-4.06	(.62)										.36	(1.18)	-1.29	(2.46)	-1.51	(3.19)	-529.46	(7.18)	-1.69	(8,10)	(1)(12)
Imperial Beach (Chula Vista is part of Imperial Beach)	15.99	(12.08)	C	-1.08	(1.57)										.03	(.39)	-.32	(2.47)	.23	(2.00)	-7.50	(.45)	-.14	(1,2)	(12)
Desert Communities																									
El Centro	29.00	(6.80)	D	1.06	(.44)	K	.26	(.05)		.07	(.08)				.36	(3.30)	.52	(.91)	.88	(1.63)	-14.94	(.84)	-.03	(1)(2)	(12)
Palm Springs	51.91	(87.12)	A,E	-.71	(.34)					.47	(.55)				.92	(10.89)	.66	(.64)	-3.11	(3.26)	-11.71	(.18)	-.04	--	(6)
Monterey Peninsula																									
Santa Cruz (inside)	11.36	(69.60)	F	-1.27	(2.12)	G	-5.59	(8.16)							.17	(3.50)	-.03	(.46)	.11	(2.16)	-22.44	(3.35)	-.51	(1)	(6,12)
Santa Cruz (outside)	13.16	(57.06)	F	2.40	(3.70)	G	-7.25	(10.10)							.05	(1.36)	-.06	(1.05)	.09	(1.70)	-23.13	(6.92)	-.73	(1)	(6,12)
Northern Inland California																									
Paradise	31.20	(5.78)	H	-11.96	(3.15)	L	2.42	(.57)							.30	(2.72)	.02	(.15)	-.19	(2.49)	-9.87	(2.79)	-.02	(1,3,6)	(1,4)(12)
Susanville		DF(1)	C	1.91	(.52)										.54	(5.23)	.09	(.20)	-1.92	(3.79)	-6.72	(.52)	-.06	--	--
Marysville	16.30	(17.55)	I	-3.71	(3.26)										.28	(4.86)	-.06	(.52)	.16	(1.54)	64.35	(1.36)	.34	--	(1,12)
San Francisco Bay Area																									
San Jose W. W. (inside)	16.86	(57.28)	A,F	-3.73	(3.43)										.20	(2.32)	-.10	(.77)	.48	(3.42)	-19.37	(1.20)	-.28	(1,2)	(12)
San Jose W. W. (outside)	20.16	(18.31)	A,F	-5.38	(3.45)	J	.87	(2.33)							.74	(5.93)	-.44	(1.30)	.52	(1.51)	6.86	(.28)	.08	(4)	(1)(12)
San Leandro	13.75	(378.92)	I	.46	(1.69)	J	-7.95	(26.58)				L	5.33	(5.41)	.11	(4.10)	-.04	(.84)	.13	(3.39)	-18.77	(1.46)	-.24	(4)	(1)(6,12)
Alameda County (inside)	12.92	(9.71)	I	-.67	(.68)	J	-.36	(.35)				L	.44	(.18)	.15	(4.00)	-.02	(.50)	.04	(.80)	5.06	(.16)	.06	(6)	(1)(12)
Oakland	12.01	(27.31)	I	.25	(.43)	J	-.23	(.37)				L	1.29	(.99)	.08	(3.05)	-.04	(.94)	.05	(1.27)	-12.07	(.70)	-.17	--	(1)(6,12)
Emeryville	15.87	(10.97)	I	-1.27	(1.01)	J	.72	(.55)				L	15.06	(5.01)	.09	(1.77)	.01	(.11)	.04	(.77)	-209.04	(5.47)	-2.23	--	(1)(12)
Piedmont	16.88	(393.02)	I	1.76	(4.95)	J	-1.30	(3.24)				L	9.65	(8.33)	.16	(3.39)	-.17	(1.70)	.27	(2.98)	-43.77	(2.92)	-.46	(4)	(1,2)(6)
Berkeley	12.39	(636.71)	I	-.92	(5.78)	J	-.54	(2.82)				L	4.03	(7.63)	.07	(3.50)	-.02	(.63)	.06	(2.52)	-11.44	(1.69)	-.16	(4)	(1)(6)
Albany	8.49	(13.69)	I	-.41	(.81)	J	-.20	(.37)				L	1.59	(1.40)	.10	(4.60)	-.03	(1.09)	.06	(2.58)	.18	(.01)	0	(4)	(1)(12)
Walnut Creek	30.90	(24.09)	I	-1.35	(.51)	J	-12.05	(4.37)				L	29.28	(5.33)	.44	(3.67)	-.18	(1.23)	.25	(1.99)	-362.58	(5.05)	-2.02	--	(1)(6,12)
Lafayette	22.95	(31.57)	I	-1.36	(.94)	J	2.77	(1.62)				L	15.72	(4.84)	.54	(4.96)	-.13	(1.11)	.15	(1.43)	-103.14	(2.30)	-.79	--	(1,2,4,12)
C. C. Co. Inside-Walnut Creek Office	22.04	(101.17)	I	-1.90	(2.41)	J	-2.66	(2.82)				L	18.16	(8.14)	.50	(5.90)	-.01	(.10)	.19	(3.80)	-121.24	(3.98)	-.97	--	(1,4)(6,12)
Alameda	15.68	(254.68)	I	.43	(1.65)	J	.57	(1.82)				L	5.95	(8.20)	.02	(1.03)	-.16	(3.17)	.17	(3.17)	-23.70	(2.35)	-.27	(1)	(4,6,8)
Richmond	11.09	(28.71)	I	-.48	(.85)	J	-.79	(1.23)				L	3.37	(2.09)	.06	(2.23)	-.02	(.59)	.03	(.86)	-33.41	(1.69)	-.52	(36)	(1)(6,12)
El Cerrito	11.35	(38.13)	I	.74	(.96)	J	-1.04	(1.21)				L	3.77	(2.01)	.04	(.89)	.01	(.14)	.08	(1.47)	-30.73	(1.20)	-.48	--	(1)(6,12)
San Pablo	12.62	(31.27)	I	1.19	(1.83)	J	-.94	(1.41)				L	.37	(.26)	.08	(2.97)	-.07	(1.94)	.06	(1.75)	-7.03	(.38)	-.10	(8)	(1)(6,12)
Pinole-Hercules	14.61	(17.77)	I	1.70	(1.45)	J	.37	(.30)				L	-.20	(.08)	.18	(4.17)	-.14	(1.77)	.06	(.84)	7.60	(.22)	.09	--	(1)(6,12)
Crockett	8.84	(94.34)	I	-.40	(1.46)	J	-.88	(2.54)				L	4.45	(5.80)	.06	(2.68)	-.05	(1.26)	.01	(.33)	-34.67	(3.14)	-.70	--	(1,4)(6,12)
C. C. Co. Inside, Richmond Office	12.45	(15.30)	I	-.29	(.40)	J	3.50	(2.64)				L	-2.86	(1.06)	.14	(2.69)	-.01	(.15)	.07	(1.05)	40.34	(1.12)	.56	--	(1)(6,12)
Ventura County																									
Ventura	18.84	(25.40)	C	-1.74	(1.03)										.23	(2.03)	-.05	(.36)	.08	(.68)	-5.75	(.16)	-.09	(6)	(1)

Community	Mean Est. Coef.	Mean t‑Value	T1 Code	T1 Est. Coef.	T1 t‑Value	T2 Code	T2 Est. Coef.	T2 t‑Value	T3 Code	T3 Est. Coef.	T3 t‑Value	T4 Code	T4 Est. Coef.	T4 t‑Value	Temp. Est. Coef.	Temp. t‑Value	Rain Est. Coef.	Rain t‑Value	Rain(t‑1) Est. Coef.	Rain(t‑1) t‑Value	Price Est. Coef.	Price t‑Value	Elasticity	MA	MA	AR
Carpinteria	66.03	(49.69)	B	-9.41	(2.96)	--	9.92	(1.90)							1.02	(3.49)	.60	(1.33)	1.02	(2.58)	-280.92	(3.74)	.63	(1,4)		(1,2)
Ventura County																										
Ventura	51.59	(22.55)	C	-11.42	(2.16)	--	3.75	(1.07)							.12	(.30)	.48	(.91)	.18	(.35)	-337.03	(3.98)	-1.89	(5,7)		(1,4)
Greater Los Angeles																										
Burbank	69.53	(69.51)	C	-1.21	(.44)										.61	(9.49)	.30	(1.96)	.19	(1.39)	-66.46	(1.67)	-.17	(1)(2)(12)		(1,4)
Greater San Diego																										
San Diego	129.88	(34.77)	A	-1.61	(.22)										1.94	(3.13)	2.85	(1.75)	3.45	(2.19)	-96.22	(1.38)	-.19	(12)		(1)
Oceanside	63.14	(16.94)	C	6.36	(1.03)										1.84	(4.41)	.27	(.27)	1.20	(1.26)	-98.39	(1.15)	-.19	(24)		(1)
Escondido [DF (1)]			B	3.71	(.55)	K	-1.96	(.27)							.17	(.91)	.51	(1.21)	.58	(1.56)	-420.27	(6.64)	-2.13			(2,12)
Imperial Beach (Chula Vista is part of Imperial Beach)	75.84	(47.61)	C	-3.41	(.85)										.35	(1.45)	.68	(1.14)	1.01	(1.79)	-323.94	(6.86)	-1.31	(4,6,12)		(1)
Desert Communities																										
El Centro	62.39	(7.14)	O	57.99	(5.86)	K	-3.48	(.28)							.46	(2.72)	.48	(.23)	.43	(2.19)	-1213.80	(9.30)	-1.68	(12)		(1)
Palm Springs	115.97	(52.88)	A,E	-2.19	(.34)										1.31	(7.83)	1.11	(.60)	5.27	(2.92)	-243.91	(1.96)	-.33			(1)
Monterey Peninsula																										
Santa Cruz (inside) [DF (1)]			F	3.66	(.67)	G	-15.66	(7.52)	L	5.65	(.91)				.61	(2.65)	.62	(1.82)	.56	(1.79)	-272.10	(3.47)	-1.21	(2,12)		
Santa Cruz (outside) [DF (1)]			F	-1.21	(.16)	G	-12.92	(1.85)	L	1.03	(.27)				.59	(2.30)	.47	(1.40)	.71	(2.20)	-91.07	(2.57)	-.60			(2,4,6,8)
Northern Inland California																										
Susanville	67.81	(3.76)	B	48.35	(1.45)										1.81	(1.92)	-19.29	(2.57)	1.22	(.17)	-2831.1	(4.39)	-3.56	(1)		
Marysville	37.76	(25.50)	C	-4.70	(2.80)										.46	(4.25)	.22	(1.00)	.18	(.90)	-98.93	(1.07)	-.19			(1,12)
San Francisco Bay Area																										
San Jose W. W. (inside)	74.34	(141.4)	A,F	-10.12	(9.09)										1.31	(13.64)	1.21	(3.26)	1.03	(2.86)	-7.39	(.38)	-.03	(1)		(3)
San Jose W. W. (outside)	70.12	(36.43)	A,F	-16.11	(6.19)	J	-4.35	(6.67)							1.80	(6.27)	1.18	(1.44)	2.25	(2.93)	58.06	(1.22)	.22			(12)
San Leandro	36.01	(497.98)	I	.70	(1.32)				L	-12.04	(21.37)	L	11.15	(6.15)	-.01	(.14)	.21	(1.91)	.34	(3.55)	-131.03	(5.65)	-.62	(2,4)		(3)(6)
Alameda Co. (inside)	35.32	(16.58)	I	-.50	(.19)	J	-8.88	(3.26)	L	-.08	(.02)	L	30.15	(6.34)	.39	(3.79)	.21	(1.30)	.08	(.48)	-476.89	(8.03)	-2.33	(14)		(1)
Oakland	40.17	(247.07)	I	-3.56	(6.53)	J	-.75	(1.14)	L	-13.94	(21.11)	L	7.96	(4.99)	.05	(1.34)	.20	(2.32)	.24	(3.16)	-54.88	(2.57)	-.23	(1)		(6)
Piedmont	41.43	(4.85)	I	8.16	(2.00)	J	-5.82	(1.42)	L	2.53	(.53)	L	31.95	(4.59)	.29	(2.20)	.03	(.15)	.19	(.90)	-498.83	(5.78)	-2.54	(6,12)		(1,2)
Berkeley	38.68	(14.97)	I	1.54	(1.16)	J	-.01	(.01)	L	-4.92	(2.92)	L	5.03	(1.70)	.66	(1.83)	.04	(.79)	.03	(.56)	-30.50	(.90)	-.13			(3)(6)
Albany	53.84	(6.88)	I	-.66	(.11)	J	20.08	(3.17)	L	1.37	(.19)	L	22.10	(2.05)	.66	(2.73)	.56	(2.09)	.17	(.71)	-310.54	(2.71)	-1.02			(3)(12)
Walnut Creek	73.05	(39.71)	I	16.24	(4.82)	J	4.32	(1.20)	L	-32.43	(7.23)	L	22.92	(4.73)	.81	(2.94)	.80	(2.47)	.62	(2.11)	-190.29	(2.54)	-.44			(1,6)(12)
Lafayette	29.89	(14.63)	I	4.03	(1.97)	J	-3.37	(1.69)	L	.39	(.17)	L	9.79	(3.00)	.10	(1.64)	.01	(.12)	.09	(1.32)	-139.74	(4.09)	.86			(3)(6)
C.C. Co. Inside‑Walnut Creek Office	102.03	(38.98)	I	1.49	(.21)	J	-16.09	(2.17)	L	-27.17	(2.94)	L	36.29	(3.55)	1.36	(3.23)	.35	(.69)	.57	(4.24)	-450.34	(3.20)	.74			(1)(6,12)
Alameda	39.61	(660.59)	I	-2.29	(3.81)	J	-3.40	(4.14)	L	-14.0	(15.53)	L	11.49	(6.39)	.20	(2.62)	.18	(1.29)	.27	(2.36)	-67.70	(2.47)	.29	(4,28)		(1,2,6)
Richmond	47.52	(116.06)	I	9.51	(5.92)	J	-8.52	(4.27)	L	-16.46	(8.54)	L	12.39	(2.89)	.22	(1.44)	.75	(3.16)	.74	(3.94)	-79.57	(1.24)	.77			(1)(4,6)
El Cerrito	43.12	(17.28)	I	2.42	(.61)	J	-8.38	(2.28)	L	-3.04	(.74)	L	14.28	(1.97)	.10	(.70)	.59	(2.80)	.44	(2.07)	-185.48	(2.07)	.72			(1)(6)
San Pablo	60.00	(10.19)	I	5.95	(1.62)	J	4.07	(1.06)	L	-2.48	(.46)	L	5.31	(.65)	.31	(2.45)	.42	(2.42)	.10	(.64)	-86.33	(.88)	.28			(1)(12)
Pinole‑Hercules	35.30	(9.62)	I	12.78	(1.78)	J	-6.07	(.89)	L	.62	(.01)	L	-13.83	(1.55)	.74	(3.40)	.51	(.90)	.24	(.43)	42.35	(.48)	.21	(10)		(1)
Crockett	17.64	(11.67)	I	-3.45	(2.07)	J	-1.20	(.74)	L	-4.71	(2.49)	L	14.83	(3.57)	.07	(.50)	-.18	(1.32)	.26	(2.26)	-178.35	(3.04)	-1.78	(2)		(3)(12)
C.C. Co. Inside‑Richmond Office	85.41	(62.25)	I	10.42	(2.74)	J	-8.30	(1.91)	L	-2.36	(.34)	L	13.99	(2.94)	.27	(1.33)	1.70	(3.76)	2.08	(5.01)	-387.86	(3.83)	.76	(1)		(6,12)
Emeryville	59.46	(10.66)	I	3.18	(.52)	J	-23.14	(3.85)	L	-4.97	(.65)	L	22.33	(1.48)	.05	(.27)	.6?	(3.17)	.60	(2.41)	-372.43	(2.05)	-1.04	(1)(6)		(1)(6)

INDUSTRIAL

Santa Barbara County

Community	Mean Est. Coef.	t-Value	Code	Treat. 1 Est. Coef.	t-Value	Code	Treat. 2 Est. Coef.	t-Value	Code	Treat. 3 Est. Coef.	t-Value	Code	Treat. 4 Est. Coef.	t-Value	Temp. Est. Coef.	t-Value	Rain Est. Coef.	t-Value	Rain (t-1) Est. Coef.	t-Value	Price Est. Coef.	t-Value	Elasticity	MA	AR
Carpinteria	318.01	(11.17)	B	-88.85	(1.52)		-31.23	(.46)		......			......		5.92	(2.48)	5.74	(1.45)	4.91	(1.39)	-1622.42	(1.96)	-.62	(6)	(1)
Ventura County																									
Ventura	2502.12	(3.72)	C	409.41	(.52)		......			......			......		15.14	(.58)	.51	(.03)	8.65	(.28)	-24,329.73	(4.37)	-2.07	--	(1)
Santa Paula	270.22	(21.86)	D	-45.04	(1.68)		......			......			......		5.77	(4.75)	-4.72	(2.53)	3.44	(1.92)	1230.9	(1.69)	.67		(1)
Greater Los Angeles																									
Burbank	658.59	(6.16)	C	-3.44	(.08)	K	68.01	(.57)		......			......		4.50	(1.56)	-1.96	(.44)	.68	(.16)	-39.59	(.03)	0	--	(12)
Greater San Diego																									
San Diego	1085.0	(18.83)	A	-157.73	(1.33)	K	-1.06	(.16)		......			......		1.20	(.13)	13.19	(.44)	-25.28	(.85)	-1663.4	(.98)	-.35	(8,11,12)	(1)
Escondido			B	9.43	(1.48)	K	-1.06	(.16)		......			......		.04	(.29)	.18	(.47)	-.32	(.94)	-1271.72	(10.16)	-6.15	--	--
Imperial Beach (Chula Vista is part of Imperial Beach) [DF(1)]			C	-3.44	(.08)	K				......			......		.43	(.30)	.09	(.02)	2.18	(.43)	607.36	(.59)	1.63	(2)	--
Monterey Peninsula																									
Monterey (Carmel, Sand City, Pacific Grove, Del Rey Oaks were coded as part of Monterey)	429.93	(43.38)	M	-47.30	(2.42)	G	20.73	(.88)		......			......		.47	(.26)	6.63	(2.04)	2.75	(.79)	-560.09	(2.81)	-.31	(1)	--
Santa Cruz (inside)	954.75	(6.34)	F	-313.02	(2.04)	G	-103.80	(.68)		......			......		20.19	(2.41)	.08	(.01)	.72	(.10)	6673.47	(3.67)	1.12	--	(1)(12)
Santa Cruz (outside) [DF(1)]			F	43.62	(2.01)	G	-90.47	(4.13)	L	221.75	(1.17)		3.22	(.14)	.96	(.30)	-1.21	(1.46)	-.65	(.78)	444.89	(7.36)	-1.03	(2)	(4)(2,12)
Northern Inland California																									
Susanville	757.90	(3.32)	B	32.63	(.08)		......			......			......		14.02	(1.22)	-57.34	(.61)	-77.48	(.84)	-905.05	(.35)	.12	(1)	--
Marysville	356.59	(5.29)	C	110.09	(.98)		......			......			......		2.22	(1.11)	-6.45	(.93)	-2.54	(.38)	-7293.72	(1.47)	-1.61	(11)	(1,3)
San Francisco Bay Area																									
San Jose W.W. (inside)	1154.3	(10.34)	A,F	-114.81	(1.18)	J	-291.69	(6.56)	G	78.80	(1.24)	L	-65.01	(1.27)	7.42	(.90)	-20.69	(1.20)	-12.42	(.74)	769.47	(.48)	.15	(1)	(12)
San Jose W.W. (outside)	574.17	(13.36)	A,F	-8.37	(1.31)	J	16.30	(.43)	G	106.5	(2.03)	L	58.27	(1.62)	8.48	(3.58)	4.24	(.59)	-13.32	(1.79)	1338.7	(1.59)	.50	--	(1)
San Leandro	526.92	(6.49)	I	-10.21	(.29)	J	-8.06	(.22)	G	-72.43	(1.04)	L	-130.82	(1.17)	.75	(.68)	.46	(.25)	-1.87	(1.07)	-155.00	(.24)	-.06	(2)	(1)(12)
Alameda Co. (inside)	361.51	(3.31)	I	118.03	(1.54)	J	63.82	(.89)	G	64.87	(.74)	L	7.28	(.82)	-1.43	(.82)	-4.22	(1.32)	3.09	(1.03)	-778.98	(1.49)	-.33	(2,4)	(1)
Oakland	642.40	(10.81)	I	192.45	(4.01)	J	40.54	(.83)	G	-28.42	(.28)	L	35.14	(.64)	5.68	(.07)	-4.15	(.20)	.20	(.08)	430.10	(.57)	-.16	(12)(24)	(1)
Emeryville	458.74	(34.52)	I	-42.09	(.52)	J	-38.68	(.50)	G	-51.31	(.36)	L	14.62	(.19)	8.07	(1.85)	-1.29	(.27)	-1.98	(.45)	-686.02	(.45)	-.16	(12)	(1)(12)
Berkeley	126.87	(10.69)	I	27.36	(1.01)	J	52.08	(1.95)	G	28.42	(.59)	L	.77	(.03)	.16	(.19)	.96	(.82)	.36	(.31)	-833.51	(2.02)	-.37	(12)	(1)(2)
Albany			I	26.16	(1.26)	J	-48.22	(2.33)	G	-47.13	(1.88)	L	-16.65	(.72)	-.35	(.52)	.70	(.71)	.31	(.33)	68.31	(.28)	.09	(2)(16,28)	(1)(2)
Walnut Creek			I	-271.46	(1.48)	J	-110.28	(.59)	G	236.81	(.99)	L	182.21	(.88)	.57	(.19)	2.65	(.43)	.98	(.17)	-2848.32	(1.74)	-.72	(1)	--
Lafayette			I	15.69	(4.01)	J	2.83	(.71)	G	-10.58	(1.30)	L	-45.74	(5.13)	.07	(.59)	.23	(1.28)	.10	(.62)	527.21	(6.65)	7.45	(2,12)	--
C. C. Co. Inside-Walnut Creek Office	239.41	(22.79)	I	82.26	(1.55)	J	-291.69	(6.56)	G	78.80	(1.24)	L	-65.01	(1.27)	3.68	(2.45)	4.33	(2.43)	.18	(.10)	-2351.66	(6.07)	-1.65	(1)	(12)
Alameda	3774.21	(37.16)	I	44.01	(1.21)	J	15.30	(.43)	G	106.5	(2.03)	L	58.27	(1.62)	.09	(.08)	-.02	(.01)	-1.74	(.76)	-1453.49	(3.47)	-.88	(2)	--
Richmond	80.98	(3.87)	I	94.83	(.40)	J	-805.26	(2.63)	G	-573.85	(2.63)	L	-130.82	(1.17)	14.74	(1.62)	-27.79	(1.81)	-22.04	(1.50)	-5436.93	(.89)	-.20	--	(1)
El Cerrito	424.13	(4.23)	I	98.37	(1.19)	J	-90.12	(1.25)	G	80.01	(1.25)	L	109.84	(.30)	8.11	(2.09)	10.41	(1.46)	8.61	(1.25)	-2116.61	(1.11)	-4.55	--	(1)(2)(3)
San Pablo			I	56.27	(.29)	J	-223.66	(1.25)	G	-27.04	(.15)	L			1.73	(.21)	-1.04	(.08)	4.39	(.33)	-3169.25	(.85)	-1.13	--	(1,2,3)(12)
Pinole-Hercules			I	-253.57	(.21)	J	3061.89	(1.93)	G	8092.31	(1.55)	L	921.88	(.20)	18.69	(.82)	-111.57	(1.58)	-21.19	(.30)	-74062.5	(1.56)	.91	(12)	(2)
Crockett	31,836.96	(3.91)	I	-7974.29	(1.32)	J	-5687.32	(.79)	G	-17,065.93	(.87)	L	1273.86	(.20)	-71.29	(.56)	317.06	(.94)	-5.17	(.02)	215381.0	(1.23)	.90	(20)	(1)(4)
C. C. Co. Inside-Richmond Office [DF(1)]	497.40	(1.26)	I	1276.29	(3.09)	J			G	3169.07	(4.84)	L	697.66	(1.68)	18.12	(1.76)	23.80	(1.41)	33.72	(2.06)	-43455.80	(6.95)	-1.29	--	--

Community	Mean Coeff.	Mean t-Value	T1 Code	T1 Coeff.	T1 t-Value	T2 Code	T2 Coeff.	T2 t-Value	T3 Code	T3 Coeff.	T3 t-Value	T4 Coeff.	T4 t-Value	Temp Coeff.	Temp t-Value	Rain Coeff.	Rain t-value	Rain(t-1) Coeff.	Rain(t-1) t-Value	Price Coeff.	Price t-Value	Elasticity	MA	AR
Carpinteria	140.39	(7.84)	B	-107.78	(4.35)	K	10.35	(.41)						3.49	(2.89)	-1.80	(1.43)	-2.76	(2.25)	-1217.17	(4.87)	-1.14	(10)	(1)(12)
Ventura County																								
Santa Paula	169.90	(26.90)	D	-14.61	(1.01)									7.51	(8.26)	4.07	(2.61)	6.01	(3.98)	-356.97	(1.26)	.31	--	(1)
Ventura	157.19	(7.02)	C	-78.50	(1.65)									-3.93	(1.28)	1.90	(.33)	7.70	(1.46)	-2257.13	(5.16)	-3.74	(1)	--
Greater Los Angeles																								
Burbank	DF(1)		C	12.14	(.35)									6.22	(8.15)	-7.45	(3.51)	-2.21	(1.10)	-1539.40	(3.69)	-1.02	(1,2,6)	--
Greater San Diego																								
Oceanside	82.59	(3.87)	C	-57.68	(1.47)									5.15	(2.54)	-7.84	(1.75)	-7.55	(1.82)	-192.57	(.52)	.24	--	(1)(15)
Escondido	DF(1)		B	34.19	(.79)	K	60.21	(.45)						.25	(.08)	12.72	(1.46)	11.33	(1.48)	-4309.95	(3.72)	-2.49	(2)	--
Imperial Beach (Chula Vista is part of Imperial Beach)	353.60	(28.75)	C	-18.12	(.61)									13.60	(7.17)	-5.67	(1.04)	-13.85	(2.42)	130.18	(.43)	.11	(1,6,7,10)	--
Desert Communities																								
El Centro	182.11	(20.01)	D	-59.10	(1.87)									2.78	(3.47)	11.38	(.91)	-2.77	(.22)	1073.4	(2.18)	.65	(19)	(1,6)
Palm Springs	273.47	(110.26)	A,E	-26.03	(1.69)	K	62.58	(2.25)						2.81	(4.40)	-8.61	(2.70)	-11.73	(3.52)	-576.41	(3.68)	.31	--	(1,6)
Monterey Peninsula																								
Monterey (Carmel, Sand City, Pacific Grove, Del Rey Oaks were coded as part of Monterey)	172.64	(10.70)	M	6.31	(.35)	G	-71.74	(3.09)						3.51	(2.31)	-4.82	(2.08)	5.38	(2.40)	53.4	(.29)	.08	(6)	(1)(12)
Santa Cruz (inside)	29.12	(5.75)	F	1.71	(.33)	G	.22	(.04)	L	-1.76	(.30)			.55	(2.25)	.13	(.55)	.39	(1.73)	-79.73	(2.89)	.47	(6)	(1)(12)
Santa Cruz (outside)	708.66	(2.03)	F	415.82	(1.02)	G	-1232.33	(3.20)	L	248.88	(.52)			59.59	(2.00)	-1.16	(.04)	10.62	(.34)	-2747.29	(2.06)	.92	--	(1,12)
Northern Inland California																								
Susanville	348.80	(10.76)	C	71.62	(1.08)									15.48	(6.26)	9.38	(.57)	-14.91	(.93)	-2176.3	(1.81)	.57	--	(1,3)
Marysville	127.18	(12.77)	C	-33.47	(1.91)									4.38	(6.80)	-1.43	(.84)	-2.61	(1.64)	719.48	(.90)	.47	--	(1,12)
San Francisco Bay Area																								
San Jose W.W. (inside)	339.53	(12.24)	A,F	-105.58	(5.13)									11.05	(4.85)	-7.71	(1.75)	9.31	(2.29)	-287.78	(.84)	.20	(1,5)	(12)
San Jose W.W. (outside)	394.73	(9.56)	A,F	-117.31	(4.96)									12.83	(4.38)	-21.03	(3.94)	8.37	(1.71)	79.55	(.21)	.05	--	(12)
San Leandro	180.08	(89.93)	I	-35.62	(3.37)	G	-24.06	(2.10)	L	-67.45	(4.15)	48.54	(2.46)	2.09	(2.41)	-1.22	(.84)	3.26	(2.55)	-1215.10	(4.71)	-1.11	(8)	(1)(4,6)
Alameda Co. (inside)	273.88	(13.46)	I	38.81	(1.64)	J	33.22	(1.35)	G	22.85	(.68)	3.17	(.12)	1.81	(1.88)	.56	(.43)	.97	(.82)	-1639.24	(5.90)	.94	(6)	(1)(12)
Oakland	231.81	(662.94)	I	18.70	(7.03)	J	16.46	(5.11)	G	-102.53	(11.02)	38.33	(9.06)	1.14	(1.83)	-1.07	(.99)	2.91	(3.24)	-452.42	(3.59)	.32	(4)	(1,2,6)
Emeryville	128.08	(3.69)	I	-70.03	(3.17)	J	32.14	(1.84)	G	-86.20	(4.72)	-20.08	(.86)	.67	(.96)	-.09	(.10)	-1.27	(1.37)	-510.56	(2.54)	.78	(14,18)	(1)(6)
Piedmont	51.62	(87.29)	I	6.21	(2.64)	J	2.45	(.80)	G	-27.19	(9.49)	10.71	(1.67)	.48	(1.63)	.95	(1.81)	-1.11	(2.33)	10.64	(.11)	.03	--	(1,2)(6)
Berkeley	296.84	(85.48)	I	17.71	(1.28)	J	72.28	(5.27)	G	-37.90	(1.37)	43.87	(2.81)	2.73	(2.23)	-3.78	(2.21)	3.58	(2.24)	-1178.65	(3.58)	.64	--	(1)(2,4,6)
Albany	492.39	(10.18)	I	124.51	(3.19)	J	53.43	(1.03)	G	-74.90	(.81)	-20.96	(.40)	5.67	(3.17)	5.09	(2.20)	1.02	(.46)	-1181.10	(1.40)	.38	(12)	(1)
Walnut Creek	104.49	(25.95)	I	.12	(.01)	J	8.23	(.86)	G	-53.38	(4.73)	53.67	(4.20)	2.54	(4.67)	.41	(.61)	1.35	(2.23)	-812.11	(4.42)	-1.30	--	(1)(6,12)
Lafayette	128.28	(7.29)	I	7.15	(.32)	J	8.33	(.36)	G	43.58	(1.95)	60.62	(1.86)	2.61	(2.70)	.58	(.50)	.43	(.42)	-1892.70	(6.00)	-2.31	(8)	(1)(12)
C. C. Co. inside-Walnut Creek Office	217.02	(39.15)	I	10.56	(.66)	J	-15.59	(.93)	G	-57.47	(2.30)	66.26	(3.48)	4.86	(4.00)	-.59	(.41)	1.98	(1.53)	-1370.58	(4.92)	-1.04	--	(6,12)
Alameda	702.38	(39.79)	I	13.37	(.37)	J	-2.22	(.06)	G	-217.23	(3.10)	103.58	(2.74)	7.03	(3.98)	-7.99	(3.19)	-4.10	(1.73)	224.19	(.40)	0.05	--	(12)
Richmond	182.53	(26.82)	I	2.21	(.14)	J	12.87	(.76)	G	-64.71	(1.70)	12.95	(.77)	.31	(.41)	.96	(.88)	1.53	(1.57)	-486.11	(1.10)	.45	--	(1)(6,12)
El Cerrito	188.73	(23.01)	I	5.47	(.57)	J	9.34	(.97)	G	-71.89	(7.35)	-31.86	(2.11)	.23	(.45)	.79	(1.07)	.15	(.24)	643.23	(3.77)	1.18	--	(1)(6,12)
San Pablo	121.36	(2.06)	I	41.42	(1.67)	J	36.59	(1.53)	G	30.07	(.93)	7.40	(.29)	.90	(.87)	.68	(.51)	.71	(.55)	-773.97	(3.42)	.71	(6)	(1)(12)
Pinole-Hercules	123.53	(11.74)	I	-36.45	(1.19)	J	-70.12	(2.24)	G	-2.24	(.06)	163.04	(3.58)	3.33	(3.17)	2.73	(.80)	3.50	(1.09)	-2918.89	(5.67)	-3.89	--	(1)
Crockett	116.47	(40.54)	I	7.98	(.91)	J	12.19	(1.20)	G	.37	(.01)	37.03	(3.65)	2.26	(2.92)	1.08	(.78)	2.16	(1.78)	-599.04	(1.78)	.88	--	(1,4)(6,12)
C. C. Co. ... (row cut off)																								

COMMERCIAL
RESIDENTIAL

Community	Mean		Treatment 1			Treatment 2			Treatment 3			Treatment 4		Temperature		Rain		Rain (t-1)		Price		Elasticity	Noise Model	
	Estimated Coefficient	t-Value	Code	Estimated Coefficient	t-Value	Code	Estimated Coefficient	t-Value	Code	Estimated Coefficient	t-Value	Estimated Coefficient	t-Value	Estimated Coefficient	t-Value	Estimated Coefficient	t-Value	Estimated Coefficient	t-Value	Estimated Coefficient	t-Value		NA	AR
Santa Paula	20.44	(35.19)	D	- 4.37	(4.04)	--			--					.59	(12.25)	.35	(3.73)	.39	(4.28)	- 35.24	(2.35)	.35	--	(1,5)(9)
												Ventura County												
Monterey (Carmel, Sand City, Pacific Grove, Del Rey Oaks were coded as part of Monterey)	11.14	(10.38)	M	.42	(.64)	G	- .50	(.56)	--					.12	(2.78)	.06	(1.30)	- .09	(1.87)	- 6.20	(1.08)	- .13	(2)	(1),(12)
												Monterey Peninsula												
												Santa Barbara County												
Goleta	29.07	(253.78)	M	- 2.73	(4.61)	C,F	- 4.77	(6.85)	K	1.64	(2.46)			.37	(4.24)	- .23	(2.52)	- .48	(5.55)	- 7.99	(1.32)	- .06	(11)	(1,4,8,12)
Montecito	40.07	(93.10)	M	- 17.94	(11.07)	A	- 5.62	(2.32)	K	3.62	(3.00)			1.79	(8.66)	.12	(.34)	- 2.08	(6.55)	- 71.58	(1.97)	- .28	(7)	--
Summerland	18.17	(67.57)	M	.81	(1.18)	A	- 2.18	(2.32)	K	2.89	(2.85)			.38	(7.21)	- .16	(1.62)	- .31	(3.42)	- 28.60	(3.25)	- .35	(1,2)	--

IRRIGATION

Community	Treatment 1 Estimated Coefficient	t-Value	Code	Treatment 2 Estimated Coefficient	t-Value	Code	Treatment 3 Estimated Coefficient	t-Value	Code	Treatment 4 Estimated Coefficient	t-Value	Code	Treatment 5 Estimated Coefficient	t-Value	Code	Temperature Estimated Coefficient	t-Value	Rain Estimated Coefficient	t-Value	Rain (t-1) Estimated Coefficient	t-Value	Price Estimated Coefficient	t-Value	Elasticity	Noise Model MA	AR
Santa Barbara County																										
Goleta	566.41	(79.54)	M	- 64.98	(3.70)	M	- 42.69	(1.55)	C,F	-101.19	(3.00)	K	------	------	--	.76	(.32)	4.61	(1.45)	5.38	(1.75)	-5347.2	(8.41)	- .95	(1)	(2,4,6,8)
Montecito	440.06	(27.78)	M	-188.24	(34.75)	M	-171.51	(3.90)	A	110.63	(2.24)	K	------	------	--	23.44	(7.05)	8.16	(1.61)	21.71	(4.58)	-3554.07	(5.41)	- .87	(1,12)	--
Summerland	182.17	(23.87)	M	- 66.79	(3.28)	M	6.00	(.23)	A	94.51	(3.17)	K	------	------	--	11.66	(6.04)	.54	(.14)	9.28	(2.48)	-1380.89	(7.57)	- 1.42	(1)	--
Carpinteria	DF(1)		B	- 83.32	(1.47)		- 13.84	(.23)	K	------	------		------	------		17.67	(8.20)	5.77	(1.34)	5.01	(1.15)	-2990.70	(8.14)	- .76	(1)	--
Ventura County																										
Ventura	358.86	(3.68)	C	- 75.97	(.57)		------	------	--	------	------		------	------	--	18.74	(2.64)	12.11	(1.47)	.15	(.03)	-2711.17	(.43)	- .65	(6)	(1)(12)
Santa Paula	1751.5	(40.26)	D	-354.42	(9.27)		------	------	--	------	------		------	------	--	93.20	(6.04)	-152.91	(7.09)	-102.72	(4.80)	74231.0	(2.36)	1.01	(1)(16)	--
Greater San Diego																										
Oceanside	924.28	(19.15)	C	-304.54	(2.59)		------	------	--	------	------		------	------	--	-41.55	(5.47)	-72.64	(5.30)	50.11	(3.61)	1270.4	(.58)	.22	(7)	(1)(11)
Escondido	375.16	(4.72)	B	285.83	(2.36)		- 93.96	(.59)	K	------	------		------	------	--	4.15	(.95)	-14.97	(1.64)	8.38	(1.00)	-3225.97	(2.91)	- 1.05	(10)	(1)(6)
Monterey Peninsula																										
Santa Cruz (inside)	DF(1)		F	- 11.50	(1.12)	F	- 1.36	(.13)	G	- 1.17	(.11)	L	------	------	--	.78	(1.92)	.10	(.24)	.39	(.93)	30.87	(1.05)	.14	--	(6)
Santa Cruz (outside)	204.52	(6.42)	F	- 12.85	(.32)	F	45.30	(1.07)	G	- 76.37	(1.46)	L	------	------	--	8.99	(2.74)	- 4.15	(1.43)	1.09	(.36)	-482.05	(2.78)	.44	--	(1)(12)
Northern Inland California																										
Paradise	542.65	(2.00)	H	-196.13	(2.08)		31.49	(.27)	L	------	------		------	------		1.94	(.62)	2.61	(.99)	1.71	(.66)	- 21.23	(.62)	- .01	--	(1,4)(12)

TOTAL PRODUCTION/ACCT.

Ventura County

Community	Mean Estimated Coefficient	t-value	Treatment 1 Code	Treatment 1 Estimated Coefficient	t-value	Treatment 2 Code	Treatment 2 Estimated Coefficient	t-value	Treatment 3 Code	Treatment 3 Estimated Coefficient	t-value	Treatment 4 Code	Treatment 4 Estimated Coefficient	t-value	Temperature Estimated Coefficient	t-value	Rain Estimated Coefficient	t-value	Rain (t-1) Estimated Coefficient	t-value	Price Estimated Coefficient	t-value	Elasticity	Noise Model MA	Noise Model AR
Port Number	28.70	(43.42)	A,E	- 2.73	(2.14)	--	------	------	--	------	------	--	------	------	.80	(5.97)	- .69	(2.37)	- .52	(1.82)	------	------	------	--	--
Desert Communities																									
Coachella	42.95	(56.60)	D	7.46	(3.48)	--	------	------	--	------	------	--	--	--	.76	(15.88)	- 2.26	(2.47)	- 2.78	(3.06)	- 7.63	(.24)	- .01	--	--
Indio	63.65	(38.15)	D	- 4.53	(1.83)	--	------	------	--	------	------	--	--	--	1.24	(11.85)	- 2.25	(4.24)	- 1.59	(3.16)	-125.79	(3.71)	- .22	(2)	(1)(12)
Central Valley																									
Madera	41.44	(8.07)	F	- 6.23	(1.08)	--	------	------	--	------	------	--	--	--	1.54	(5.26)	- 1.65	(1.33)	- .55	(.44)	------	------	------	--	(1)(12)
Merced	48.12	(9.50)	A	- 9.14	(3.39)	--	------	------	--	------	------	--	--	--	1.38	(7.71)	- 1.76	(3.95)	- .40	(.88)	------	------	------	--	(1)(12)
Woodland	46.10	(17.95)	B,M	- 8.66	(2.05)	--	------	------	--	------	------	--	--	--	1.42	(6.51)	- .76	(1.15)	- .31	(.48)	------	------	------	--	(1)(12)
Davis	41.07	(21.90)	C,F	- 3.63	(1.42)	--	------	------	--	------	------	--	--	--	1.25	(10.66)	- 1.21	(4.20)	- .35	(1.23)	------	------	------	(11)	(1)(12)
West Sacramento	48.68	(11.30)	C,F	- 12.31	(5.07)	--	------	------	--	------	------	--	--	--	1.26	(5.61)	- 1.33	(2.63)	- .15	(.51)	------	------	------	--	(1)(12)
Monterey Peninsula																									
Watsonville	21.04	(19.96)	A	- 1.53	(1.78)	--	------	------	--	------	------	--	------	------	.65	(7.18)	- .36	(3.07)	- .20	(6.92)	-21.66	(2.05)	- .19	--	(1)(12)
Northern Inland California																									
Grass Valley	39.55	(4.48)	A,F	- 8.56	(1.07)	--	------	------	--	------	------	--	------	------	.76	(4.33)	- .19	(1.07)	.26	(1.55)	------	------	------	--	(1)(12)
San Francisco Bay Area																									
Marin County	20.29	(26.61)	M	- 1.02	(.74)	C,F	- 4.39	(2.58)	G	- 6.50	(3.05)	L	4.0	(1.86)	.42	(5.46)	- .14	(2.27)	.10	(1.79)	- 8.84	(1.50)	- .14	(12)	(1,2)

Community	Mean		Treatment 1			Treatment 2			Treatment 3			Treatment 4			Temperature		Rain		Rain (t-1)		Price			Noise Model	
	Estimated Coefficient	t-Value	Code	Estimated Coefficient	t-Value	Code	Estimated Coefficient	t-Value	Code	Estimated Coefficient	t-Value	Code	Estimated Coefficient	t-Value	Estimated Coefficient	t-Value	Estimated Coefficient	t-Value	Estimated Coefficient	t-Value	Estimated Coefficient	t-Value	Elasticity	MA	AR
Oxnard	30.38	(3.79)	0	- .44	(.46)	--	------	------	--	------	------				- .02	(.33)	- .17	(2.68)	- .13	(2.19)	23.72	(.43)	.21	(10)	(11)(2)
													Greater Los Angeles												
Alhambra	23.54	(27.2)	0	- 4.44	(5.38)	--	------	------	--	------	------				.29	(2.82)	.09	(.63)	.07	(.50)	-31.9C	(1.61)	- .19	--	(1,4)(6)
													Desert Communities												
Blythe	46.79	(41.33)	A	- 2.69	(1.02)	--	------	------	--	------	------				1.53	(15.93)	.80	(.25)	.21	(.22)	-34.5C	(1.43)	- .03	(2,12,19)	--
													Humboldt County												
Arcata	131.11	(66.13)	A	- 1.70	(2.84)	--	------	------	--	------	------				.24	(3.00)	- .19	(2.35)	.03	(.30)	10.2E	(2.12)	.22	--	(1)(5)
Cutten	126.53	(16.33)	A	- 1.23	(.79)	--	------	------	--	------	------				.15	(1.50)	- .22	(2.84)	.13	(1.71)	-21.6C	(3.28)	.42	--	(1)(9,11)
Eureka	13.18	(18.36)	A,F	- 2.30	(3.88)	--	------	------	--	------	------				.24	(3.50)	- .18	(3.40)	.13	(2.52)	48.3C	(2.32)	.61	--	(1,12)

Code Sheet for Treatments 1–4

Code	Explanation
A	Conservation literature sent with bill.
B	Conservation literature sent with bill, and toilet kits made available.
C	Educational programs, water kits, and conservation literature sent with bills.
D	No specific measures.
E	Educational programs on how to conserve water.
F	Ordinances passed to restrict water use.
G	Water rationing.
H	Restrictions on use and rationing.
I	Comprehensive water management plan passed.
J	Program to detect and correct water leaks.
K	End of the drought.
L	End of rationing.
M	Moratorium on installation of new water hookups.

NOTES

Chapter One

1. On the average, about 200 million acre-feet (MAF) of water from precipitation falls on California each year. (An acre-foot is the amount of water required to cover an acre of land with a foot of water; one acre-foot equals 325,851 gallons.) About 20 percent of this total is eventually used by state residents either directly or through goods and services consumed, with approximately half coming from groundwater and half from surface water. About 85 percent of the water used in the state can be attributed to agricultural consumption; most of the remainder is consumed by various kinds of "urban" users (Phelps et al. 1978).

2. For those unfamiliar with the economics and politics of water use in California, it is well known that historically, economic principles have not played a sufficiently important role in the development of state water (for example, see Lipson 1978). In addition, water purveyors have been loath to apply economic principles in establishing an efficient system of allocation of water to consumers. Basically, instead of making the most of potential efficiencies that result from the market, water development and distribution have been constrained by state laws, legal decisions, and administrative regulations that seriously distort the market for water. To quote a recent assessment:

> Is water being used efficiently in California? This study concludes that water use throughout the state is *not* efficient. The lack of efficiency is not due to mismanagement or waste by water users (agriculture, business, and households) but rather to a myriad of legal and institutional restrictions on water pricing, transfer, sale and use. In general, water users individually appear to use water efficiently, *given the circumstances they face,* but those circumstances (the body of water law, water supply institutions and legal rulings) essentially dictate that water use be inefficient from a statewide perspective. More important, improvement in the efficient use of state water supplies could forestall or even eliminate the need for construction of expensive new water development facilities now being considered by the legislature. The current system generates annual losses to California conservatively estimated to be $60 to $370 million, which is equivalent to a once-and-for-all wealth loss of $1 to $5 billion. It is this loss that should be contrasted against legal, political, and economic costs associated with a move to efficient water use. (Italics are in the original.) (Phelps, Moore, and Graubard, 1978, p. v)

3. To those unfamiliar with the consequences of determining prices in terms of the real cost of the "next unit" consumed (the marginal cost), this may seem an all too casual solution to a knotty problem. Basically, we are arguing that if water were priced appropriately, one could at the same time reduce the quantities demanded and maximize the net benefits to the people of California. We are *not* saying that the increases in the real cost of water are unimportant or that they are inherently desirable. What we *are* saying is that, given existing inefficiencies, there is a genuine problem, but if water management

policies followed sound economic principles, the state could easily absorb significant increases in the real price of water.

4. These pricing issues are extremely important for a general understanding of current water-pricing policies in California. Moreover, the issues are far more complicated than our summary suggests. We will return to the question of appropriate water-pricing strategies later, although our discussion will be more narrowly focused on difficulties raised by acute shortages, such as those associated with the 1976–1977 drought. Readers interested in an excellent consideration of water-pricing policies in California should consult Phelps, Moore, and Graubard (1978).

5. The list of practical obstacles that need to be overcome before water is supplied in an economically efficient manner is staggering, and the political battles implied should give pause to even the most fervent reformers (Phelps et al. 1978).

6. The region served by the Ogallala Aquifer is one of the most important examples and because of the nationwide implications has recently received front page coverage in the *Wall Street Journal* (Frazier and Schlender 1980). The Ogallala Aquifer provides water that supports much of the agricultural economy from South Dakota to Texas, and is being "mined" at rates far in excess of the natural pace at which the water is replenished.

7. About 75 percent of California's annual precipitation is lost through evaporation or transpiration (Kahrl et al. 1979, p. v).

8. Water districts vary enormously in size and function. Some serve only a few hundred accounts, while others serve millions. As for diversity, Kahrl (1979, p. 63) lists twenty kinds of water districts, many of which are irrelevant to this research. The water districts we examine are of interest because they are the immediate suppliers of water to consumers. Such districts may purchase water from outside (for example, from the State Water Project), draw on their own local supplies (for example, from local groundwater), or even develop supplies from beyond their borders (for example, water supplied to Los Angeles from the Owens Valley). However they obtain their water, they are "urban" in the sense that they are associated with one or more municipalities. In contrast, some water districts may only serve a number of large farms. Readers interested in learning about water districts in more depth should consult the excellent discussion in Phelps et al. (1978).

9. The initial target of fifty districts was also partly determined by the cost of data collection and analysis. Technical and economic considerations typically interact in large-scale studies. In this case the major cost involved sending research assistants into the field to collect data.

10. The major practical constraint was the lack of adequate data. Sometimes the necessary historical time series simply did not exist; in other instances the data were recorded in a form that would have made aggregation into monthly

totals prohibitively time-consuming. Unfortunately, it was difficult to know without firsthand exposure to a district's data whether they would measure up or not.

11. In terms of total withdrawals from California's developed water supplies, 87 percent goes to irrigation; 8.5 percent to domestic, commercial, and institutional uses; 2 percent to manufacturing; and 2.5 percent to other purposes (Kahrl 1979).

12. The fieldwork was overseen by a full-time administrator who made travel arrangements, kept project records, was routinely available to answer emergency phone calls from the field (for example, a local official wanting to talk to someone "in authority" back at the university), and made sure that fieldwork was proceeding as planned. We also found it helpful to have a ninth field worker "in reserve" to bolster any two-person teams that needed extra help and to be available for scouting or follow-up missions.

Chapter Two

1. This chapter is an expanded version of the theoretical section in "Reducing Consumption in Periods of Acute Scarcity: The Case of Water" (Berk et al. 1980).

2. We distinguish here between pure public goods of the Samuelsonian type and "crowdable" public goods.

3. Economists define efficiency as that state where no one can be made better off without making someone else worse off. The application of marginal cost pricing to the water industry is outlined in Appendix 2. For more details, see Hirshleifer, DeHaven, and Milliman (1969). For practical applications, see Hanke (1978) and Cooley and LaCivita (1979).

4. This assumes that the producer is operating in an area of increasing costs. Hirshleifer DeHaven and Milliman (1969, chapter 5) and Cooley and LaCivita (1979, pp. 216–218) argue that this is the case for water purveyors.

5. For this and other reasons, existing legislation does not allow public water agencies to take in more revenue than required to cover their historical costs. In other words, pricing practices are constrained to yield an approximate equivalence between revenues and account costs, which results in an inefficient allocation of water.

6. Becker (1965) and others consider the household a productive unit; as such the household demand for water is a derived demand.

Chapter Four

1. It is probably worth noting in passing that variation in the number of accounts served over time for particular locales will, in principle, introduce het-

eroskedasticity into our standardized consumption time series, because the aggregate monthly estimates will be based on varying sample sizes. However, the number of accounts served from month to month rarely varied. Moreover, when we occasionally made adjustments for heteroskedasticity, the story was unchanged.

2. Readers who are familiar with Box-Jenkins time series procedures may wonder about the simplicity of the model. However, in this case and in most to follow, there was rarely any evidence in the residuals of changes in levels or slopes, even when seasonal nonstationarity was considered. In other words, whatever the nature of our specification errors, there was rarely any evidence that temporal trends or seasonal patterns were being neglected. When such problems occasionally surfaced, they were handled with differencing. There was also no evidence of the need for fancier parameterizations, particularly the inclusion of delta parameters to capture dynamic effects. In fact, when we occasionally tried to force such parameters into the models just to see what might happen, they never added significantly to the variance explained. The usual consequence was a dramatic increase in multicollinearity.

3. It is apparent that our causal relationships are linear. Other functional forms are of course possible (e.g., a log-log relationship). However, there seemed to be no particular theoretical reason to employ more complicated causal forms, and there was nothing in our inductive procedures to suggest that we had misspecified the functional form.

4. This is a conservative procedure, since most of our hypotheses were one-tailed. For one-tailed tests, t-values of 1.64 are statistically significant at the .05 level, while t-values of 1.98 are statistically significant at the .01 level. Basically, we are allowing for counter-intuitive results to be statistically significant.

Chapter Five

1. Actually, ignored is far too strong a word. We spent a great deal of time examining the data and trying a number of different strategies to moderate the impact of outliers. It was eventually apparent that one could obtain a rather different story, depending on the outlier strategy employed, and that many of the stories made no sense. Consequently, we have not burdened the text with a discussion of these results.

2. Recall that commercial consumers were generally less responsive than residential users to conservation programs, once we standardized for mean consumption. What we are saying here is that variation around average effects unstandardized for mean consumption is about the same for both residential and commercial users *as a function of the number of conservation programs introduced*, once the impact of average consumption is controlled. In view of the vulnerabilities in the analyses presented in this chapter, perhaps the most reasonable conclusion is the most simple one: the differential effectiveness of conservation programs for both residential and commercial consumers is

partly a function of the number of programs introduced. More precise comparisons may border on the fatuous.

3. This ignores, of course, the patterns for agricultural and industrial consumers. In this context, the presence of outliers for industrial use almost by definition means that the coefficients are *not* drawn from a single underlying distribution. Given only eleven communities for which agricultural breakdowns were available, it is difficult to say much one way or the other.

Chapter Six

1. More generally, current methods of forecasting too often extrapolate from past trends. Such procedures are almost certain to provide significant *overestimates* of future demand for water, in part because the impact of increases in the real price of water are neglected (Flack 1967). One result in California was the unnecessary expansion of an already overbuilt water supply system.

2. Our argument here is just a special application of a more general and devasting critique of procedures used to justify the development of water supply systems in California, perhaps stated most forcefully by Hirshleifer, DeHaven, and Milliman (1969). For example, there is solid evidence that the Colorado River Aqueduct Project has resulted in a major economic loss to the Los Angeles area, and that this loss, paid for by taxpayers, has hindered the growth of many important local industries (Hirshleifer, DeHaven, and Milliman 1969, pp. 135–136).

3. We will argue shortly that the commons dilemma disappears if marginal cost pricing is used.

4. What we are claiming is that marginal cost pricing *may* produce unsatisfactory distributional outcomes if a severe drought of short duration occurs. To avoid these outcomes, public policy might be effectively served by providing subsidies to the endangered region. However, such subsidies should be made available *only* until the local economy returns to normal. Alternatively, if the local supply system is operating in the region of increasing costs (which is likely), another option is to distribute agency profits to consumers in dire need. We will have more to say about this shortly, when we discuss other distributional issues.

5. It is important to emphasize that one can obtain the same distributional result and an approximation of economic efficiency with appropriate increasing-block pricing structures. In brief, levels of consumption are organized into "blocks" from low to high levels of use. The price per unit of water used increases as one moves from lower to higher blocks. Thus, modest use (presumably to meet necessities) is less costly, and this addresses the distributional problem. Now assume that one could determine in the aggregate the average quantity of water used by individual consumers if the per-unit price accurately captured the real marginal cost of supplying the next unit of water. That is, suppose one could estimate the intersection point of the supply and

demand curves. Then the increasing-block price structure could be set so that the price of water within the block containing this equilibrium level of consumption was equal to the real marginal cost. An approximation of economic efficiency would follow.

6. In addition, very few water districts document the specific timing and content of their various conservation efforts.

7. If marginal cost pricing is used, efficiency problems are automatically solved, and there is no need for benefit-cost analyses.

Appendix 2

1. Parts of this appendix have appeared in Cooley and LaCivita (1979).

2. In what follows, we explain how marginal cost pricing can be applied by water suppliers. We note, however, that efficient water use can also be attained through central planning of water use and supply, or by enabling water users to buy and sell water in a competitive market. For more on these two alternatives, see Phelps et al. (1978).

3. Other less common sources of subsidies are federal revenue-sharing funds and state and federal grants.

4. It is interesting to note that water agencies in general have consistently overforecast the demand for water by as much as 40 percent. See Hirshleifer et al. (1969), Flack (1967), and Hanke and Boland (1971).

5. For an application, see Hanke (1978).

REFERENCES

Adler, J., and Agrest, S. 1981. Drought in the Northeast. *Newsweek* (January 5): 20.

Bain, J. S.; Caves, R. E.; and Margolis, J. 1966. *Northern California's Water Industry: The Comparative Efficiency of Public Enterprise in Developing a Scarce Resource.* Baltimore: The Johns Hopkins Press.

Becker, G. S. 1965. A Theory of the Allocation of Time. *Economic Journal* 75, no. 299: 493–517.

Berk, R. A. et al. 1979. An Introduction to Estimation Procedures for Pooled Cross-Sectional and Time Series Data. *Evaluation Quarterly* 3, no. 4: 385–410.

————. 1980. Reducing Consumption in Periods of Acute Scarcity: The Case of Water. *Social Science Research* 9 (June): 99–120.

Box, G. E. P., and Jenkins, G. M. 1976. *Time Series Analysis: Forecasting and Control.* San Francisco: Holden-Day.

Box, G. E. P., and Tiao, G. C. 1975. Intervention Analysis with Applications in Economic and Environmental Problems. *Journal of the American Statistical Association* 70, no. 1: 70–79.

Brechner, K. C. 1977. An Experimental Analysis of Social Traps. *Journal of Experimental Social Psychology* 13: 552–564.

Brewer, M. B. Forthcoming. Ingroup Bias in the Minimal Intergroup Situation: A Cognitive-Motivational Analysis. *Psychological Bulletin.*

Bruvold, W. 1978. Consumer Response to Urban Drought in Central California. Technical report. University of California, Berkeley.

California Department of Water Resources. 1976a. An Urban Water Conservation Conference. Proceedings. January 16–17, Los Angeles, California.

————. 1976b. Water Conservation in California. Bulletin 198 (May).

————. 1977. The Continuing California Drought. August.

————. 1978. The 1976–1977 California Drought—A Review. May.

Campbell, D. T., and Stanley, J. 1963. *Experimental and Quasi-Experimental Designs for Research.* Chicago: Rand McNally.

Cooley, T. F., and LaCivita, C. J. 1979. Allocative Efficiency and Distributional Equity in Water Pricing and Finance: A Post–Proposition 13 Analysis. Proceedings of the Santa Barbara Tax Limitation Conference, December 1978. *National Tax Journal* 32, no. 2: 215–228.

Dawes, R. M. 1975. Formal Models of Dilemmas in Social Decision Making. In *Human Judgement and Decision Processes,* M. F. Kaplan and S. Schwartz, eds. New York: Academic Press.

Dawes, R. M.; McTavish, J.; and Shaklee, H. 1977. Behavior, Communication, and Assumptions About Other People's Behavior in a Commons Dilemma Situation. *Journal of Personality and Social Psychology* 35: 1–11.

Flack, J. E. 1967. Meeting Future Water Requirements Through Reallocation. *Journal of the American Water Works Association* 59, no. 11: 1340.

Frazier, S., and Schlender, B. R. 1980. Huge Area in Midwest Relying on Irrigation Is Depleting Its Water. *Wall Street Journal.* August 6.

Gottlieb, M. 1963. Urban Domestic Demand for Water: A Kansas Case Study. *Land Economics* 39, 2: 204–210.

Granger, C. W. J., and Newbold, P. 1977. *Forecasting Economic Time Series.* New York: Academic Press.

Grima, A. P. 1972. *Residential Water Demand: Alternative Choices for Management.* Toronto: University of Toronto Press.

Hanke, S. H. 1978. Pricing as a Conservation Tool: An Economist's Dream Come True? In *Municipal Water Systems*, D. Holtz and S. Sebastian, eds. Bloomington: Indiana University Press.

Hanke, S. H., and Boland, J. J. 1971. Water Requirements or Water Demands? *Journal of the American Water Works Association* 63: 677–681.

Hanushek, E. A., and Jackson, J. E. 1977. *Statistical Methods for Social Scientists.* New York: Academic Press.

Hardin, G. 1968. The Tragedy of the Commons. *Science* 162: 1243–1248.

Haver, C. B., and Winter, J. R. 1963. *Future Water Supply in London: An Economic Appraisal.* London, Ontario: Public Utilities Commission (January).

Headley, J. C. 1963. The Relation of Family Income and Use of Water for Residential and Commercial Purposes in the San Francisco–Oakland Metropolitan Area. *Land Economics* 39, 4: 441–449.

Hirshleifer, J.; DeHaven, J. C.; and Milliman, J. W. 1969. *Water Supply: Economics, Technology and Policy.* Chicago: University of Chicago Press.

Hoffman, M.; Glickstein, R.; and Liroff, S. 1979. Urban Drought in the San Francisco Bay Area: A Study of Institutional and Social Resiliency. *Journal of the American Water Works Association* 71 (July): 356–363.

Howe, C. W. 1979. *National Resource Economics.* New York: John Wiley.

Howe, C. W., and Linaweaver, F. P., Jr. 1967. The Impact of Price on Residential Water Demand and Its Relation to System Demand and Price Structure. *Water Resources Research* 3, 1: 13–22.

Hume, E. 1980. Wastes Imperil Drinking Water in 3,600 Areas. *Los Angeles Times*, July 24.

Jaquette, D. L. 1978. Efficient Water Use in California: Conjunctive Management of Ground and Surface Reservoirs. Report No. R-2389-CSA/RF. Santa Monica, California: Rand Corporation.

Jaquette, D. L., and Moore, N. Y. 1978. Efficient Water Use in California: Groundwater Use and Management. Report No. R-2387/1-CSA/RF. Santa Monica, California: Rand Corporation.

Jenkins, G. M. 1979. Practical Experience with Modeling and Forecasting Time Series. In *Forecasting*, O. D. Anderson, ed. New York: North Holland.

Johnston, J. 1972. *Econometric Methods.* New York: McGraw Hill.

Jones, R. A. 1980. State Water Project Faces Major Hurdles. *Los Angeles Times*, June 8.

————. 1980b. Equity of Water Project Cost Questioned. *Los Angeles Times*, June 9.

Kahrl, W. L., ed. 1979. *The California Water Atlas.* Sacramento: Office of Planning and Research, Governor's Office.

Kelley, H. H., and Grzelak, J. 1972. Conflict Between Individual and Common Interest in an n-Person Relationship. *Journal of Personality and Social Psychology* 21: 190–197.

Kmenta, J. 1971. *Elements of Econometrics.* New York: Macmillan.

Latane, B., and Darley, J. H. 1968. Group Inhibition of Bystander Intervention in Emergencies. *Journal of Personality and Social Psychology* 10: 215–221.

Leventhal, H. 1970. Findings and Theory in the Study of Fear Communication. In *Advances in Experimental Social Psychology,* vol. V, L. Berkowitz, ed. New York: Academic Press.

Leventhal, H.; Singer, R. P.; and Jones, S. 1965. Effects of Fear and Specificity of Recommendation upon Attitudes and Behavior. *Journal of Personality and Social Psychology* 2: 20–29.

Linder, D. E. 1977. Patterns of Energy Utilization and Conservation: A Social Trap Perspective. Symposium paper presented at the American Psychological Association Annual Convention, Toronto, September.

Lipsey, M. W. 1977. Personal Antecedents and Consequences of Ecologically Responsible Behavior. Journal Supplement Abstract Service, Ms. 1521.

Lipson, A. J. 1978. Efficient Water Use in California: The Evolution of Groundwater Management in Southern California. Report No. R-2387/2-CSA/RF. Santa Monica, California: Rand Corporation.

McClelland, L. 1977. Encouraging Energy Conservation as a Social Psychological Problem. Paper presented at the American Psychological Association Annual Convention, Toronto, September.

McGuire, W. J. 1969. The Nature of Attitudes and Attitude Change. In *Handbook of Social Psychology,* Vol. III, G. Lindzey and G. Aronson, eds. 2nd ed. Reading, Mass.: Addison-Wesley, pp. 136–314.

Madalla, G. S. 1977. *Econometrics.* New York: McGraw Hill.

Marascuillo, L. A., and McSweeney, M. 1977. *Nonparametric and Distribution-Free Methods for the Social Sciences.* Monterey, California: Brooks/Cole.

Marwell, G., and Ames, R. E. 1979. Experiments on the Provision of Public Goods. Part I: Resources, Interest, Group Size, and the Free-Rider Problem. *American Journal of Sociology* 84: 1335–1360.

Messick, D. M. 1973. To Join or Not to Join: An Approach to the Unionization Decision. *Organizational Behavior and Human Performance* 10: 145–156.

———. 1974. When a Little "Group Interest" Goes a Long Way: A Note on Social Motives and Union Joining. *Organizational Behavior and Human Performance* 12: 331–334.

Miller, P. D. 1979. Stability, Diversity and Equity: A Comparison of Coal, Oil, Shale, and Synfuels. *Sociopolitical Effects of Energy Use and Policy.* Washington, D.C.: National Academy of Sciences, pp. 176–177.

Moore, N. Y.; Graubard, M. H.; and Shishko, R. 1978. Efficient Water Use in California: Water Supply Planning. Report No. R-2390-CSA/RF. Santa Monica, California: Rand Corporation.

Phelps, C. E.; Moore, N. Y.; and Graubard, M. H. 1978. Efficient Water Use in California: Water Rights, Water Districts, and Water Transfers. Report No. R-2386-CSA/RF. Santa Monica, California: Rand Corporation.

Phelps, C. E. et al. 1978. Efficient Water Use in California: Executive Summary. Report No. R-2385-CSA/RF. Santa Monica, California: Rand Corporation.

Platt, J. 1973. Social Traps. *American Psychologist* 28: 641–651.

Schelling, T. 1971. On the Ecology of Micromotives. *The Public Interest* 25: 59–98.

Seligman, C.; Darley, J. M.; and Becker, L. J. Forthcoming. Behavioral Approaches to Residential Energy Conservation. *Energy and Buildings*.

Sewell, W. R. D., and Rouche, L. 1974. Peak Load Pricing and Urban Water Management: Victoria, B.C., A Case Study. *Natural Resources Journal* 14, no. 3: 383–400.

Spector, M., and Kitsuse, J. I. 1977. *Constructing Social Problems*. Menlo Park, California: Cummings Publishing.

Stern, P. C. 1976. Effects of Incentives and Education on Resource Conservation Decisions in a Simulated Commons Dilemma. *Journal of Personality and Social Psychology* 34: 1285–1292.

Talarowski, F. S. 1977. Effects of Moralizing and Individual Incentive in Decomposed Commons Dilemmas. Unpublished M.A. thesis. University of California, Santa Barbara.

Talarowski, F. S., and McClintock, C. G. 1978. The Conservation of Domestic Water: A Social Psychological Study. Final report to the Water Resources Center, University of California, Davis.

Taylor, L. 1975. The Demand for Electricity: A Summary. *The Bell Journal of Economics* 6: 74–110.

———. 1980. Some Problems and Issues in Building Econometric Models of Energy Demand. Department of Economics, University of Arizona. Mimeo.

Thompson, P. T., and McTavish, J. 1976. Energy Problems: Public Beliefs, Attitudes and Behaviors. Allendale, Michigan: Urban Environmental Studies Institute, Grand Valley State College.

Turnovsky, S. S. 1969. The Demand for Water: Some Empirical Evidence on Consumers' Response to a Commodity in Uncertain Supply. *Water Resources Research* 5, no. 2: 350–361.

Ward, R. C. 1975. *Principles of Hydrology*. New York: John Wiley.

Watkins, G. A. 1974. Developing a "Water Concern" Scale. *The Journal of Environmental Education* 5: 54–58.

Wetzel, B. 1978. Efficient Water Use in California: Economic Modeling of Groundwater Development with Applications to Groundwater Management. Report No. R-2388-CSA/RF. Santa Monica, California: Rand Corporation.

Wong, S. 1972. A Model on Municipal Water Demand: A Case Study of Northeastern Illinois. *Land Economics* 48, no. 1: 34–44.

INDEX

Adler, J., 8
Advertising, 31
Agrest, S., 8
Agricultural users
  commons dilemma approach to, 148
  consequences of drought on, 1
  conservation measures and, 2
  demand for water among, 29
  differential effects of conservation programs on, 127–128
  marginal prices and, 93
  in Montecito, 102–105
  monthly consumption figures for, 96
  price elasticities and, 30, 156
  relative effectiveness of conservation programs and prices and, 157, 158
  time series analyses of, 102–105, 113–115
Alhambra, California, 81
American Water Works Association (AWWA)
  declining-block rate structure of, 24–25
  materials available from, 51, 52–53, 71, 81
Ames, R. E., 21
Arcata, California, 71
Association of Water Agencies (AWA), 81
Attitudes toward consumption
  demand and changes in, 31–32
  perception of conservation and, 22

Becker, L. J., 22, 23
Berk, R. A., 3, 4, 13
Berkeley, California, public water authority use in, 107–109
Billing
  demand and types of, 31–32
  surcharges used in, 64
Blythe, California, 84
Boland, J. J., 32

Box, G. E. P., 97, 98, 101, 155
Bradley, Mayor, 82
Brechner, K. C., 21
Brewer, M. B., 21
Bruvold, W., 22
Burbank, California
  commercial water use in, 105–106
  Public Works Department, 81

California-American Water Company (Cal-Am), 77
California Department of Water Resources (CDWR)
  categories of conservation programs and, 38
  implementation of programs and, 39
  Marin Municipal Water District (MMWD) programs and, 35, 36
  materials available from, 51, 52–53
California Health and Safety Code, 64
California State Water Project, 1, 5
Campbell, D. T., 3
Carpinteria County Water District, 77
Central Valley programs, 1, 4, 73
Citations, for water overuse, 64
Climate
  agricultural users and, 29
  demand for water and, 26, 29
  within sample districts, 46, 48–49
Coachella Valley County Water District, 84
Code changes, for plumbing, 39, 45, 64, 66, 154
Colorado River
  complications from dependence on, 4
  consequences of drought and, 1
  conservation programs and reliance on, 85
  San Diego's reliance on, 2, 83
  water quality and, 5
Commercial users
  in Burbank, 105–106
  demand for water among, 26–27

differential effects of programs for, 134–136, 161
price elasticities and, 156
relative effectiveness of conservation programs and price and, 157, 158
time series analyses of, 105–106, 115–116
Commons dilemma, in water use, 20, 21, 148
Community Emergency Drought Relief Act of 1977, 76
Conservation programs
  aggregate reduction figures from, 3–4
  American Water Works Association materials for, 51, 52–53
  assessments of, 2
  attitudes toward, 22, 31–32
  belief in shortage and, 21–22
  categories of, 38
  causal model of water use and, 3
  Central Valley, 73
  community characteristics and commitment to, 68–71
  conflicts in public interest and, 20
  consequences of drought and, 2
  demand affected by, 30–31
  Desert Communities, 84–85
  differential effects of, 124–140
  during drought in sample districts, 51, 57–60, 65
  education used in, 44, 45
  evaluation of success of, 155–159
  factors affecting response to, 67–68
  feedback to users and, 33
  gaps between targets and procedures in, 154
  greater Los Angeles, 81–83
  greater San Diego, 83–84
  Humboldt County, 71–72
  implementation of, 38–39
  irrigation in, 39, 41–42, 45
  leak detection and repair in, 42, 45
  local variations in, 2
  Marin Municipal Water District (MMWD), 35–37
  metering in, 43, 45
  methods used in, 39–45

  microeconomic perspective on, 23–33
  Monterey Bay area, 76–77
  native landscaping used in, 42, 45
  new technology in, 39, 41
  Northern Inland communities, 72
  number of, in sample districts, 66–67
  overview of, 51–71
  postdrought, in sample districts, 51, 61–63
  predrought, in sample districts, 51, 54–56, 65, 153
  pricing in, 43, 45
  relative effectiveness of pricing and, 157–159
  residential consumers as primary targets of, 86–87
  responses after drought and, 4
  retrofitting in, 39, 40–41
  social psychological perspective on, 19–23
  San Diego, 38
  San Francisco Bay area, 73–76
  Santa Barbara County, 77–79
  sewer charges in, 43, 45
  summaries of, by sample communities, 71–85
  summary and conclusions for, 85–87
  surcharges in, 30, 31
  typology of, 38–46
  unanswered questions in, 162–164
  variation in number and kind of, 153–154
  Ventura County, 79–81
  water-saving plumbing used in, 39, 45
Consumption
  aggregate reduction figures for, 3–4
  attitude changes and billing and, 31–32
  causal models of, 3, 147–152
  commons dilemma in, 20, 21
  conflicts in public interest and, 20
  feedback to users on, 33
  leak repair and, 45
  microeconomic perspective on, 23–33

Consumption (*continued*)
  monthly figures in, 94–96
  postdrought, 4, 156–157
  social psychological perspective
    on, 19–23
  social traps in, 20, 21
  time series analyses of, 13, 88–122
  underpricing and, 149
Cooley, T. F., 149
Costs
  declining-block rate structure and,
    24
  economic inefficiencies of water
    policy and, 5–6
  price patterns and, 179–181
  pricing policies and, 6
  public works projects and, 4
  of water quality, 5
Cutter, California, 71

Darley, J. H., 22, 23
Data base in survey, 12–13
Data collection in survey, 14–15
  questionnaire used in, 165–177
Davis, California, 73
Dawes, R. M., 20, 21
Declining-block rate structure, 24–25,
  91–93
DeHaven, J. C., 3, 6, 9, 149
Demand
  agricultural users and, 29
  attitude changes and, 31–32
  climate and, 26
  among commercial users, 26–27
  conservation measures and, 30–31
  family income and, 26
  feedback to users and, 33
  industrial users and, 28
  moratoriums and, 30–31
  politics of water and, 4–5
  price elasticities and, 29–30
  pricing and decrease in, 25–26
  public authority water use and,
    28–29
  among residential users, 26
  surcharges and, 30, 31
  type of user and, 26–29
  viability of existing supplies and, 4
  water shortages and, 11, 145–146

Differential effects of programs,
    124–140, 160
  commercial users in, 134–136
  importance of study of, 125–126
  price in, 160–161
  public users in, 137–139
  residential users in, 128–134
  summary and conclusions of, 139–
    140
  variables in analyses of, 127
Drought
  consequences of, 1
  definitions of, 2–3, 9–12
  hydrologic balance model in, 9–10

East Bay Municipal Utility District
    (EBMUD)
  conservation programs of, 74–76
  leak repair programs of, 45
  Marin programs and, 37
  model for local response to pro-
    grams and, 68–71
  predrought programs in, 65
  PROJECT WATER of, 75
  recycling programs of, 64
East Coast water shortage, 8
Economic development, and water
    supplies, 144
Economic factors, and commitment
    to programs, 87
Education, 31
  advantages and disadvantages of,
    44
  in conservation programs, 44, 45
  within sample district programs,
    51, 64
  Spanish-speaking consumers and,
    87, 154
  water use choices and, 21
  see also Years of schooling
El Centro, California, 84
Energy crisis, 8, 144
  conservation programs for, 33
  social psychological perspective
    on, 21–22
Environmental factors, in pricing, 6
Environmental movement, 4, 128
Environmental Protection Agency, 7,
    144

Escondido, California, 83
Eureka, California, 2, 71, 72

Family income, *see* Income
Federal government, and subsidies, 6, 149, 178
Feedback in programs, 33
Flat-rate billing, 31–32
Forecasting, 146
Frazier, S., 148

Glickstein, R., 74
Goleta County Water District, 78–79
    attitudes toward conservation in, 22
    marginal cost of water in, 149
Gottlieb, M., 93
Government subsidies, 6, 149, 178
Granger, C. W. J., 97, 99, 100
Grass Valley, California, 72
Graubard, M. H., 149
Grima, A. P., 181, 182
Groundwater
    conservation program adoption and amount of, 131
    population growth and, 4
    pricing policies and, 6
    water quality and use of, 5
Grzelak, J., 20

Hanke, S. H., 32
Hanushek, E. A., 131
Hardin, G., 20
Haver, C. B., 93
Hirshleifer, J., 3, 6, 9, 149, 179, 181
Hoffman, M., 74
Howe, C. W., 2–3, 5, 6, 39
Humboldt County programs, 71–72
Hume, E., 7

Imperial Beach, California, 83
Implementation of programs, 153
    types of, 38–39
    voluntary programs in, 39
Income
    demand for water and, 26
    differential effects of programs and, 129
    response to programs and, 68

within sample communities, 46, 48–49
Income tax, 178
Indio, California, 84
Industrial users
    demand for water among, 28
    differential effects of programs on, 128
    marginal prices and, 93
    monthly consumption figures for, 96
    price elasticities and, 156
    relative effectiveness of conservation programs and price and, 157, 158
    in San Diego, 106–107
    time series analyses of, 106–107, 116–117
    water quality and, 7
Irrigation, 39, 41–42, 45

Jackson, J. E., 131
Jenkins, G. M., 97, 98, 99, 101, 155
Johnston, J., 97
Jones, R. A., 5

Kahrl, W. L., 1, 2, 4, 12
Kelley, H. H., 20
Kits, in conservation programs, 64
Kitsuse, J. I., 3
Kmenta, J., 97

LaCivita, C. J., 149
Lake Tahoe, California, 5
Landscaping, in conservation programs, 42, 45
Latané, B., 22
Leak detection and repair, 42, 45
Leventhal, H., 22
Linder, D. E., 21
Lipsey, M. W., 22
Liroff, S., 74
Local governments
    price subsidies among, 6
    responses to drought among, 34–87
Los Angeles, 81–83
    area programs, 81–83
    Department of Water and Power, 82–83

Los Angeles (*continued*)
  leak repair in, 45
  rainfall variations in, 2
Los Angeles Times, 4–5, 7
Love Canal, 144

McClelland, L., 33
McClintock, C. G., 22
McGuire, W. J., 22
McSweeney, M., 111
McTavish, J., 20, 21
Madalla, G. S., 129
Madera, California, 73
Marascuillo, L. A., 111
Marginal cost of water, 5
Marin Municipal Water District (MMWD), 73
  consequences of drought in, 1
  conservation programs of, 2, 35–37, 153
  rationing program in, 36–37
  response to drought in, 35–37, 38
  retrofit program of, 36
Market mechanisms, and pricing, 7, 86
Marwell, G., 21
Marysville, California, 72
Merced, California, 73
Messick, D. M., 20
Metering, 43, 45
  advantages and disadvantages of, 43
  demand changes and, 31–32
  in sample districts, 51, 66, 154
Mexican-American consumers, 87
Microeconomic theory, 15, 23–33
Miller, P. D., 8
Milliman, J. W., 3, 6, 9, 149
Montecito County Water District, 78
  agricultural water use in, 102–105
Monterey, California, 64, 77
Monterey Bay area programs, 76–77
Moore, N. Y., 149
Moratoriums
  agricultural use in Montecito and, 103
  demand for water and, 30–31
  in sample districts, 65

Newbold, P., 97, 99, 100
New Jersey water shortage, 8
New York City water shortage, 8
Northern Inland communities, 72

Oceanside, California, 83–84
  residential water use in, 99–102
Office of Economic Opportunity, 73
Ogalla aquifer, 144, 148
Oil industry, and water supplies, 8, 144
Oxnard, California, 79, 80

Palm Springs Desert Water Agency, 84–85
Paradise, California, 72
Platt, J., 20
Plumbing code changes, 39, 45, 64, 66, 154
Policymaking
  causal model of water use in, 3
  differential effects of programs and, 126
  economic inefficiency and, 5–6
  forecasting problems in, 146
  marginal cost pricing in, 149–151
  underpricing and, 149
Political factors
  conservation programs and, 38
  demand and, 4–5
Pollution, and water quality, 5, 7, 144
Pomona, California, 81
Population
  demand for water and growth of, 4
  response to programs related to, 68, 70
  within sample districts, 46, 48–49
Port Hueneme, California, 79–80
Precipitation, *see* Rainfall
Pricing policies
  advantages and disadvantages of using, 43, 45
  conservation program use of, 43, 45
  declining-block rate structure in, 24–25, 91–93
  demand decrease and, 25–26
  differential effects of conservation programs and, 126, 128–129, 136, 137, 160–161

distributional consequences of, 151

economic inefficiencies and, 5–7

elasticities for types of water use and, 29–30, 156

environmental consequences of, 6

impact of, 146

marginal cost pricing in, 149–151

market mechanisms and, 7

microeconomic perspective on, 23–26

real cost of water and, 6

relative effectiveness of programs and, 157–159

revenue needs of local agencies and, 86

subsidies and, 6

supply and demand in, 26–27

surcharges used in, 64

surplus revenues from, 151–152

theoretical considerations in, 178–182

time series analyses and, 93

underpricing and, 149

PROJECT WATER, 75

Property tax, 178

Psychology, social, *see* Social psychology

Public water use, 28–29

in Berkeley, 107–109

differential effects of programs on, 137–139, 161

marginal prices and, 93

relative effectiveness of conservation programs and price and, 157, 158–159

responsiveness to, 156

time series analyses of, 107–109, 117–118

Public welfare, and conservation programs, 19–20

Public work projects, 4

Questionnaires in sample, 4

copy of, 165–177

Quality of water

costs of, 5

problems in insuring, 5, 7

Rainfall

response to programs related to, 68

in sample districts, 46, 48–49

time series analyses with, 91, 92

variations in, 2

Rates, *see* Billing; Metering

Rationing, 36–37, 64

Reclamation, 64, 66

Recycling, 64, 66, 154

Residential users

demand among, 26

differential effects of programs on, 128–134, 161

marginal prices and, 93

monthly consumption figures for, 96

in Oceanside, 99–102

price elasticities and, 29

as primary targets of programs, 86–87

relative effectiveness of conservation programs and price and, 157–158

responsiveness to, 156

Spanish-speaking consumers as, 87

time series analyses of, 99–102, 112–113

Retrofitting programs, 39, 40–41

advantages and disadvantages of, 40–41

kits used in, 64

in Marin program, 36

Sample water districts

Central Valley, 73

characteristics of, 46–50

climate within, 46, 48–49

community characteristics and commitment to programs in, 68–71

conservation program during drought in, 51, 57–60, 65

data base in, 12–14

data collection in, 14–15, 165–177

desert communities, 84–85

differential effects of conservation programs of, 124–140

factors affecting response in, 67–68

Sample Water Districts (*continued*)
    greater Los Angeles, 81–83
    greater San Diego, 83–84
    Humboldt County, 71–72
    Monterey Bar area, 76–77
    Northern Inland communities, 72
    number of conservation programs
        in, 66–67
    population within districts in, 46,
        48–49
    postdrought conservation pro-
        grams in, 51, 61–63
    predrought conservation programs
        in, 51, 54–56, 65
    program summaries by commu-
        nities for, 71–85
    public water districts used in,
        12–14
    questionnaires used in, 14
    San Francisco Bay area, 73–76
    Santa Barbara County, 77–79
    summary and conclusions of pro-
        grams in, 85–87
    variations among, 13
    Ventura County, 79–81
San Diego, California, 83–84
    conservation programs in, 2, 38,
        83–84
    industrial water use in, 106–107
San Francisco Bay area, 73–76
    conservation programs in, 64–65,
        73–76
    predrought policies of, 153
San Jose Water Works (SJWW), 73, 74
Santa Barbara County, 77–79
Santa Clara Valley Water District, 74
Santa Cruz, California, 76
Santa Paula, California, 79
Schelling, T., 20
Schlender, B. R., 148
School, years of, *see* Years of school-
    ing
Seligman, C., 22, 33
Sewage, and water quality, 5, 7
Sewer charges, in conservation pro-
    grams, 43, 45
Shaklee, H., 20, 21
Shishko, R., 149

Social psychology, 16, 19–23
    attitudes toward conservation in,
        22
    belief in resource shortage in,
        21–22
    commons dilemma in, 20, 21
    conflicts in public interest in, 20
    policy recommendations from,
        148–149
    social traps in, 20, 21
Social traps, in consumption, 20, 21
Spanish-speaking consumers, 87, 154
Spector, M., 3
Stanley, J., 3
State government, and subsidies, 6,
    149
Stern, P. C., 21
Subsidies, and pricing, 6, 149, 178–
    179
Summerland, California, 77–78
Surcharges, 64, 86
    effects of, 30, 31

Talarowski, F. S., 20, 21, 22
Taxes, 178–179
Taylor, L., 91
Technology, in conservation pro-
    grams, 39, 41
Temperature
    in sample districts, 46, 48–49
    time series analyses with, 91, 92
Thompson, P. T., 21
Tiao, G. C., 98
Time series analyses, 13, 88–122
    agricultural users summary results
        in, 113–115
    agricultural water use in Montecito
        in, 102–105
    combined user categories results
        in, 118–119
    commercial users summary results
        in, 115–116
    commercial water use in Burbank
        in, 105–106
    conclusions from, 119–122
    for full sample, 183–191
    industrial users summary results
        in, 116–117

industrial water use in San Diego in, 106–107

measures of conservation efforts in, 93–94

monthly consumption figures in, 94–96

public authority users summary results in, 117–118

public authority water use in Berkeley in, 107–109

residential users summary results in, 112–113

residential water use in Oceanside in, 99–102

statistical procedures used in, 96–99

summary of results of, 110–119

total water production in Watsonville in, 109, 110

variable construction in, 90–96

Turnovsky, S. S., 32

Twin Rivers, New Jersey, 22, 33

Ventura County programs, 45, 79–81

Voluntary programs, 39, 153

Ward, R. C., 9

Warnings, for water overuse, 64

Wastewater reclamation, 64, 66

Water districts
basic records kept by, 90–91
see also Sample water districts

Water quality, *see* Quality of water

Watersheds, and industrial expansion, 7–8

Water shortage
belief in, and conservation practices, 21–22
definitions of, 9–12, 145–147
demand and, 11
hydrologic balance model in, 9–10

Water supplies
changes affecting, 7–8
economic inefficiencies and, 5–6
factors affecting, 144, 145
insuring adequate, 4–5

Water use, *see* Consumption

Watkins, G. A., 22

Watsonville, California, 76
total water production in, 109, 110

West Sacramento, California, 73

Winter, J. R., 93

Woodland, California, 73

Years of schooling
differential effects of conservation programs and, 137–138
in sample districts, 46, 48–49